BECOMING EUROPE

BECOMING
EUROPE

Economic Decline, Culture, and How America Can Avoid a European Future

SAMUEL GREGG

Encounter Books New York • London

First American edition published in 2013 by Encounter Books, an activity of Encounter for Culture and Education, Inc., a nonprofit, tax exempt corporation. Encounter Books website address: www.encounterbooks.com

Manufactured in the United States and printed on acid-free paper. The paper used in this publication meets the minimum requirements of ANSI/NISO Z39.48 1992 (R 1997) (*Permanence of Paper*).

FIRST AMERICAN EDITION

LIBRARY OF CONGRESS CATALOGING-IN-PUBLICATION DATA
Gregg, Samuel, 1969–
Becoming Europe: economic decline, culture and how America can avoid a European future/Samuel Gregg.
page cm
Includes bibliographical references and index.
ISBN 978-1-59403-637-8 (hardcover: alk. paper)
ISBN 978-1-59403-650-7 (ebook) (print)
1. Europe—Economic conditions—21st century. 2. Europe—Economic policy. 3. Europe—Social conditions—21st century. 4. Europe—Social policy. 5. United States—Economic policy—2009–6. United States—Social policy—1993– I. Title.
HC240.G656 2013
330.973—dc23

2012038913

Contents

AS ALWAYS, FOR INGRID AND MADELEINE.

THE GREATNESS OF AMERICA LIES NOT IN BEING MORE
ENLIGHTENED THAN ANY OTHER NATION,
BUT RATHER IN HER ABILITY TO REPAIR HER FAULTS.

—*Alexis de Tocqueville*

Acknowledgments

The topic of this book is one I have been thinking about for many years. But a book about America and Europe owes a great deal to the insights of friends, colleagues, and critics on both sides of the Atlantic. In Europe, thanks are owed to Antonio Arcones, Leszek Balcerowicz, Philip Booth, János Csák, João Espada, Peter Gonda, Lord Brian Griffiths, Kishore Jayabalan, Oskari Juurikkala, Bishop Kęstutis Kevalas, Jan Kłos, Bishop Jean Lafitte, Heinrich Liechtenstein, Alexandre Pesey, Monsignor Martin Schlag, Andrea Schneider, Ondrej Socuvka, Manfred Spieker, Paweł Toboła-Pertkiewicz, Paula Olearnik, Rita Seabra Brito, Damian von Stauffenberg, Alexander Trachta, Raquel Vaz-Pinto, Andreas Widmer, Michael Zoeller, and Christof Zellenberg.

Likewise, in America, gratitude is extended to Dennis Bark, Alejandro Chafuen, John Couretas, Ross Emmett, Paul Kengor, Ted Malloch, Father C.J. McCloskey, Michael Matheson Miller, Kris Alan Mauren, Juha and Mary Ann Merikoski, John Moore, Michael Novak, Amity Shlaes, Father Robert A. Sirico, and James Stoner.

Some of the ideas in this book were developed in a number of forums, most notably the *American Spectator*, *National Review*, and *Public Discourse*. For that, I extend thanks respectively to Wlady Pleszczynski, Kathryn Jean Lopez, and Ryan Anderson.

Jeremy Beer is also thanked for his thoughts about the original proposal and for contributions to its development. In my native Australia, my thanks go to my extended family—Jeannette Gregg, Nigel and Sarah Watson, Matthew and Susannah Merrigan and their wonderful children—for their continued love, despite the great geographical distance. Elena Leontjeva must be especially singled out for urging me—for several years now—to write something about the truths and goods we care about for a broader audience. My publishers, Encounter Books, are owed much for their willingness to commit to this project. Thank you to Roger Kimball, Nola Tully, Heather Ohle, Katherine Wong, and their team for seeing the potential for this book. Kacey Chuilli is also thanked for her editing work and for saving me from several errors.

My greatest debt, however, is recorded in the inscription.

Prologue

The lights are going out all over Europe: we shall not see them lit again in our lifetime.

—SIR EDWARD GREY, BRITISH FOREIGN SECRETARY, AUGUST 3, 1914

It is uncertain whether Sir Edward Grey actually uttered these words on the eve of World War I. But whether or not he said them, they did reflect a sense of foreboding among many statesmen of the time: a conviction that Europe—the very heart of Western civilization—was about to launch itself upon a path of self-destruction from which there might be no return.

Almost one hundred years later and with the fading of time, it is hardly surprising many of us have lost a sense of what World War I did to Europe. The military death toll alone should give room for pause. The minimal estimates are chilling: Germany, 1,800,000 deaths; Russia, 1,800,000; France, 1,384,000; Austria-Hungary, 1,290,000; Britain, 743,000; Italy, 615,000; Romania, 335,000.

America did not enter the Great War until April 1917. This followed two and a half years of efforts by President Woodrow Wilson to maintain the United States' neutrality. Between that time and the signing of the armistice that silenced the guns on the western front on November 11, 1918, forty-eight thousand Americans were killed in combat.[1]

This last figure is a tragic number. Yet it was far less devastating than the human and material destruction inflicted upon Europe by four years of modern warfare that drew upon all the might of industrial capitalist economies turned against each other. No American city was occupied. America suffered no naval blockade. Trenches bristling with sharp wire and lethal machine guns were not dug for thousands of miles across American soil. And when it was over, millions of American soldiers went home. Whether they numbered among the victors or the defeated, Europeans remained, surrounded by living memories of what had been twentieth-century Europe's first civil war.

Europe would never be the same. Within twenty-one years of the 1918 armistice, World War II took the European continent once again to the brink of self-immolation. Though Europe slowly recovered after 1945, its days as the center of world power were over. European colonial empires gradually disappeared from the globe. Until 1989, half of Europe was subject to Communist tyranny. Europe's lights, it seems, did indeed go out.

When the victors and losers of World War I gathered to make peace in Versailles, the seventeenth-century palace built by France's Sun King, Louis XIV, the agenda went beyond issues such as border changes, the recognition of new nations, or the carving-up of Germany's former colonial possessions. An intense awareness of dramatic economic changes in the offing permeated the Peace Conference. Socialist and Marxist political movements, characterized by a deep hostility to capitalism, were in the ascendancy. Lenin's Bolshevik revolutionaries had seized power in Russia. Germany's government was in the hands of Europe's largest social democratic party.

Even without these developments, economic issues were going to be central to the negotiations at Versailles. As well as ceding territory, Germany and the defeated nations were expected to pay reparations to the victors. This was understood as punishment of the losers and compensation for the winners. The sheer scale of reparations demanded by the Allied powers, however, was a severe shock to Germany. It quickly became a festering source of burning resentment among Germans of all political stripes. Germany's final reparations payment was not to be made until October 4, 2010.

Germans were not alone in their dismay. The burden of reparations that the Allies wanted to impose upon Germany was just as astonishing to a small number of officials serving as members of the Allied delegations at Versailles. One such delegate, a young British civil servant named John Maynard Keynes—later to become perhaps the twentieth century's most famous and influential economist—was so appalled that he resigned from the British Treasury in protest. Within months of doing so, in 1919 Keynes vented his misgivings in the book that first gave him celebrity status: *The Economic Consequences of the Peace*.

Read by thousands across Europe and America, Keynes's short and frankly polemical text shocked and titillated British, European, and American opinion with its pithy, even irreverent portraits of the statesmen who had led the Allies to victory. Figures such as Britain's David Lloyd George ("ill-informed"), France's Georges Clemenceau ("dry in soul, empty of hope"), and America's Woodrow Wilson ("slow and unadaptable") were presented as men with feet of clay, veering between utopian idealism and Machiavellian cynicism. Yet beneath the iconoclasm permeating Keynes's book was a far more serious message: that the economic conditions being imposed upon the defeated nations by these politicians were economically foolish, morally indefensible, likely to destabilize an already shattered German economy, and fertile ground for demagogues of the Left and Right.

The deeper background to Keynes's *Economic Consequences* was his conviction that Europe's economic landscape was about to change forever. At the beginning of the text, Keynes wrote almost winsomely about pre-1914 Europe as a world in which free trade prevailed, passports were unnecessary to cross borders, economic upward mobility was the norm, and people could invest virtually anywhere across the globe with relatively little interference.

Keynes may have been exaggerating, but his description of pre-war European economic life was not far from the truth. Moreover, the economies of Europe *did* undergo dramatic transformations over subsequent decades, as governments—and not just those led by Socialists and Social Democrats—steadily assumed an ever-increasing part in Europe's economic life, not least, ironically enough, because of economic theories Keynes himself developed in the 1930s as Europe and the world struggled to find a way out of the Great Depression.

Another subterranean theme pervading Keynes's *Economic Consequences* was his immense disappointment with the performance of America's President Woodrow Wilson at Versailles. It may have been, Keynes conceded, partly a question of inflated expectations. President Wilson, in the eyes of Keynes and many other Europeans with progressive dispositions, had traveled to Europe enjoying "a prestige and a moral influence unequaled in history."[2] Yet almost from the beginning of the Peace Conference, it became clear to Keynes that Wilson simply did not understand Europe. Wilson, Keynes wrote, "not only had no proposals in detail, but he was, in many respects, perhaps inevitably, ill-informed as to European conditions."[3]

Not all Americans were as naïve about Europe's postwar economic conditions in 1919 as Keynes considered Wilson to be. Plenty of Americans were aware that economic problems were contributing to the deaths of thousands of noncombatants in Germany through mass starvation and disease. Few today know that the future American president, Herbert Hoover, was responsible for organizing the transfer of several million tons of food supplies from America to Germany and other starving areas of Central Europe immediately following World War I. "Europe," Keynes himself acknowledged, "should never forget the extraordinary assistance afforded her during the first six months of 1919 through the agency of Mr. Hoover and the American Commission of Relief." A few lines later, Keynes added: "The American Relief Commission, and they only, saw the European position during these months in its true perspective."[4]

In many history books Herbert Hoover is dismissed as an unsuccessful president: a leader who did too little too late as the Great Depression's effects crashed their way through every home and business across America. From Keynes's perspective, however, the prepresidential Hoover *was* an American who understood Europe, and considered it important enough to be worth helping in its hour of need.

Americans have, of course, been thinking about and influenced by Europe for a long time. Today the rise of China and India presents new mirrors through which Americans can reflect upon themselves. Nevertheless, Europe has been an external focus for America in ways that India and China have not, and may never be. Political correctness and the ideology of multiculturalism notwithstanding, America's persistent attention to Europe owes much to the simple fact that contemporary America's cultural origins do not lie in China, India, or Africa. Buddha and Confucianism are not significant reference points for the overwhelming majority of Americans in the way that Magna Carta and Christianity are. When it comes to its dominant political ideas, iconic figures, legal institutions, religious culture, and economic history, America is very much Europe's child. To be sure, America is a bigger, more powerful, grown-up child. And, like all children, it has determined much of its own destiny and is not a clone of its parents. But for all that, America remains an offspring of Europe.

In part, this reflects economic links. Before the American Revolution, many of the thirteen colonies enjoyed closer economic links with Britain than with each other. Today, the amount of trade between the United States and European nations remains extraordinarily high, as does the degree of capital invested by Americans and Europeans in each others' economies.

Nor can we discount the political connections between the two continents. Despite strong isolationist impulses in America, the twentieth century saw millions of American soldiers travel to Europe twice in the short space of twenty-seven years. Postwar economic and political engagements, such as the Marshall Plan, the formation of NATO in 1949, and the stationing of American troops in Europe, have helped keep the "Old Continent" at the forefront of many Americans' minds.

Taken together, these cultural, economic, and political realities present America with some distinct opportunities. One is that social and economic developments in Europe can give Americans insights into possible scenarios for their own future. Americans are so accustomed to hearing Europeans talk, often with a tone of complaint or resignation, about the "Americanization" of their cultures that they rarely consider the ways in which America has become, or is becoming, *economically Europeanized*.

To be sure, no two European nations are exactly alike. Finland is not Belgium, France is not Germany, Britain is not Greece, and Poland is not Portugal. Nevertheless, part of this book's argument is that, when it comes to the economy, there is enough of a European "canary in the coal mine" to help Americans with decisions about their economic future that, once made, would be increasingly difficult to retreat from.

To put the point in somewhat dramatic terms:

- Do Americans want to embrace *modern European economic culture*? Do they want to live in a set of economic expectations and arrangements that routinely prioritizes economic security over economic liberty; in which the state annually consumes close to 50 percent of gross domestic product;

where the ultimate economic resource (i.e., human beings) is aging and declining in numbers; where extensive regulation is the norm; and perhaps above all, where economic incentives lie not in hard work, economic creativity, and a willingness to take risks, but rather in access to political power?

- Or do Americans want to embrace the opposite? Do they want to live in an economy in which economic entrepreneurship is rewarded; where the government's economic responsibilities are confined to a number of important but limited functions; and where the stress is upon economic liberty, rather than remorseless efforts to equalize economic outcomes through state action?

That is the choice increasingly facing America: a form of "cuddle capitalism"—the European social model—presided over by an all-pervasive European-like political class and associated insider groups wielding bureaucratic power; or, alternatively, a dynamic market economy that takes liberty seriously and understands that government intervention in the economy must and can be limited. As we will see, the decision is not as simple as it might seem. Among other things, it involves trade-offs, the prioritization of different values, differences about ends and means, and fundamental disagreements about the nature and functions of government.

The debate about which road to take is not a new one. Its origins go back to Europe's Middle Ages. There is, however, nothing like a crisis to focus the mind. And this, many would say, is precisely what happened in 2008, when the United States entered a period of economic instability of such severity that it is known today as the Great Recession.

We're Becoming Like Europe

All educated Americans, first or last, go to Europe.

—RALPH WALDO EMERSON

As anyone who lived through the financial crisis that rocked Wall Street with ever-increasing intensity throughout 2008 will attest, the sense of *systematic* failure pervading American society at the time was palpable. The self-doubt of many Americans in their economic system was personified by former Federal Reserve chairman Alan Greenspan, who confessed during congressional testimony that his faith in free markets had been shaken. "I have found a flaw," Greenspan stated. "I don't know how significant or permanent it is. But I have been very distressed by that fact."[1]

That something was fundamentally awry with American capitalism was a view shared—and loudly expressed—by many prominent Europeans in the last four months of 2008. In a widely publicized speech, Germany's then finance minister, Peer Steinbrück, castigated the American economic system. "The financial crisis," he insisted, "is above all an American problem." Steinbrück continued: "The U.S. is the origin and the clear focal point of the crisis, but it is now spreading worldwide like a poisonous oil spill."[2]

Similar statements echoed across Europe's political spectrum. Their common theme was summed up in a few short sentences by France's then president, Nicolas Sarkozy. "Self-regulation as a way of solving all problems is finished," Sarkozy claimed. "Laissez-faire is finished. The all-powerful market that always knows best is finished."[3]

To some more detached observers, however, America's 2008 economic crisis seemed to confirm what they already thought: that the twenty-first century's economic future did not lie in America. Instead, that future would be found in the European Union.

In 2004, for example, the American economist Jeremy Rifkin published an international best seller, *The European Dream: How Europe's Vision of the Future Is Quietly Eclipsing the American Dream*. That same year, the journalist T. R. Reid authored *The United States of Europe: The New Superpower and the End of American Supremacy*. Six years later, in 2010, the political scientist Steven Hill published *Europe's Promise: Why the European Way Is the Best Hope in an Insecure Age*.

The content of these books should be self-evident from their titles. While they differed in their degree of advocacy and the sharpness of their contrasts drawn between the European and American economies, there was little question which economic model these authors considered superior.

Whether the American economy of 2008 was as "unregulated," "laissez-faire," or "finished," as some Americans and Europeans imagined at the time, is questionable. What is clear is that just over one year after Wall Street's meltdown, many member states of the EU were well into their own phase of pronounced economic instability.

At the beginning of 2010, Portugal, Ireland, Greece, and Spain found themselves staring into an economic abyss, as they desperately sought to stave off the humiliation of sovereign debt default. Such were the debt levels of these countries (which acquired the unfortunate acronym of "PIGS") that in May 2010 the EU effectively abandoned its previous "no bailout" stance and joined the International Monetary Fund in creating a massive safety net for the PIGS. Images of rioters burning tires, looting shops, and attacking police in the streets of Athens in protest against austerity measures introduced by Greece's embattled government symbolized many Europeans' shock and anger at what was happening. The extent of the crisis was such that *The Wall Street Journal*'s Daniel Henninger was moved to write that "Any U.S. politician purporting to run for the presidency of the United States should be asked why the economic policies he or she is proposing won't take us where Europe arrived this week."[4]

The contrast between American and European reactions to their respective crises, as they played out over 2009 and 2010, could not have been more different. After the initial panic subsided, many Americans found themselves growing gradually uneasy—and increasingly enraged—at the suddenness and extent of the federal government's growth in response to the economic downturn. The equally dramatic rise of the Tea Party movement as a force in American politics during this period cannot be understood without this background.

To a good number of Americans, the bailout of banks, Congress's apparently insatiable appetite for spending, the passing of Obamacare into law, the new regulatory regime for the financial industry, and the government's rescue of American car companies increasingly looked like a wider pattern. Something seemed to be changing—and not for the better—in American economic and political life.

This book is about those changes, and how they resemble prominent features and trends in Western European economic life. At a deeper level, it is about understanding these developments through the medium of what is called *economic culture*: the value commitments, attitudes, rules, and institutions that shape and characterize economic life in a given society.

Social Democracy in America

A careful look at American economic history over the twentieth century suggests that many of the transformations noted above have a longer and deeper pedigree in the United States than many Americans realize. In an insightful 2011 article, the political analyst Yuval Levin argued that one of the most formative forces upon twentieth-century Western economic development—including America's economy—was the dream of the social democratic welfare state. He described the content of this vision in the following terms:

> From birth to death, citizens should be ensconced in a series of protections and benefits intended to shield them from the harsh edges of the market and allow them to pursue dignified, fulfilling lives: universal child care, universal health care, universal public schooling and higher education, welfare benefits for the poor, generous labor protections for workers, dexterous management of the levers of the economy to ease the cycles of boom and bust, skillful direction of public funds to spur private productivity and efficiency, and, finally, pensions for the elderly. Each component would be overseen by a competent and rational bureaucracy, and the whole would make for a system that is not only beneficent but unifying and dignifying, and that enables the pursuit of common national goals and ideals.[5]

Levin maintained that one of the stories of American economic life from the 1930s onward has been of a slow stumble toward a halfhearted semi-embrace of elements of this vision: a stumble that occasionally turned into a rush in particular circumstances, such as the 1929 Great Depression and the 2008 Great Recession.

The general slowness of this shift toward aspects of social democracy, Levin argued, may be partly attributed to an ingrained skepticism about government that pervades American culture and facilitates considerable pushback against efforts to turn social democratic ideals into reality. The American Center Left has consequently opted to explain expansions of the welfare state as a matter of pragmatism rather than an expression of ideological commitment. These circumstances have helped bequeath America with a hodgepodge of welfare state arrangements tilted, Levin noted, "disproportionately toward the elderly" in the form of America's two biggest entitlement programs (Social Security and Medicare), as well as dozens of smaller and targeted programs such as Rural Rental Assistance, the Summer Food Service Program for children, and the Low Income Energy Assistance Program.

But however fragmented and pragmatic their approach, many American liberals have no doubt that realization of the social democratic vision should be the economic end goal. As Levin observed, it was telling that when President Barack Obama signed his health-care legislation into law on March 23, 2010, he described it as the culmination of "almost a century of trying" and an expression of "reforms that generations of Americans have fought for and marched for and hungered to see." This also explained, Levin added, why then House Speaker Nancy Pelosi called the final vote to a close by banging the same gavel used when the House of Representatives voted to enact the Medicare and Medicaid programs in 1965. The calculated use of such language and symbols, Levin suggested, was to emphasize that these were all elements of a larger, more expansive project.[6]

Europeanization

These developments and history made it all the more ironic that, by late 2009, some European governments were responding to Europe's own economic crisis by choosing a path that looked decidedly "un-European" and "un-social democratic." After responding to the initial crisis with bank bailouts and stimulus packages, they began—to the dismay of prominent American apostles of interventionism such as Nobel Prize winner Joseph Stiglitz[7]—opting for budget cuts, restraints in public-sector spending, and even attempts at welfare reform throughout 2009, 2010, 2011, and 2012. Indeed, some European politicians, including Germany's Chancellor Angela Merkel, openly resisted pressures from the Obama administration to employ more expansionist measures in their response to the crisis.

The reaction of many Europeans to even limited attempts by their governments to deal with their nations' mounting fiscal problems through the policies of austerity was most revealing. Between May and November 2010, for example, France endured an ongoing series of protests and work stoppages in response to Nicolas Sarkozy's ultimately successful effort to lift the retirement age from sixty to sixty-two. That will not strike many people as a radical reform, but many French citizens considered it a deeply unjust move.

Likewise, on September 29, 2010, Spain experienced its first nationwide strike in eight years, in response to Prime Minister José Luis Rodríguez Zapatero's introduction of reforms designed to liberalize Spain's notoriously rigid labor market. Two months later, Portugal witnessed its first general strike in more than two decades, following government spending cuts.

Toward the end of that same year, central London witnessed some of its worst rioting in years, as university students and left-wing activists protested against the British government's decision to raise university fees. And throughout May 2011, young Spaniards effectively occupied the main squares of major cities including Madrid, Barcelona, and Valencia to protest rampant unemployment (which had reached 50 percent among those in their twenties and thirties in some parts of Spain) and the effects of the government's austerity measures.

Perhaps the most noteworthy aspect of the economic policies provoking such widespread protest from so many Europeans was the *way* in which European political leaders chose to sell them to the public. *None* of Europe's governments seemed especially interested in using their country's economic problems as a circuit breaker that would enable them to articulate a grand moral and political vision, one of freeing up the economy and society more generally from the dead hand of the state. More often, politicians such as Spain's Zapatero, France's Sarkozy, and Britain's David Cameron presented their reforms as necessary evils, embarked upon with considerable reluctance.

One explanation for this absence of effort to explain the changes in terms of positive *value* may be that Europe's political leaders believed that explicit moral appeals for greater economic liberty and a less expansive state simply would not resonate with large numbers of Western Europeans. This reluctance to go beyond technicalities when explaining the need for reform points to the saliency of economic culture as a way of understanding what has happened to Europe, and what may lay ahead for America.

In an unconscious way, Americans themselves seem aware of the importance of this factor. One indication is the spread of the word *Europeanization* in everyday American conversation from 2009 onward. It is shorthand for describing what people think is happening to America's economy, from the Bush administration's heavy spending and fiscal stimulus programs to the acceleration of deficit spending and a general expansion of government economic intervention during President Obama's.

"We're becoming," the sentiment runs, "like Europe."

By "Europeanization," people mean something that goes beyond ideological positions such as socialism or social democracy. Phrases such as "Europeanization"—or, for that matter, "Americanization"—encapsulate realities that include but also transcend political commitments. Instead, they point to a *cultural* dimension to the economy: a culture of expectations, beliefs, values, and institutions that themselves are embedded in a history that is economic, but also more than economic.

Culture Matters

Culture is one of those phenomena to which we all refer, but often with little precision about what we mean. On one level, culture is employed to describe the importance of symbols, rituals, and collective memory.

At the root of culture, however, are human beings. Unlike plants and animals, humans can consciously *cult*ivate ideas, things, and the natural world through their choices and actions. Hence, in its broadest sense, culture encapsulates everything that humans develop through their minds and work.

Over time, these choices and habits may become concretized in various products, protocols, and even institutions that themselves shape our choices, sometime without us being especially conscious of these influences. Any one culture therefore embraces more than simply the material things and technology created by people. It also includes recognizable ways of living and acting that emerge from a distinguishable set of attitudes, customs, conventions, laws, ways of working, methods of communication, learned and learnable patterns of behavior, and practices of religion. Taken together, these features of life constitute a more or less lasting and recognizable cultural reality.

But at the heart of all the distinct historical features and social, political, and economic formations that are central to a culture's identity are the intentions, principles, ideas, and beliefs to which a given society ascribes high value. A market economy, for example, relies on processes such as market prices and the exchange of goods and services, institutions such as private property and rule of law, as well as actions such as innovation and economic entrepreneurship. Note, however, how every single one of these economic processes, actions, and institutions assumes a commitment to *freedom*. The mundane business of deciding the price at which I will sell my house is based on the assumption that I am at *liberty* to do so. Absent economic freedom, the process of free exchange and the free formation of prices both grind to a halt.

The centrality of values to any culture is no guarantee that all cultures will embody the right commitments or be conducive to human flourishing. In fact, most cultures embody some habits and practices that, in retrospect, appear positively antihuman. The institution of slavery is a good example. Nor does the reality of culture mean that people are somehow prisoners of their social, political, and economic environments. In times of crisis, it is entirely possible for a given culture to change quickly, for better *and* for worse.

Above all, the saliency of culture should not blind us to the fact that all humans share much in common with the rest of humanity. Given the universality of human reason, we should not be surprised at the remarkable consensus among cultures when it comes, for example, to many moral questions. Very few cultures regard stealing as good. Certainly, different cultures have rationalized particular forms of stealing at various points of history; they have also often disagreed on the precise details of what constitutes theft in different circumstances. But very few cultures have claimed that stealing in itself is good.

Culture and the Economy

Cultures are complex. They are untidy, usually in a state of flux, and do not lend themselves easily to certain types of scholarly analysis. That may be one reason why much of mainstream economics, dominated by mathematically-centered forms of analysis since the 1940s, often treats culture as a somewhat mysterious subject and consequently tends to ignore it.

No doubt applying mathematical and empirical analysis to the study of economic life has its uses. Yet it also tempts people to believe that those things that cannot be quantified either do not exist or are of marginal relevance. That culture is sometimes difficult to quantify does not mean that it is not real, or that it does not have immense implications for economic life.

Consider the different views taken by Americans and Europeans on a subject such as health care. Whatever people think of the Obama administration's 2010 health-care legislation, it is difficult to deny that many Americans' profound opposition to Obamacare was based on more than a cold cost-benefit analysis.

No doubt many Americans were concerned about the economic inefficiencies associated with any government monopoly. But many also believed that Obamacare would unreasonably constrict people's economic choices, incentivize them to take less responsibility for their own lives, facilitate the further bureaucratization of health care, and expand the government's control of the American economy. A strong value component was central to *all* these concerns. No one who attended any of the anti-Obamacare rallies or town hall meetings debating the subject could doubt that the opposition was at least partially derived from many Americans' sense that Obamacare simply did not accord with American expectations about the values, practices, and institutions that should underlie and inform American economic life.

Americans, Europeans, and Solidarity

Empirical research has its limitations in what it can tell us about reality. But in his 2010 book, *The Battle: How the Fight Between Free Enterprise and Big Government Will Shape America's Future*, the social scientist Arthur C. Brooks drew upon a large amount of data to demonstrate the consistent attachment of significant majorities of Americans to a positive view of free enterprise, entrepreneurship, free markets, and low tax rates, and a preference for a limited economic role for government.[8] In this light, the intensity and persistence of many Americans' hostility to Obamacare is unsurprising.

However, Brooks went on to point out, the same data indicated that high-income, high-education individuals working in what Brooks calls the "intellectual industries"—universities, law, the media—had far less favorable views of the values, preferences, and institutions associated with free markets. He also observed that, on average, Americans below the age of forty tended to be less wary of government intervention.

Brooks's findings receive some confirmation from research conducted into the attitudes of the Occupy Wall Street movement. The embrace by young occupiers (defined as being in their twenties) of slogans such as "freedom" and "responsibility," and their attacks on "crony capitalism," were found to be "solely surface-level and hollow." Beneath the rhetoric, they turned out to be overwhelmingly concerned with issues of economic security and safety, relatively hostile to free markets, and highly susceptible to "any movement or leader that offers to decrease the uncertainty and level of risk in the present-day society."[9]

If these analyses of the data are correct, then numerically speaking, Americans with a favorable view of free enterprise and free markets remain a majority. But numbers are not everything. No one should have any doubt about the disproportionate cultural influence of what Brooks called "the 30 percent coalition" upon American life.

In this context, it is telling that the depth of many Americans' opposition to Obamacare was a source of puzzlement to this 30 percent coalition. Equally revealing is that many Europeans at the time—including many conservative Europeans—simply could not understand why anyone would morally or economically oppose the state's assumption of such a central part in the provision of health care. However one views the economic arguments for and against state provision of health care, many Europeans regard the state's heavy involvement as the most effective and, more importantly, the most just way of institutionalizing people's responsibilities to those in need: what might be called the good of solidarity.

In much of Western Europe, the language of solidarity and social justice permeates public discourse to an extent that can surprise

Americans. It is widely assumed by many Western Europeans that this moral responsibility should primarily be realized through state action. This is partly what Europeans have in mind when they refer to "Social Europe" or the "European social model." Even minor efforts to reform social welfare programs, let alone reduce the welfare state's size, are regarded by many Europeans as a heartless assault on the weak and marginalized, and a betrayal of the commitments widely associated with Social Europe.

By contrast, America has given a somewhat different institutional expression to the idea that we should help our neighbor in need. America certainly does have a large—and growing—welfare state. But it also has a long history and contemporary practice of private associations addressing social and economic problems.

Americans are often regarded as more individualistic than Western Europeans. This was one of the distinguishing features of America that struck the French social philosopher Alexis de Tocqueville when he visited the United States between 1831 and 1832. He also marveled at the relative absence of government from American life.

Tocqueville quickly realized, however, that this individualism and absence of the state was not symptomatic of a callous disregard by Americans of their fellow citizens. Though Americans tended, he observed, to dress up their assistance to others in the language of enlightened self-interest, Tocqueville underscored how they usually expressed those values through the habits and institutions of free and voluntary association. Some of these associations (like churches) had a more or less permanent presence in American society. Others lasted only as long as a particular economic or social problem persisted. As a consequence, the pressures for centralized top-down government-led solutions that prevailed in Tocqueville's native France were not present in the young American republic.

The moral of the story is this: *Economic culture matters.* At the most basic level, it matters whether the people living in a given economic setting prefer, for instance, liberty to security, or if they prioritize equality of outcome over access to opportunity. It also matters *how* we give institutional expression to particular universal values (such as concern for those in need) in economic life. Depending on the nature of these values and institutions, they can either be a boon to wealth creation and growing prosperity, or they can become what the economists Arnold Kling and Nick Schulz call "invisible liabilities," impeding and undermining economic innovation, adaptation, and efficiency.[10]

Economic Culture: Toward a Definition

Economists are often parodied as suffering from a bad case of maths envy. Yet in more recent decades, some economists have begun paying significant attention to the importance of values, rules, and institutions when explaining economic trends or elucidating different economic models' strengths and weaknesses. Some have even made the case for the superiority of one set of beliefs and institutions over others, at least in terms of their ability to contribute to growing prosperity over sustained periods of time.

This approach appears in the work of the man widely regarded as the first modern economist. Adam Smith's pathbreaking *The Wealth of Nations* was a systematic exercise in abstract analysis of economic life, and an elaboration of what should be done in policy terms if society's overall material enrichment is deemed desirable. Nonetheless, Smith's political economy was attentive to how beliefs, ideas, and events shaped the character of economic practices and systems.[11]

Over the past twenty years, the economist who has presented perhaps the most penetrating case for the importance of economic culture in understanding the functioning of economies is the 1993 Nobel Prize winner Douglass North. North is widely associated with the emergence of what is called "new institutional economics":[12] the study of the nature of institutions, how they develop, and their effects upon the economy over long periods of time.

North himself acknowledges that he has long since moved beyond the bounds of much of mainstream economics. Economics, North argues, cannot be separated from disciplines such as sociology and political science, because, in his words, "all the interesting issues are on the borders between them." In the real world, North insists, moral, political, and economic questions are all mixed up. While some degree of separation can be useful for analytical purposes, it all needs to be brought together at some point.

For North, it comes together in the idea of *institutions*. As he stated in his 1993 Nobel Prize lecture:

> Institutions are the humanly devised constraints that structure human interaction. They are made up of formal constraints (rules, laws, constitutions), informal constraints (norms of behavior, conventions, and self imposed codes of conduct), and their enforcement characteristics. Together they define the incentive structure of societies and specifically economies.[13]

Observe how North weaves together what most of us think of as institutions (rules, laws, constitutions) with values (norms of behavior, conventions, self-imposed codes of conduct) as well as the means by which they are upheld and protected (enforcement characteristics). Though North uses the phrase "institutions" to describe this conglomerate, it amounts to as good a summary of the idea of economic culture as you are likely to find.

The last part of the citation above is also important. It explains *how* a society's given economic culture influences people's choices. Any one economic culture will provide *incentives* for people to act in particular ways.

We often think of incentives primarily in terms of financial rewards. But incentives can be nonfinancial. The desire to do good and be seen as a good person can sometimes incentivize people to act in one way rather than another, even if, objectively speaking, it is the wrong moral choice. Incentives can also assume a coercive character. People may choose to act in particular ways because they fear that failure to act in such a manner will result in the application of arbitrary force, legal punishment, or stigmatization.

What does this mean for economic culture? It means that if a given economic culture locates financial rewards in, for instance, proximity to political power, we should not be surprised that many businesses will focus their efforts upon getting as close as possible to government officials and regulators. Likewise, if being seen as a good person by your peers is intrinsically associated with supporting a big welfare state, then some people will vote for extensive welfare programs despite the fact that, economically speaking, it may not be in their best interests. Similarly, if the path to social ostracism lies in arguing that people should be helped to take care of themselves, the incentives for being a prominent advocate of limiting government power are much lower.

If this is true, then economic culture has immense implications for how we understand economic development and the possibility of change. Certainly, changing policies is vitally important to altering a society's incentive structure. There is every difference in the world between the rules that govern economic life in a Communist command economy and a relatively market-oriented economy. But as North cautions, "Both institutions *and belief systems* must change for successful reform since it is the mental models of the actors that will shape choices." Such are North's convictions on this matter that he argues, "Informal constraints (norms, conventions and codes of conduct) favorable to growth can sometimes produce economic growth *even with unstable or adverse political rules.*"[14]

These "mental models," one might add, need not be explicit in people's minds. Much of the content of a given economic culture can consist of what the philosopher Karl Polanyi called *tacit knowledge.*

Language is a good example of tacit knowledge. Up to a point, language can be formally taught and learned. It cannot, however, be fully understood by reading a book of grammar. The more intangible aspects of language (such as knowing when to use particular tones, or what words are appropriately used in certain contexts) are communicated tacitly: through personal experimentation, through watching others, through "breathing in" the context of any given language. This knowledge is thus internalized in people's behavior and choices through habit and practice, to the point whereby people act almost unconsciously.

So it is with much economic culture. The informal, unstated ways in which people interact in the economic setting of, for instance, a Southern European country, compared to an economy with distinctly "Anglo-American" features, like Australia, may be difficult for Italians or Australians to express precisely, because they are so ingrained in their daily economic life.

Economic culture does not explain everything. American and European economic successes and failures are attributable to more than just institutions and values as North understands them. Plenty of authors have illustrated the importance of factors such as war, peace, technological change, politics, or religion when seeking to understand why one economy differs from another. This being the case, this book does not seek to explain everything about the character of economic life in Europe and America in terms of economic culture. It does, however, illustrate that economic culture plays a singularly important role that we neglect at our peril.

Culture and Attitudes: Europe and America

Whether the knowledge is explicit or tacit, the importance of the attitudes and values at the core of North's "mental models" cannot be underestimated when it comes to understanding any economic culture. This proposition is at the heart of arguments made by another Nobel Prize economist, Edmund Phelps, who has devoted considerable time to seeking to explain some of the differences in economic performance between America and continental Europe.

Like many others, Phelps concluded long ago that contemporary continental European economies are less productive than America's because of the prevalence of factors in Europe that discourage productivity, such as heavy regulation of labor markets, and weaknesses in those factors that help encourage growth, such as vibrant capital markets.

Yet, Phelps thought, this couldn't explain everything. Modern European nations, to use his pithy phrase, "were not a bunch of banana republics." Nor was it clear, Phelps claimed, that they were somehow lagging behind America when it came to classic predictors of growth such as rule of law and strong property rights protections.[15]

Phelps's intuition was that the differences came down to America's economy being closer to one in which a private-ownership system was "structured for cutting-edge innovation, . . . *fertile* in coming up with innovative ideas with prospects of profitability; *shrewd* and *adept* in selecting among these ideas for development; finally, *prepared* and *venturesome* in evaluating and trying the new products and methods that are brought out."[16] This in turn, Phelps reasoned, was influenced by a *culture* which valued entrepreneurs, in which financiers were more willing to give different ideas a genuine evaluation and then risk backing them with capital, and where neither entrepreneurs nor financiers needed the tacit approval of social groups and established businesses to try out their new products and services.

By contrast, Phelps maintained, continental European economies were closer to a model in which private property arrangements were supplemented with a strong emphasis upon protecting established social groups—communities and regions, existing businesses, organized labor and professions—from the creative destruction of free markets. This focus upon security and stability made it possible for new entrepreneurs to be blocked if they failed to gain the consent of existing "stakeholders": i.e., employees, customers, even rival companies. This was further underpinned by the priority many

Europeans accorded to social cohesion over individual engagement and personal growth.

Drilling down into a range of data that surveyed the attitudes of Americans and citizens of major European countries toward variables such as change, acceptance of new ideas, views of competition, and the desirability of freedom to make decisions, Phelps found that, with minor exceptions, Americans had more favorable views than Europeans. "I came away," Phelps commented, "with the impression that differences across countries with respect to certain well-defined institutions were not as important as the prevailing differences in economic culture."[17] As Phelps put it in his 2006 Nobel Prize lecture, "various attributes of a country's economic culture serve to animate entrepreneurs and, more broadly, to encourage them by offering them a willing workforce and a receptive marketplace for their innovations."[18]

Phelps even speculated that an economic culture can become so entrenched over time that the minds of its human inhabitants become closed to other possibilities. "It may be," he argued, "that the French, having long since despaired of having more freedom and more initiative, have learned not to care much about those values. Similarly, it may be that Americans, having assimilated large doses of freedom and initiative for generations, take initiative and freedom for granted."[19]

Even key EU institutions such as the Brussels-based European Commission have become increasingly conscious of the significance of economic culture in explaining important differences between Europe and America. In 2003 the European Commission published a green paper entitled *Entrepreneurship in Europe*. It focused on two questions: Why did relatively few Europeans set up their own businesses? And why were so few European businesses growing?

As it studied these subjects over the following five years, the commission increasingly focused upon different *attitudes* toward entrepreneurship as a key factor. In a 2010 survey of views in Europe,

America, and China entitled *Entrepreneurship in the EU and Beyond*, the commission found:

> EU citizens appeared to be almost evenly divided in their prefer-
> ence for being self-employed or for having employee status: 45%
> would prefer the former and 49% the latter. . . . In the US, a
> majority of respondents would opt for self-employment, while
> just over a third would prefer to be an employee (55% vs. 36%).
> Similar results were seen in Iceland (52% "self-employment" vs.
> 38% "employee status"), Turkey (51% vs. 46%) and South Korea
> (51% vs. 37%). Respondents in China, however, were the most
> likely to say they would prefer to be self-employed rather than an
> employee (71% vs. 28%).[20]

In other words, a slight majority of Europeans preferred to work for others. It is worth noting that these results were gathered in 2009, in the midst of a global economic downturn that would surely moti-vate even many entrepreneurially-minded people to opt for security and stability. And yet, despite the turmoil, Americans and Chinese remained far more positive about entrepreneurship than Europeans.

Empirical data and attitudinal surveys are important, especially when it comes to satisfying social scientists with a penchant for numbers. But these results are also compatible with the observations of historians familiar with the life and history of both America and Europe.

In his 2007 study of similarities and differences between Ameri-cans and Europeans, the historian Dennis Bark drew upon compara-tive history; his own experience of living, working in, and writing about both continents; and the insights of European and American intellectuals, politicians, journalists, and CEOs. Bringing together this variety of sources, Bark concluded that an essential economic and political difference was that "Europe was constructed from the top-down and America was made from the bottom-up."[21]

Other factors, Bark acknowledged, have obviously made an impact. His conclusion, however, is quite compatible with the evidence marshaled by Phelps. In societies where less value is attached to the freedom to make decisions for ourselves, it is hardly surprising that an emphasis on top-down coordination by the state prevails. In other words, it comes back to beliefs, expectations, and values.

The Way Ahead

Economic culture, then, is the primary lens through which this book tells its story. It does so in three parts.

In part 1, we explain how contemporary Europe's economies—specifically those which characterize Western Europe—"came to be" what they are today. This involves an excursion into longer-term European economic history, followed by an examination of developments since World War II.

This sets the stage for part 2. Here we examine some particular features of contemporary European economic life: specifically, how the European model creates insiders and outsiders; the challenges facilitated by modern European welfare states; the dynamics driving the EU's debt and currency problems; and, finally, Europe's response to globalization.

Our goal in part 2 is not to provide a blow-by-blow account of the European social model's current problems. Rather, the focus is upon giving readers deeper insights into particularly revealing aspects of contemporary European economic culture, and then comparing them with features of American economic life today. This serves to highlight existing and ongoing divergences, as well as some increasingly troublesome similarities in the two economic cultures' respective trajectories.

In parts 1 and 2, our emphasis is upon the interplay in the economy between values, the institutions that embody these beliefs and attitudes, the incentive structures they create, and the forces they set in motion. To this end, this book employs particular concepts and considers various pieces of historical and empirical data that, while relatively familiar to specialists, are not as widely known among the broader audiences for whom this book is written. The aim is to produce a narrative for interested nonspecialists that highlights the essential elements and trajectory of European economic culture, and illustrates the instances where America's economic life appears to be becoming "European" in its direction and emphases.

The endgame of this narrative is direct, practical in its implications, and forms the subject matter of part 3. Having demonstrated the ways in which America's economic culture has drifted further in a European direction than many Americans have hitherto realized, we consider how—at the level of values—America can avoid further drift and, perhaps, even reverse some of these developments.

This assumes, of course, that economic Europeanization would be a mistake for America. One does not have to accept the rather breathless claim of another Nobel Prize-winning economist, Paul Krugman, that postwar Europe contains some of "the most decent societies in human history, combining democracy and human rights with a level of individual economic security that America comes nowhere close to matching,"[22] to agree that European economic life has some admirable features. For example, a World Bank report released in early 2012 pointed out that Europe's share of the world's GDP was still one-third, and yet it had just 10 percent of the world's population. Moreover, the standard of living enjoyed by many Europeans, especially in Mediterranean countries, is light-years away from the nadir of 1945.[23] Such achievements should not be dismissed lightly.

Nonetheless, this book argues that it would be a grave error for America to go down the European economic path, and not simply because it would result in less economic prosperity. The moral and political cost, in terms of reduced freedom, is simply not worth it.

Qualifications and Objections

As noted, it would be a mistake to imagine that Europe and America are completely dissimilar in terms of their economic cultures. After all, the two continents have been economically intertwined ever since North America's colonization by European countries—primarily Britain, but also France, Spain, and the Netherlands.

It is not as if prominent features of market economies do not exist in Western Europe. Moreover, there are plenty of individuals within Europe itself who would prefer a more "American" economic culture to prevail in their own countries, and not all of them can be dismissed as fringy libertarians who have read too much Ayn Rand. Likewise, what we will call *dirigiste* policies (efforts by the government to directly manage the economy) and "neo-corporatist" ideas (practices and institutions often considered "European") have had a considerable impact upon the United States, the New Deal being perhaps the most prominent example.

But is it even possible to speak of a European economic model or economic culture? Surely, it might be said, there are enough differences between, say, Southern and Northern European economies to render talk of a European economic culture somewhat artificial. Indeed, throughout the 2000s and especially following the Great Recession, evidence mounted of significant and growing disparities between "Northern Europe" and "Southern Europe" in areas such as productivity, unemployment levels, debt levels, innovation, and exports, as the "South" ceased to catch up with, and increasingly fell behind, the "North."[24]

As anyone who has visited the Old World knows, to speak of "Europe" can be a misnomer. There are in fact many "Europes." Linguistically, Europe is a staggeringly diverse continent. In January 2007, the EU recognized twenty-three official and working languages. This list excluded the sixty-plus indigenous "regional and minority languages" spoken on a daily basis by more than forty million Europeans (Catalan being the most widely used of these, with Sorbian and Sardinian among the more exotic).[25]

Then there are the often very distinct histories of many European nations. The histories of France and Slovakia, for instance, are different in ways that the histories of Michigan and California are not. Regionally speaking, European political commentators such as Timothy Garton Ash have illustrated how we may legitimately speak about Western, Central, Central East, Scandinavian, Baltic, South, South East, Balkan, and Iberian regions of Europe as distinctive realities. It is even possible to refer to cultural differences between "Latin," "Germanic," "Nordic," and "Slavic" parts of Europe. Britain—with its long, unique, and at times ambiguous relationship with the rest of Europe (as well as its special relationship with America and continuing ties to former colonies such as Australia and New Zealand)—adds yet more complexity to an already rich mosaic.

All of these factors have played their part in creating resistance to closer political and economic integration in Europe. Charles de Gaulle's wariness of Britain's particular ties to America was one element in France's choice to twice veto Britain's entry into the European Economic Community (EEC) in the 1960s. In more recent times, unwillingness in significant sections of both elite and popular European opinion to dilute national sovereignty beyond a certain point has obstructed deeper pan-European unification.

Nor can one discount the significant dissimilarities between European countries in variations in economic institutions and patterns of development. Many of these flow from the differing influences of often disparate economic philosophies and histories. Long-standing differences between France and Germany in their conduct of monetary policy, for instance, owe something to France's extensive history of economic *dirigisme,* and also to Germany's unhappy memories of the social, political, and economic damage inflicted by the severe inflation of the 1920s.

Even these dissimilarities pale in comparison to the different economic legacies bequeathed by Communism to those European countries that were subjected to Marxist-Leninist regimes from the late 1940s until the Berlin Wall's fall in 1989. The visible effects can be observed by comparing economic conditions in the *lander* of the former East Germany with their West German counterparts.

And Yet There Remains a Europe

To varying degrees, all of these dissimilarities, divergences, differences, and divisions are real, and have implications for economic life in Europe. They should not, however, blind us to those realities that make it possible and legitimate to refer to a European economic model and European economic culture.

The *first* such reality are those influences in the Old Continent that transcend national, ethnic, and regional boundaries and which form a common cultural backdrop to contemporary European economic life. Linguistically speaking, there has always been a lingua franca in much of Europe, especially at the level of elites. For centuries, it was Latin. Between approximately 1700 and 1950, it was French. Today it is English.

Another cultural commonality—however much some Europeans may dislike it—is the indelible imprint left upon Europe by two thousand years of Christianity. This impact goes beyond religious belief and practice. Despite the real and important differences between Catholicism, Eastern Orthodoxy, and Protestantism, Christianity's unique integration of biblical faith, Jewish wisdom, Greek reason, and Roman law forged likewise unique intellectual, cultural, and institutional bonds between various European ethnic groups and nations. The idea of Christendom, for instance, had real political and legal manifestations that persisted until its crackup, following the rise of the nation-state, monarchical absolutism, and the religious schisms of the sixteenth century. Notwithstanding many European countries' currently low rates of formal religious practice, Christianity remains by far the majority faith to which most Europeans (even in deeply secularized nations such as Britain and Sweden) nominally adhere. As we will see, it also played a central part in shaping the two dominant approaches to economic life that have characterized European economic culture since the early Middle Ages.

Another element of common European cultural formation is the Enlightenment. Like Christianity, this was not a monolithic phenomenon. We can speak, for instance, of Scottish, English, French, and German enlightenments, some of which bequeathed very different economic legacies. It's also true that the origins of ideas promoted by many Enlightenment thinkers—the natural sciences, natural philosophy, mathematical inquiry, and the concern for utility—all predate the Enlightenment. That said, the impact of the enlightened intellectual movements that began emerging in the late seventeenth century was felt all across Europe. Today they continue to function as significant common cultural points of reference in European life.

The *second* reality is that, for all their differences, Europe's economies have been intimately intertwined for centuries. Intra-European trade did not have to wait for the formation of the EEC, following the signing of the Treaty of Rome by six Western European countries in 1957, to take off.

The *third* reality attesting to the existence of a European economic culture is the existence of the EU as an identifiable political, legal, and economic entity. Today's EU has two presidents, a foreign minister, a council, a commission, a parliament, a judiciary, a central bank, a civil service, a diplomatic corps, and a common currency. Many of these organizations possess considerable powers that can legally bind EU member states to the pursuance of specific political, economic, and legal goals.

Though, as chapter 4 demonstrates, the primary goal of some of these institutions—and the modern European experiment as a whole—has always been political unification, one way (if not the main means) for realizing this agenda has been through efforts to integrate Europe's economies. This has been pursued via a combination of (1) top-down *dirigiste* coordination by European-wide institutions and national governments, (2) the selective liberalization of different economic sectors across the EU, and (3) the adoption of particular social welfare and neo-corporatist policies at the EU, national, and regional levels. Though reflecting different and often contradictory aspects of European economic thinking and history, this combination has, for better or worse, encouraged a certain commonality, and even facilitated a high degree of what economists call "convergence" in economic conditions across much of the EU.[26]

But what perhaps, above all, makes it legitimate to treat Europe as a distinct political and economic entity is a *fourth* reality: that sizable numbers of Europeans, especially among Europe's political and intellectual classes, *want* Europe to be treated as a single economic unit. They *want* to promote an economic model and culture for Europe that differs in important respects from what they perceive to exist in America and the rest of the world.

In some instances, they will speak of this culture's superiority compared to that of America's. The late British historian Tony Judt famously claimed that the European social model "binds Europe together" in a way that makes it distinct from the "American way of life." Judt went on to argue that "The Anglo-American model with its cult of privatisation is not only ethically dysfunctional, but will soon be seen to be economically dysfunctional."[27] Though undoubtedly sharpened by the sense of crisis that permeated the last months of 2008, comments like those by Sarkozy and Steinbrück about the American economic system did not emerge from a cultural vacuum. They reflect many Europeans' sense that their economic culture is *distinct from* and *better than* what exists in America, especially in terms of its realization of values.

And so, for all these reasons, it is legitimate to speak of a European economic culture. For precision's sake, however, we primarily focus upon the EU, and even more particularly upon the economies of Western Europe not subject to Communism after 1945.

Within this set of countries, distinctions are often made between what are often called "core" economies (Germany or France) and "peripheral" nations (Greece, Portugal, or Ireland). "Core" versus "peripheral" is not so much about geography, but primarily about the size of one nation's economy compared to others.

Yet being a peripheral EU economy does not mean it is of marginal importance for the EU, or insignificant in telling us certain things about European economic culture. The panic throughout the entire EU induced in early 2010 by the escalating financial problems of Greece — a country that numbers approximately eleven million in an EU of almost 502 million people—illustrated that some European nations are not as marginal to the EU's overall economic well-being as we might imagine. In some instances, these peripheral nations also highlight significant problems associated with European economic culture.

A European in America

In the prologue to this book, the point was made that, culturally speaking, America is Europe's child. This truth, as well as the ongoing economic and political links between the United States and the European Union, will make developments in Europe a source of continuing fascination for Americans, no matter how important China and India might loom in the twenty-first century.

Nevertheless, the American-European mirror has never been a one-way reflection. European travelers to America have been observing and writing about the American Republic from its very beginning. Like America's Founding Fathers, many of these thinkers were acutely aware that while the United States had its roots in Europe, it also represented something new.

The first significant writer of this description was J. Hector St. John de Crèvecoeur, an eighteenth-century French aristocrat who settled in Orange County, New York, after serving in the French and Indian War. His *Letters from an American Farmer*, published first in London in 1782, portrayed the nascent American society as a distinct nation rather than a collection of British colonies. It helped to establish in many Europeans' imagination some of those characteristics regarded as distinctly "American": a zest for change, an indomitable restlessness, and a focused determination to bring under cultivation that which was previously wild and untamed. The implied contrast with European societies—stable, established, and full of tradition—was unspoken, but would undoubtedly have made an impression upon Crèvecoeur's readers.

But it was another Frenchman who did the most to capture for many Europeans the uniqueness of what has been called the American experiment in ordered liberty. On this occasion, part of his purpose in studying America concerned a desire to provide Europeans with insights into the character of their own political, social, and economic cultures. Once we accept that America is Europe's child, the inevitable question becomes: "And whose child is Europe?" This was always of central interest to that other, more famous French observer of America—perhaps *the* most insightful commentator on America ever—known to most people today simply by his surname: Tocqueville.

I

A Tale of Two Europes

2

Free Markets, Guilds, and the State

The European navigator is cautious about venturing onto the high seas. He sets sail only when the weather is inviting. If an unforeseen event occurs, he returns to port. At night he partly furls his sails, and when the ocean turns white with the approach of land, he slows his course and checks the sun.

The American neglects these precautions and braves these dangers. He sets sail while the storm still rages; by night as well as by day he spreads his full canvas to the wind; he repairs his storm-damaged ship while still under way; and when at last he comes to the end of his voyage, he continues to make for the coast at full speed as if he already has his port in sight.

—ALEXIS DE TOCQUEVILLE[1]

At eight o'clock on the evening of May 9, 1831, a French ship out of the port of Le Havre dropped anchor in the harbor of Newport, Rhode Island, en route to New York. On board was a short, frail-looking 25-year-old Frenchman who had been sent by his government to study the American penitentiary system. After thirty-eight days sailing the Atlantic in a poorly provisioned ship, most people would have wanted to rest and recuperate. The young man, from one of France's oldest aristocratic families, would have none of that. From almost the beginning of his 286 days in the New World, Alexis de Tocqueville displayed an apparently unquenchable thirst for knowledge about this society so different from that of his native France.

The fruit of Tocqueville's travels and reflection was borne four years later when the first volume of his *Democracy in America* was published, on January 23, 1835. It was immediately acclaimed as a masterpiece of social inquiry. Years later, the high and mighty of French society were still talking about the book. In 1848, for instance, King Louis Philippe I of France was engaged in endless discussions with various politicians in a futile attempt to prevent the overthrow of his throne during what later came to be called Europe's Year of Revolutions. Eventually, it was Tocqueville's turn to be summoned to a private interview with the king. To his surprise, Louis Philippe began the conversation with the words, "Since you're here, Monsieur de Tocqueville, I'd like you to tell me a little about America."[2]

Tocqueville was never quite sure why, in the midst of revolutionary turmoil, Louis Philippe suddenly wanted to talk about America. Perhaps the soon-to-be-deposed king sensed that America's story might provide clues to what was happening in his own country.

In this and the following two chapters, we reverse this comparison in order to explore another story: that of the development of European economic culture. For if Americans want to understand, say, why many Europeans insist that employees must be formally represented on the boards of private companies, or why other Europeans assume that state action should be the first means of addressing economic problems, they must first comprehend the deeper forces shaping economic culture in Western Europe over many centuries.

Though we are often reluctant to admit it, recency and relevance are not the same thing.

From the beginning of the Middle Ages until the present, Europe has been the scene of an ongoing clash between two sets of values, priorities, and institutions. One of these sets may be described as *market culture*. The other consists of those expectations and their organizational expressions that have been given a variety of names— guild, mercantilist, corporatist, social democratic—but that generally seek the same thing: the progressive realization of economic security through social organizations wielding political and legal power, backed up and guided by a state committed to a top-down coordination of economic life.

Between Two Worlds

It's not clear Tocqueville anticipated that his book about the young American republic would be greeted with such praise in France. One reason for *Democracy in America*'s success was that the book was, in its own way, as much about France as it was about America. It is easy to forget that Tocqueville was not writing for an American audience. His primary intended readership was France's political and social elite, and thus, by extension, the rest of 1830s continental Europe. They, he knew, would be struck by just how different the United States portrayed in *Democracy in America* was from their European world.

Today Tocqueville's book continues to be treated primarily as a work of political sociology. *Democracy in America*, however, is replete with economic observations. One of the most significant was Tocqueville's astonishment at "the spirit of enterprise"[3] that characterized much of the country. Americans, Tocqueville quickly realized, were "a commercial people."[4] The nation hummed with the pursuit of wealth and riches. Economic change was positively welcomed. "Almost all of them," Tocqueville scribbled in one of his notebooks, "are real industrial entrepreneurs."[5]

As a consequence, America's social structures—with the notable exception of the slave-holding states—were far more fluid than those of France. Hard work and meeting consumer demand was the path to economic success. Profit making was celebrated and encouraged, rather than treated as something best not discussed in polite company. Even bankruptcy, Tocqueville found, did not carry the same degree of social stigma as in continental Europe.[6] It was simply part of life in an economy that rewarded audacity, and indicative of a society marked by a profound restlessness of spirit. In fact, Tocqueville commented, if you had made your fortune in America and were content to do nothing more, you would be better off living in Europe![7]

Of course, it was not as if 1830s France was immune to the siren calls of commerce and trade. Throughout the 1830s and 1840s, France underwent the same industrialization occurring in much of Western Europe. The expression used to characterize the period—*enrichissez-vous!*—indicates that many Frenchmen were just as interested in acquiring wealth as Tocqueville's Americans. Indeed, the bedrock of King Louis Philippe's rule was France's wealthy, untitled middle class.

Plenty of Frenchmen, however, were unhappy with this state of affairs. On one end of the spectrum, many Frenchmen regarded a single-minded focus on the acquisition of wealth as somehow unworthy of *la grande nation* that had played such a prominent part in Europe for more than two centuries. At the other end was seething discontent among left-wing intellectuals and the emerging industrial working class with the growing economic inequality that seemed to follow industrialization.

Tocqueville himself was rather ambiguous about the desirability of this emerging commercial order. He was certainly attached to the institution of private property and the liberties associated with it—so much so that he had no hesitation in supporting the use of the French army to suppress the more revolutionary, explicitly socialist elements that helped overthrow Louis Philippe's regime in 1848.[8]

Nor was Tocqueville interested in returning to a lost economic past, or opposed in principle to economic growth and free enterprise.

But as one perceptive commentator on Tocqueville's economics, Richard Swedberg, points out, Tocqueville himself held mildly protectionist views. While he conceded the intellectual argument for free trade, Tocqueville was skeptical about the political prospects of advancing it, partly because he doubted that France could compete with Britain under conditions of free trade.[9] Another prominent Tocqueville scholar, Seymour Drescher, notes that Tocqueville's position on many economic questions was sometimes the exact opposite of prominent French free marketeers of the time, most notably the political economist and journalist Frédéric Bastiat.[10]

Economics, Corruption, and Social Disintegration

Tocqueville was also ill at ease with many of the political changes he associated with emerging capitalist societies in Europe. Eighteen years after the 1830 revolution that sent Louis Philippe's predecessor, King Charles X, into exile, Tocqueville wrote:

> In 1830, the triumph of the middle class was decisive and so complete that the narrow limits of the bourgeoisie encompassed all political powers, franchises, prerogatives, indeed the whole government, to the exclusion, in law, of all beneath it and, in fact, what had once been above it. Thus the bourgeoisie became not only the sole cultivator of society, but, one might say, its cultivator. It settled into every office, prodigiously increased the number of offices, and made a habit of living off the public Treasury almost as much as from its own industry.[11]

This is not the analysis of a proto-Marxist. Nor was Tocqueville a romantic restorationist hankering after the *ancien régime*. Rather, his concern was with the French middle class's use of state power to solidify its position, to lock out other social groups from political participation and economic opportunity, to utilize government offices as a form of patronage, and to live increasingly at others' expense. How different this was from Tocqueville's America, where the striving after wealth seemed far less associated with efforts to capture state power, let alone attempts to use the government to promote narrow sectional interests.

At the same time, Tocqueville was particularly interested in a subject that attracted increasing attention from across the political spectrum of mid-nineteenth-century France: the social effects of industrialization and the spread of commerce. Socialists celebrated the emergence of "pauperization" as providing fertile territory for wider revolutions; conservatives worried about it for the same reason. Though not opposed in principle to economic growth, the latter were especially disturbed by the breakdown of institutions such as guilds, which they believed had provided society with sufficient ballast to weather the effects of economic change.[12]

Industrial capitalism's emergence thus had more than economic implications. Tocqueville understood how it was helping to reconfigure the fault lines of French and European politics. For Europe, however, this was nothing new. Tensions about which habits, practices, and institutions should drive economic life have influenced European political and cultural life for centuries.

Prior to exploring this historical background, we need to make a detour that addresses a vital question relevant to all subsequent discussion: *Why* did the world's first capitalist economies, and the associated sustained growth in wealth, first emerge in Europe—especially Western Europe—rather than China, India, or Africa?

Why Europe?

The answers given to this question range from factors such as geography, financial entrepreneurship, Catholicism, the natural environment, technological innovations, disease, Protestantism, population growth, the Scottish Enlightenment, church-state rivalry, accidents of history, and the proliferation of small states to competition between nation-states. The discussion is further complicated by ongoing arguments about whether capitalism is essentially a product of modernity, or if its origins first crystallized and acquired momentum in the Middle Ages. There are also cause-and-effect disagreements between those who think that ideas have their own force and those who believe ideas largely reflect economic change.

Perhaps the most important point to keep in mind when considering these debates is the folly of looking for monocausal explanations. The economic historian Eric Jones, author of the influential 1981 book *The European Miracle*, prudently advises that there is "no single explanatory key"[13] to Europe's economic success. "I found none in my researches," Jones writes, "and do not believe that such a complicated set of processes can be accounted for so neatly."[14] Those who think they have found the "trigger," or a "master variable," Jones believes, tend to decide what it is beforehand, construct a theory around it, and then find as many supporting facts as possible.[15]

Instead, Jones stresses the importance of paying attention to very long-term developments in assessing the impact of ideas, the growth of institutions, technological change, the effects of environment, and ongoing interactions between all these factors when seeking to explain capitalism's emergence in Western Europe. In Jones's view, the most likely answers are to be found between what he calls "simple materialism" and the undiluted history of ideas.[16]

Jones focuses on the period between 1400 and 1800, primarily because his interest is in exploring the period of acceleration during which Europe's economic growth began to quickly outpace that of China, India, and the Middle East. In terms of what might be called the simple material factors, Jones lists the following as crucial elements at work during this period:

- Integrated Markets: Markets in commodities, but more importantly land and especially labor, became integrated.

This helped to dissolve cultural and political impediments to development, innovation, and growth.

- Location: Western Europe was located a long way from the central Asian epicenters of great military invasions, such as those of Genghis Khan, that at different times devastated large swaths of India, China, and the Middle East.
- Location: Western Europe was conveniently situated near some of the richest seas and most naturally resourced parts of the world: the Atlantic, Africa, and the Americas.
- Capital Accumulation: European marriage patterns permitted the long-term amassing of capital, which helped fuel rising living standards.
- Innovation: Europe had a persistent tendency for tinkering, inventing, and innovating.
- Competition: The persistence of internal and external competitive pressures made resource allocation in post-1400 Europe more efficient than anywhere else in the world.
- Peace . . . : Despite very real external threats (such as from the Ottoman Empire) and internal European disputes that turned into war, European states were relatively good at defending themselves from military aggression.
- . . . and Easy Taxes: During the Middle Ages, a struggle began to curb predatory governmental taxes and arbitrary power that was ultimately successful. Contrary to historical mythology, Western European rulers were never able to do "whatever they wanted," even during the age of eighteenth-century absolutism. While there were many instances of rulers breaking their own laws, Jones stresses these were exceptions, rather than the norm.
- Political Centralization . . . : The emergence of nation-states, Jones suggests, reduced the potential for the exercise of growth-killing arbitrary power by lesser lords.

- ... and Political Decentralization: It was highly important that the number of European nation-states was never reduced to just one, despite the efforts of the likes of Emperor Charles V, King Louis XIV, and Napoleon I. A competitive political environment was maintained within Europe after the fall of the Western Roman Empire, unlike the vast centralized empires that emerged at different times in China, Asia, India, and the Middle East. When combined with relative freedom of movement between European nation-states and the economic reality that more and more people could simply opt to leave a jurisdiction if they became unhappy with tax rates or frustrated with inefficient justice systems, the effects were twofold: rulers had incentives to improve their institutional competitiveness; and they became more open to advice on how to rule.

- Disaster Response and Public Goods: Europe came to outclass the rest of the world in the policies it put in place to avert or cope with disasters ranging from disease to famine. This reflected the willingness and ability of European states to assume responsibility for what economists call "public goods": those goods from the use of which no one can be excluded, such as the administration of justice (including the enforcement of contracts and protection of property rights), national defense, and public works such as roads and bridges.[17]

Some Qualifications

Jones's list is compelling. While some have quibbled with the saliency of various factors, it remains a good checklist for any society, European or otherwise, interested in economic growth and maintaining a competitive economy. There are, however, four important contextual qualifications that should be made to Jones's picture.

First, the conditions he lists did not suddenly appear *ex nihilo* in the early 1400s. Jones stresses that they began slowly emerging as early as the high Middle Ages.[18] Jones also points to relatively conclusive findings illustrating that, in strict growth terms, Europe began taking off as early as 1000 A.D.[19]

This conclusion is shared by economic historians from different schools of thought. In their history of business in the medieval world, Edwin Hunt and James Murray comprehensively demonstrate how, through the efforts of merchants, lawyers, rulers, clergy, bankers, and entrepreneurs, medieval Europe not only reduced the incidence of famine, disease, and war; it also developed ideas, technologies, and organizational and financial techniques that produced the surplus capital, purchasing power, innovation, and institutions that laid the groundwork for Europe's accelerated economic expansion in the sixteenth century.[20]

In a similar fashion, the medieval historian Robert Lopez goes so far as to describe the economic changes of the Middle Ages as nothing less than a Commercial Revolution. The growth of population in tenth-century Western Europe, Lopez argues, necessitated an expansion of agriculture and the development of new agricultural techniques. This provided enough in the way of surpluses for commercial activity with a strong profit orientation to undergo rapid development, especially in northern Italy. The increased pace of market exchange led in turn to the emergence of more convenient financial tools, including more sophisticated contractual arrangements for sharing risks and profits, a refined banking system, and most importantly, easier means of credit.

All this was brought to a temporary halt in the mid-fourteenth century by the outbreak of protracted wars in Western Europe and, above all, the Black Death, which instigated a temporary demographic collapse. Fortunately, Lopez notes, the Commercial

Revolution's foundations were sufficiently resilient for the primary conditions for accelerated growth to remain in place.[21]

The *second* qualification to Jones's analysis is that none of the factors he identifies emerged seamlessly, without opposition, or unaccompanied by competing ideas, institutions, and practices that inhibited economic growth. The temptation for governments to try to influence investment and innovation—and not always in the interests of growth—is hardly new. Hunt and Murray illustrate that this tendency gathered pace in the mid-sixteenth century, following many European governments' concerted efforts to exert more control over economic life.[22]

This reality is especially relevant to our *third* qualification. As Jones cautions, we need to remember that "Economies are politically embedded, and this is decisive for the way they perform."[23] Political embeddedness means more than simply the presence of governments. It also means that any given economic setting—including the factors listed by Jones himself—is influenced by a range of value commitments, ideas, and movements. The sociologist Rodney Stark has argued it is impossible to understand Western European capitalism's development without acknowledging the commitment to reason and progress espoused by Christianity from its very beginning. Contrary to popular Dark Ages mythology, Stark argues, these Christian commitments were indispensable to numerous intellectual, cultural, political, and economic breakthroughs in premodern Europe.[24]

The *fourth* qualification is that "political embeddedness" does not mean that all the values and institutions permeating economic life are necessarily compatible with each other. The coexistence of very different ideas and practices in a given culture can result in an economy being propelled in often contradictory directions.

And herein lies the story of two distinct European economic cultures. Both enjoy some common roots, assumed concrete form in the medieval period, and continue to influence European economic life today. For as much as many of us like to imagine that the past is the past, the past exercises a grip on our economic imaginations far more than we realize.

Market Culture, Guild Culture

When writing about economic culture, Edmund Phelps presents two ideal types between which, he suggests, contemporary Western economies oscillate. The first is a private-ownership system that stresses entrepreneurship, innovation, and the willingness to match new people and ideas with financial capital. The second is a private-ownership system that tends to limit innovation to established entities, values long-term relationships between recognized businesses and long-standing financial firms, emphasizes mediation over competition, tries to compensate for weak entrepreneurship with top-down coordination, and is underpinned by a strongly egalitarian streak in the sense of equal outcomes.[25]

Being ideal types, there is no economic culture in Europe or North America that conforms exactly to either of these models. As ideal types, however, we encounter echoes of them in two economic cultures that first emerged side by side as distinct entities in medieval Europe.

The most comprehensive work on this subject is by the English sociologist and historian Antony Black. Drawing on sources ranging from economic history and political and theological texts to medieval legal documentation, Black illustrates how two sets of values and institutions—guild-corporatist culture and market culture—emerged throughout Europe with varying degrees of strength and weakness, always in tension and never isolated from each other.

Guilds and the Medieval World

Though we often associate guilds with medieval societies, Black observes that the ultimate roots of medieval guilds lie in mutual aid societies that were already present in pre-Christian Roman times, but which gradually came to embrace an unending variety of mutual protection and insurance functions during the slow-motion collapse of the Roman Empire. Over time, they became Christianized, and more closely associated with crafts and other related forms of economic activity.[26]

In value terms, medieval guilds were dominated by the Christian emphasis upon brotherly love. This was interpreted as bestowing upon the guild's members certain rights and duties that fostered a particular understanding of justice in the sense of *security* for the guild's members, and an emphasis upon *equality of outcome*. As Black writes, this produced an economic way of life focused upon

> the duty to produce work of a certain standard and the right
> to secure employment. The chief means to do this was the
> restriction on craft entry. Rules stipulating maximum hours and
> so on comprised a large part of guild regulations. . . . The main
> purpose of the corporate legal rights claimed by guilds was to
> ensure a secure livelihood. In this way their sense of justice led to
> a belief in approximate equality of output and of the returns due
> to all craft members; their main opponent here was the merchant-
> capitalist . . . who, by employing more men and working them
> harder, undercut their price and ruined their livelihood.[27]

Immediate economic, legal, and political effects flowed from these commitments. It resulted in guilds seeking to establish monopolies over their particular trades in a given area, efforts to fix prices by insulating them from market competition, centralized approaches to deciding wage levels, and the spread of negative attitudes toward businesses owned by independent entrepreneurs, which might undermine a guild's monopoly.[28] In these respects, Lopez points out, the activities of medieval guilds increasingly resembled certain behavioral features of modern cartels and labor unions.[29]

Legally speaking, medieval guilds invested considerable energy in attempting to secure formal legal status as corporate entities whose choices and preferences would be enforced by law. To this extent, Lopez argues, guilds gradually shifted away from their original religious and social priorities and became more focused on the promotion of "mere collective self-interest." They subsequently sought to establish themselves as privileged corporations exercising monopolies over parts of the economy, and aggressively promoted protectionist policies. By the fourteenth century, some of the more powerful guilds in Italy and Flanders had achieved partial control of regional and city governments, and were using their political muscle to the disadvantage of consumers, individual merchants, and members of smaller, less powerful guilds.[30]

These developments were complemented by the efforts of a number of contemporary intellectuals to integrate the idea of guilds as "corporate bodies" into an entire theory of a corporate state. Chief among them was Marsilius of Padua, who is most known for his intellectual backing of the subordination of the church to the state. But Marsilius also sought to develop the idea of the state as a body or "corporation of citizens" in which the ethos of mutual aid prevailed, and at the head and center of which was the secular ruler. The parts of the body (*corpus*) included different occupational categories and functional group; guilds consequently featured prominently in Marsilius's thought. He even believed they merited their own place in the legislature.[31]

The Market Challenge

Despite the spread of guild-corporatist culture throughout medieval Europe, it did not achieve dominance throughout the continent. It almost immediately encountered a rival set of ideas and practices. Black lists the values central to this *market culture* as

first, personal security in the sense of freedom from the arbitrary
passions of others. And freedom from domination in general.
This involves freedom (or security) of the person from violence,
and of private property from arbitrary seizure. But these . . . can
only be maintained if legal process is credible and successfully
enforced as an alternative to physical violence, in settlement of
disagreements, and in redressing wrongs committed by violence.
This leads to the notion of legal rights. . . . both in the sense of
the right to sue in court on equal terms with everyone else—legal
equality—and in the sense of claims, for example, to property,
recognized and upheld by the law.[32]

Some of the intellectual influences underpinning market culture came from medieval writers who had read the Roman philosopher Cicero's book *De Officiis* [*On Duties*]. One of the most widely
perused texts in medieval Europe, its pre-Christian author underscored the notion that to violate someone's property was to do enormous damage to the social order.

But Black goes to some lengths to demonstrate that market culture's stress on personal liberty as profoundly valuable came straight
from Christianity.[33] The Christian faith stressed that humans had
been liberated from sin, not just as a race, but individually as well.
Combined with the church's stress upon mankind's free will—a
theme constantly underlined by medieval theologians—and equal
dignity, a powerful cultural and political dynamic was created that
was almost irresistible.

In economic terms, this translated into many things: freedom to
create, freedom of association, freedom of exchange, and freedom to
contract. The notion of equal dignity also gave powerful grounding
to the idea of equality before the law. Growing legal recognition
of these liberties and protections encouraged the legitimacy of

relatively free-floating economic relationships, as distinct from the more communal types of connections encouraged by guilds and corporatist thought. Medieval market culture also derived support from the prohibitions in the Ten Commandments, which in their absolute condemnation of stealing, murder, lying, and unfaithfulness, highlighted the essential *wrongness* of *arbitrary* behavior.

Another Christian contribution to the growth of market liberties and practices sprang from the epic medieval clash between church and state known as the Investiture Controversy. At the core of this eleventh-century debate was an argument about who appointed bishops—the church or the monarch. The church's freedom from state control had always been implicit to the Christian faith. The famous injunction "Repay to Caesar what belongs to Caesar and to God what belongs to God" (Luke 20:25, New American Bible) had shattered the inseparability of religious beliefs and state that prevailed in the pagan world, and effectively de-divinized the state.

Once the church's liberty (or *libertas ecclesiae*) from the control of secular rulers had been formally accepted, the application of the principle to other spheres of life could not be stopped. If the church was free, many asked, then why should not other groups and even individuals enjoy similar freedom under the law, and liberty from excessive government or lordly control?

The emergence and proliferation of these ideas in many sectors of European economic and political life could not help but give a particular flavor to the Commercial Revolution. Certain rights concerning the free trade of privately-owned goods began to receive formal legal recognition in twelfth- and thirteenth-century civil and canon law. By the thirteenth century, the willingness throughout England to exercise legally recognized liberties to buy and sell property had become so widespread, facilitated such low transaction costs in the exchange of goods, and encouraged such relatively easy capital formation that the historian Alan Macfarlane has described this society as "an open, mobile, market-orientated nation."[34]

Overlap and Tensions

When thinking about these two European economic cultures, we should avoid oversimplification. In day-to-day medieval life, market ideas and institutions overlapped with those associated with guild-corporatist culture. Guilds were not opposed to profit or private property. Nor did independent merchants and bankers believe there was something intrinsically wrong with people forming fraternities. Even in Marsilius's corporatist theory of political order, free economic exchanges were not forbidden and the ruler was by no means absolute.

The two cultures also varied in their degree of impact upon different parts of Europe. Guilds were never especially strong in England. In parts of Germany, by contrast, they exercised considerable influence.

But blending and overlap could not disguise the fact that tensions existed. Medieval theologians, lawyers, and bishops were unafraid, usually in the name of liberty and equality before the law, to challenge the guilds' sway over large parts of economic life.[35] Theologians—especially those trained in the scholastic tradition associated with the most influential of medieval thinkers, St. Thomas Aquinas—did not regard guilds as morally significant communities in the way that they did the family or the church. Nor were they slow to point out the merits of fiscal impartiality or the damage done to consumers by restrictive guild practices. Aquinas and other scholastics assailed price-fixing, restrictive labor practices, and economically monopolistic tendencies on the part of anyone—merchant, guild, or state—as instances of exploitation, as facilitating artificial scarcities of goods and services, and as violations of liberty and the commandment of love.

One of their major targets was guilds. These were explicitly criticized for such practices by scholastic thinkers as early as the first decades of the thirteenth century.[36]

Not surprisingly, the guilds fought back, as part of a general reaction against the emergence of market culture and competitive economic pressures. For example, the guilds tightened their regulations to forbid people from choosing to work overtime; many joined with town governments to forbid especially skilled craftsmen from migrating to cities where they might reasonably expect to earn more.[37]

From Markets and Guilds to Mercantilism and Absolutism

As the Middle Ages gave way to the early modern period, cooperation between guilds and the state intensified, and shifted the balance of European economic culture away from market values and institutions. Much of the change was facilitated by the increasing economic role assumed by the state throughout Europe. This in turn is associated with the theory and practice of what came to be called "absolutism."

Today the word *absolutism* tends to imply tyranny, or arbitrary or despotic government. Yet the age of absolutism, which lasted from about 1600 until 1800, was something rather different. Few monarchs described as absolutist could literally do whatever they wanted. They remained bound by certain legal constraints. Economically speaking, they were limited by financial realities. Even personifications of absolutism like Prussia's most famous king and military genius, Frederick the Great, were acutely aware they could demand only so much from their subjects if they wanted to avoid popular and elite rebellion. The lesson of what happened to King Charles I of England, beheaded in 1649 at the end of his long struggle with Parliament, was not lost on monarchical audiences.

Absolutism is better understood as a theory and system of government having particular implications for economic life. Part of its early legitimation rested on the notion of the divine right of kings (a doctrine, incidentally, never accepted by the Catholic Church). Absolutism was also closely associated with the rise of the nation-state and the modern concept of sovereignty, which preceded the Reformation and accelerated following the schism that split Western Christendom in the sixteenth century.[38]

What, then, were some of the practical manifestations of absolutist government? Looking at eighteenth-century absolutist regimes, the following characteristics can be identified:

- The consolidation of political sovereignty and power in the monarchy, the diminishment of feudal powers and autonomies exercised by the aristocracy and the church, and the emasculation and subordination of other sources of authority, such as legislatures or judiciaries.
- The implementation of reforms that fused and streamlined laws, often in codified form.
- The establishment of state bureaucracies and professional armies.
- The diminishment of consents previously required before the state could raise existing taxes or implement new taxes.
- The closer regulation of communities and occupational groups by the centralized state.

The dominant motif underlying all these developments and ambitions was a *centralized* approach to creating order and addressing social and economic ills. Eighteenth-century absolutist thought repeatedly claimed that centralization of political power in the state was *the* path to a more efficient and prosperous society.[39]

While there was something distinctly new about this absolutism, it also drew upon guild-corporatist ideas and organizations surviving from the medieval period. The foremost theorist of royal absolutism, the sixteenth-century political philosopher Jean Bodin, specifically integrated guilds and other nonfamilial, nongovernmental organizations into his vision of the modern absolutist state.

These "colleges," as Bodin called them, were important, he argued, because they fostered mutual aid beyond the family, promoted stability, and helped develop a consensus of thought and action within society. Consistent, however, with the absolutist insistence upon centralization, Bodin argued that all such organizations required the king's approval, for part of their function, he maintained, was to support the exercise of royal power.[40]

In economic terms, absolutism did not seek to abolish market institutions such as private property and contracts. It did involve significantly constraining them so they could be more easily directed toward realizing state objectives. As absolutist rulers built and consolidated the nation-state's power (especially in order to enhance its capabilities to wage war), the government gradually assumed a more significant part in economic life—sometimes directly, and sometimes through guilds and other colleges.

The name given by Adam Smith to the economic system associated with absolutism (though, to be fair, it was also adopted by non-absolutist regimes) was the *mercantile system*. The essence of mercantilism was the practice of embedding private commercial activity in a web of state direction. This included the extensive imposition of tariffs upon imports, subsidizing exports, and creating government monopolies on particular trade or products that could then be sold or leased to groups of merchants. Mercantilism also manifested itself in the forced cartelization of some industries by the state, or laws requiring that everyone involved in certain trades join one of the state-authorized guilds.

Mercantilism reached its zenith in the absolutist France of Louis XIV, especially under his famous master of finances, Jean-Baptiste Colbert. *Colbertisme*, as it came to be called, involved systematically regulating virtually all aspects of economic life. Its means for doing so included protectionism against foreign imports (sometimes to the point of prohibition); the state's subsidizing of entire domestic industries (such as glass manufacturing) from scratch; according monopoly privileges (such as for lace manufacturing) to small groups of merchants; placing limits on the ability of skilled laborers to migrate in search of new opportunities; establishing an entire network of bureaucrats (*les intendants*) to monitor and enforce the growing list of state regulations; promulgating literally thousands of directives stipulating how products were to be manufactured; establishing overseas colonies; and even occasionally forbidding the use and export of new technologies that might result in intensified competition.[41]

Guilds were part and parcel of *colbertisme* inasmuch as they served as a major means for controlling the labor market, discouraging "unauthorized" innovation and entrepreneurship, keeping the size of most businesses small, and generally limiting the scale and depth of competition. They thus were among the major beneficiaries of mercantilism. Those merchants who were fortunate enough to secure a legal monopoly on a trade or product also benefited from artificially high prices and the absence of internal and foreign competition. Politically speaking, mercantilism helped the state to consolidate its power, provided endless opportunities for new revenue (not to mention numerous possibilities for state officials to use their office to secure bribes), and above all, helped to establish the government as the center of all major political and economic patronage.

No doubt, many monarchs and civil servants in seventeenth- and eighteenth-century Europe sincerely believed mercantilist policies were the best means of growing and strengthening their countries' economic position. But we should not discount the degree of self-interest at work. The path to economic success in mercantilist economies did not lie in innovation, competitiveness, or making profits through providing consumers with what they wanted in a cost-effective way. Rather, economic advancement was a matter of becoming close to government officials and other sources of state patronage in order to obtain the types of licenses needed to engage in particular economic practices. In 1771, for example, the French metal industry was dominated by just 601 investors. Of these, fifty-five were members of the clergy and 305 were aristocrats[42]—two of the elite groups in *ancien régime* absolutist France whose legally privileged status was to be swept aside seventeen years later in the upheaval and violence of the French Revolution.

And Back to Markets

By the mid-eighteenth century, mercantilist systems had begun to break down. In part, this reflected an awareness that mercantilist policies, with their emphasis upon establishing monopolies on trade with different regions of the world, had contributed to wars between the European powers as they sought to wrestle such monopolies away from each other. Britain's political leaders were particularly conscious that mercantilist policies had helped spark the revolt of the thirteen colonies in North America.

The difficulty and cost in enforcing the mercantilist system also accelerated its demise. No matter how formidable the obstacles, smugglers were adept at evading customs barriers. Moreover, despite the opportunities they accorded for the state to strengthen its financial power, mercantilist policies were never able to generate sufficient revenue for nation-states such as France or Britain to project their military power across Europe and the globe for extended periods of time, or for Spain or Portugal to pay the costs of maintaining their enormous empires.

But ideas also played a role in mercantilism's demise. The case for market-oriented policies was never quite extinguished, and sometimes found a home in unsuspected places. Moral and economic arguments in favor of free trade, low taxes, reduced public expenditures, and market-determined prices were developed, albeit unsystematically, by Spanish Catholic theologians writing in the sixteenth and seventeenth centuries—the very summit of the Spanish empire's embrace of mercantilist practices.[43]

In late eighteenth-century France, the economic school known to history as the *physiocrats* argued for the diminishment of tariffs and other mercantilist practices, which they saw as discouraging hard work and innovation. Their ideas had some influence upon Anne-Robert-Jacques Turgot, who served as finance minister under the ill-fated Louis XVI. Overcoming enormous opposition from palace courtiers, the state bureaucracy, and favored merchants, Turgot successfully established free trade in grain, and abolished a series of regulations that endowed guilds with legal privileges. Significantly, Turgot prefaced the edicts abolishing these regulations with a bold statement of every person's right to work without restriction—a clear assertion of the value of liberty against guild priorities.[44]

It was in Britain, however, that the moral and intellectual case for market economic culture was made with particular force. Britain had been among the first to embrace a mercantilist path, with the passing of the Navigation Act of 1651 and the Staple Act of 1663, both of which imposed strict regulations upon trade between England, her colonies, and continental Europe.

Yet mercantilism proved harder to realize in Britain than in some other European nations. The strength of its common-law system created obstacles to the centralized imposition of policies. It helped that England's extremely influential chief justice, Sir Edward Coke, viewed guilds as monopolies and actively sought to diminish their restrictive labor practices, not least by claiming such practices were inconsistent with the natural liberty of all the Crown's subjects. The fact that the Crown had sought to impose royal monopolies on trades and practices as an alternative source of revenue to parliament helped to link mercantilism with absolutism in many Englishmen's minds.[45]

Nevertheless, few would question that Adam Smith's *The Wealth of Nations* played *the* most important role in intellectually undermining the case for mercantilism, and providing economic and moral arguments in favor of market freedoms and institutions. Part of the intellectual power of Smith's argument against mercantilism involved his compelling case for the mutually beneficial effects of free trade. Nor did Smith hesitate to underscore the ways in which mercantilist policies benefited established interests (such as merchants who held monopolies and licenses, government officials, and the state itself)—those who might be called *insiders*—at the expense of the liberties, opportunities, and potential prosperity of the *outsiders* created by mercantilist arrangements: consumers, entrepreneurs, low-skilled laborers, and potential migrants to and from Britain.

Smith was deeply critical of guilds and other corporate bodies being accorded legal privileges. Part of Smith's objection was economic: Guilds allowed their members to escape the discipline of consumer demand and kept wages, prices, and profits artificially high. But he also considered such institutions *unjust,* insofar as they undermined the ability of individuals to offer their labor freely in the marketplace. In other words, the guilds' emphasis on security, stability, and equal outcomes for their members came at the cost of other people's liberty.

Thus it was that the gradual collapse of mercantilist practices from the mid-eighteenth century onward, accompanied by the spread of Smith's ideas, helped revive market institutions. Throughout the nineteenth century monopolies, tariffs, and regulations were gradually abolished in Britain. Restrictions on immigration and the export of technology were lifted. In continental Europe, the internal customs barriers between most German states were removed in 1833. Ironically, much of the initial impetus for this particular economic liberalization came from Prussia—the war-fighting North German nation that, under its warrior-king Frederick the Great, had been the eighteenth-century absolutist-mercantilist-militarist state par excellence.

The repeal of Britain's Corn Laws in 1849 marked the next major symbolic step toward more widespread market arrangements throughout Europe. Thirteen years later, Prussia and France concluded a tariff-reducing commercial treaty. During the same period, the guilds that had hitherto occupied a considerable part of Western Europe's economic landscape (particularly in Germany) largely disappeared, especially after the Prussian-dominated North German Confederation abolished the power of guilds to impose restrictions on occupational liberty, in 1868. Their demise was accentuated by technological changes that made it much harder for craft-based production to compete with the mass production of industrialization.

But Corporatism Rebounds

Looking back on this period of economic transformation, John Maynard Keynes marveled at the economic benefits that the industrial revolution, easy migration, free trade, and economic growth bestowed across much of Europe. Yet, while World War I helped end what some regard as economic liberalism's golden age, the temporary triumph of markets had not exorcised an attachment to guild and corporatist values from European economic culture.

In 1873, the new German Empire endured a financial and commercial crash. This was followed by a severe industrial recession, and a downturn in German agriculture's profitability in the wake of competition from American farmers. Many economists, politicians, and business leaders subsequently became skeptical of the benefits of competition and free trade. When Imperial Germany's first chancellor, Otto von Bismarck, introduced customs duties on iron and grain imports in 1879, he was taking advantage of growing dissatisfaction throughout Germany with economic liberalization.[46] This protectionist shift was accompanied by Bismarck's attempts to establish a council of corporatist organizations, designed to represent the interests of a range of business and occupational groups to the government. Though this attempt at co-option failed, it underscored Bismarck's intention to use such organs as tools to centralize more power in the executive wing of government.

More broadly, a reaction against the spread of market values had been underway for several decades. The promotion of values and institutions associated with guilds was taken up by trade unions, friendly societies, co-operatives, and associated political movements such as the German Social Democratic Party. These organizations attracted people dissatisfied with various aspects of nineteenth-century capitalism. Obviously, the type of work and technologies employed in factories differed greatly from the craft world of the guilds. Nonetheless, the ethos of groups such as unions closely paralleled that of guilds: brotherhood, solidarity, mutual aid, and opposition to economic liberalization. The influence of Marxism added a class struggle to this mixture that had not been quite as explicit or potent with the guilds.

An important related development was the rise of economic cartelization in key European economies, particularly Germany. Some businesses, like the iron and steel industry, sought to respond to competitive pressures by agreeing among themselves to fix the price of a given product rather than let it be determined via free competition. The point was to preserve each cartel member's share of the market and block outsiders from entry. Not surprisingly, this was subject to legal challenge. Eventually, however, the practice of cartelization received legal approval from the German Supreme Court in 1897, and consequently accelerated throughout the German economy.

Another contributing factor in the decline of market culture's influence was the emergence of corporatism as a distinct political philosophy and program. The intellectual roots of this movement varied; it drew upon the writings of individuals ranging from the German philosopher G. W. F. Hegel to the French sociologist Émile Durkheim. It also attracted support from sections of both the political Left and the political Right. Corporatist thinkers included socialists, Christians, nationalists, liberals, progressives, and even fascists. The basic outlines of the corporatist program may be summarized as follows:

- Private enterprise and the market economy are useful, especially as barriers to collectivism. However, they promote excessive disparities of wealth, undermine community, diminish security, create social instability, and impoverish sections of the population. In short, they undermine the value of solidarity—a word frequently used in corporatist circles from the nineteenth century onward.
- Private property and free exchange must be imbedded in an economic, legal, and political context that coordinates the building of consensus and fosters mutual assistance throughout society.
- Each industry and profession should have organizations that embrace all those who work in it. These organizations have the primary responsibility for deciding wages and conditions, and providing workers with a voice in management decisions. This helps foster some mutual identity of interests on the part of the members.
- The primary place for resolving disputes within industries should be within these corporate groups, if necessary with the assistance of special industrial tribunals that could issue binding resolutions.
- The activities of all corporate groups should be coordinated by state agencies, which accord legal recognition to these groups.

To be sure, there were variations on the corporatist agenda, particularly concerning the precise relationship between the state and these organizations. Some corporatists believed that corporatism logically extended to the development of separate, representative chambers of employers and workers who would consult and work with governments on a regular basis. Others insisted these corporate bodies should be coordinated directly by the state in order to achieve particular predetermined national goals.

Antony Black points out that corporatist theories first gained traction in societies with strong guild traditions, such as Germany. In England, the word "guild" was regularly invoked by scholars promoting recognizably corporatist ideas. While some corporatist theorists went to significant lengths to distinguish their program from the old guild system, the parallels between their ideas and medieval and early modern guilds were remarkable. The values that corporatists sought to embody in economic institutions were virtually identical to those of the guilds. Corporations, Émile Durkheim wrote, were more than just economic configurations: They were also about trying to "lead one and the same moral life together" and concerned with "living in communion."[47] And, like the guilds of old, most corporatist thinkers stressed the importance of the state granting a special legal status to the various occupational and professional groups. In some circles, there was even talk of the "co-sovereignty of the Guilds and the State."[48]

The gulf between corporatist ideas and economic reality in pre-World War II Western Europe varied. In countries such as interwar Austria, considerable effort was made to build corporatist principles into most aspects of economic life. In Mussolini's Italy, however, the emphasis was less upon reorganizing the economy along corporatist lines than upon using corporatist structures to deepen the Fascist regime's political control.

But perhaps the true significance of corporatism, along with the rise of trade unions, co-operatives, cartelization, and (as will become apparent) modern European welfare states, is that it expressed an abiding desire across much of Europe to establish protocols, institutions, and laws that gave practical effect to guild-corporatist values. In some cases, the intention was that these should more or less obviate market values and institutions. In practice, however, they encouraged the rise of corporatist practices and organizations that overlapped with those habits and formations that stressed personal liberty, entrepreneurship, and legal equality. All of this was steadily overlaid with varying degrees of state coordination—a process enhanced by the state's growing intervention into the economy, especially during and after World War I.

On the Brink of Europe

However one looks at the pattern of ideas and institutions that constituted European economic culture between the Middle Ages and World War II, we see various points of convergence and divergence with American arrangements as observed by Tocqueville.

Perhaps the most significant commonality was the presence of market values and institutions on both continents. The differences lay in the relative absence from the social and economic landscape of Tocqueville's America of highly centralized governments, strong civil service bureaucracies, and the powerful entities and ideas that sought to explicitly promote guild-corporatist values and institutions through a combination of political pressure and legal sanctions.

But as we begin to reflect upon present-day American economic culture, questions may have already begun to emerge in readers' minds. Don't certain aspects of corporatism remind us of particular features of the twenty-first-century American economy? Could it be that a type of neo-mercantilism is alive and well in contemporary America? Doesn't even brief reflection upon twentieth-century American history suggest that America has experienced persistent efforts to incorporate state-centralizing impulses into its economic life? Aren't there some American businesses which regularly seek to secure legislation that enables them to hamper real and potential competitors? Don't similar guild-like tendencies manifest themselves in the behavior of some American trade unions?

Before moving fully to compare Europe with America, we first need to develop our broad historical account of the emergence of the "two Europes." The next chapter demonstrates how the trajectory of postwar Western European economies continued to reflect the influences of—and tensions between—the two economic cultures portrayed here, as well as concerted intellectual and government efforts to forge a type of hybrid out of the two traditions: what is widely known today as the European social model.

3

Toward the European Social Model

The argument today is not at all that between laissez-faire and economic planning. . . . The conflict is a different one. One side . . . is of the opinion that the state must influence, or even directly establish, the forms and institutional framework within which the economy should work. . . . Others believe that the state must not just establish the framework, but must influence the day-to-day working of the economy on the basis of central planning.

—WALTER EUCKEN

Very few Europeans recognize his name today. Yet much of contemporary Western Europe owes its present-day prosperity to an obscure anti-Nazi German economist who, despite remaining in Germany after Hitler's rise to power in 1933, somehow managed to survive World War II. Walter Eucken was a primary intellectual architect of the "economic miracle" that took West Germany from economic ground zero in 1948 to being postwar Europe's economic strongman within ten years. Today, a united Germany is the EU's foremost economic power, and its strength and resilience owe much to the foundations established by Eucken and a small band of fellow free-market economists in the years immediately following the war.

But despite the success of the market reforms introduced into West Germany in 1948, Eucken had no illusions that either his ideas or the views associated with other prominent European free mar-keteers (such as his fellow German Wilhelm Röpke, the Austrian Friedrich August von Hayek, or the Frenchman Jacques Rueff) had achieved intellectual ascendency in Western Europe. On the con-trary, Eucken, Röpke, Hayek, and Rueff knew that their economic positions were those of an often marginalized minority. Anything that smacked of "capitalism" in postwar Europe was regarded with considerable suspicion by the Left, and also by many on the Right.

To most Americans, the word *capitalism* isn't especially contro-versial. Prominent center-left American politicians including Bill Clinton have no hesitation in speaking positively about capitalism. But in Europe, particularly Western Europe, capitalism carries very different connotations.

The former center-right French president, Jacques Chirac, once famously informed his fellow Europeans that "*Le libéralisme, ce serait aussi désastreux que le communisme*" ("Liberalism would be as disastrous as communism").[1] By "liberalism," Chirac did not have in mind what most Americans associate with the word: extensive government economic interventionism à la Franklin Roosevelt or Lyndon Johnson. Rather, he meant what many Americans under-stand by "capitalism": an economic system that stresses entrepre-neurship, free exchange, free trade, and a government that confines its economic activities to upholding private property rights and con-tracts, the provision of public works, and fulfilling minimal welfare responsibilities in a context governed by rule of law.

To equate the workings of such an economy with the intrinsic brutality of Stalinist command economies, or even the dysfunctional state-managed economies of Communist Eastern Europe, could be easily dismissed as another unfortunate instance of Chiracian hyperbole. Chirac, however, is hardly alone among West Europeans in holding such views. In many respects, his words reflected sentiments deeply rooted in modern European culture, and which find comfortable homes across the political spectrum.

This does not mean that most Europeans are rabid advocates of socialism. Few contemporary left-wing Europeans (or left-wing Americans, for that matter) insist upon the complete abolition of something as basic to the workings of markets as free prices. No significant European political party today argues that the profit motive can be done away with entirely. Proposals for the outright collectivization of private property are largely confined to fringe Marxist elements. In fact, major institutions and practices commonly associated with capitalism *do* exist in Europe, and are in no danger of disappearing altogether.

Perhaps the best general description of the type of economic system that has held sway in Western Europe since 1945 was given by the economist Barry Eichengreen. In describing Western Europe's rise from the rubble of World War II, he writes:

> Critical to Western Europe's success was the security of private
> property rights and reliance on the price mechanism. But the
> rapid growth of the postwar golden age depended on more than
> just the free play of market forces; in addition it required a set of
> norms and conventions, some informal, others embodied in law,
> to coordinate the actions of the social partners and solve a set of
> problems that decentralized markets could not.[2]

On this basis, Eichengreen describes the European economic model as one characterized by *coordinated capitalism*.

By coordinated capitalism—or what Europeans usually call the European social model—Eichengreen does not mean the type of coordination that occurs through free exchange against a background of secure property rights, contracts, and an independent judiciary which adjudicates disputes. "Coordination" in postwar European economies has from the beginning included:

- direct state interventions to stimulate or dampen economic growth;
- the establishment of extensive welfare states;
- direct subsidies to particular industries;
- state-supervised cooperation between trade unions and business;
- formal and informal intergovernmental cooperation between nation-state governments; and
- the general pursuit of redistributive policies.

As the previous chapter illustrated, attempts by the state to coordinate economic activity toward the realization of specific ends is not a new phenomenon in European life. Since World War II, however, coordination has been taken to levels that, while avoiding state socialism, reflect strongly *dirigiste* instincts and an effort to integrate market freedoms and protocols with neo-corporatist institutions, guild values, and state-managed welfare systems. This chapter examines some of the primary intellectual and political vehicles through which this form of coordination has been given expression, most notably Keynesianism, Social Democracy, Christian Democracy, and what is often—and confusedly—called neoliberalism. As a collective whole, their influence helps explain marked differences between contemporary European and American economic cultures.

Ground Zero: 1945

While ideas can often survive without significant popular affirmation, their ability to move beyond the speculations of intellectuals depends upon some affirmation from the cultures in which they emerge. Coordinated capitalism is no exception to this rule.

In the immediate aftermath of World War II, the soil for the European social model was especially fertile. The sheer amount of destruction wrought by six years of brutal modern warfare, from Normandy in the west to Stalingrad in the east, created circumstances in which significant extensions of government economic intervention proved extremely difficult to oppose politically. As one French journalist wrote, retrospectively, about the state of his own nation in 1945:

> The material situation of France, or rather of the French people, was tragic. I cannot refrain from evoking here my own memories of the children of the time, so pale that they looked as if they had been dug out of the cellars in which they had so often sought refuge; of the skeleton-like old men, who waiting for the return of men from the army or concentration camps, seemed to be stuck forever in queues, while the women worked for the whole family; of those vague crowds wandering, from an improbable train to an impossible bus.[3]

At the time, few believed Adam Smith's invisible hand would bring Europe out of the abyss. For every person who was inspired by Hayek's famous warnings about the political implications of government economic planning in his 1944 best seller *The Road to Serfdom*, ten more were convinced that extensive planning was the way of the future. The wartime leader of the Free French Forces, Charles de Gaulle, captured these sentiments in a widely reported 1944 speech to the newly liberated France:

> What we want . . . is to harness in common all that we possess on this earth and, to do this, there is no other way than what

is called the planned economy. We want the State to plan the economic effort of the entire nation to the benefit of all . . . . The collectivity, that is to say, the State, must take direction of the great sources of the common wealth and supervise certain other activities without, of course, excluding those great levers in human activity, initiative and fair profit.[4]

In the following months, the French government nationalized the coal industry, air transportation, parts of the manufacturing sector, and approximately half the banking industry. This pattern of selective nationalization while maintaining a private sector was replicated throughout much of Western Europe.

A second element at work in the European model's emergence was the experience of living in war economies. Twice in thirty years, Europeans had seen millions of people mobilized to manufacture, produce, and fight, all with the single-minded goal of defeating the enemy. The unprecedented production figures, the virtual elimination of unemployment, and the sense of common purpose attained under wartime conditions led many Europeans to imagine similar methods could be applied in peacetime.

Thirdly, the reputation of the market economy had reached catastrophic lows during the immediate prewar period. Millions of Europeans—and more than a few Americans—firmly believed that the Great Depression and Hitler's subsequent rise to power had been the result of capitalism. As a consequence, the conviction prevailed across Europe's various political groupings that there could be no going back to the allegedly unbridled capitalism of the past.

Fourthly, even before war's outbreak in 1939, many Europeans had already become accustomed to extensive economic intervention on the part of the modern state. During the interwar years, the regime of free trade that had prevailed throughout pre-1914 Europe had been undermined by a resurgence of capital controls, the end of the gold standard, and the widespread imposition of tariffs. Countries such as Nazi Germany had engaged in pump-priming of the economy on a scale that Keynes could only marvel at. Above all, there was the example of the Soviet Union. Thousands of Western European intellectuals—and not just convinced Communists—were impressed by the rapid industrialization achieved by Russia's Bolshevik masters. In some cases, they simply turned a blind eye to Stalinism's moral and human cost.

Communism itself helped to determine the types of economic policies adopted by Western European governments after 1945. Many politicians of the moderate left, center, and right were deeply worried by the strength of Communist movements in postwar Western Europe. Communists and Communist parties had played a major part in much of the underground resistance in occupied Europe (where there was much deliberate forgetfulness of their passive stance toward Nazi Germany between August 1939 and June 1941 following the shameful Molotov-Ribbentrop Pact). They subsequently proved adept at capitalizing on their wartime prestige.

In postwar elections in 1945, the French Communist party gained 26 percent of the vote. The following year, the Communists won almost 19 percent of the electorate in Italy. Amidst fears of Western Europe going the way of the Russian-occupied East, many non-Communist politicians made a conscious decision to use the state to pursue interventionist policies in the hope of diminishing Communism's appeal.[5] To their minds, simply waiting for the market to gradually resolve Europe's postwar economic shortages was not a politically realistic option.

Lastly, and perhaps most importantly, we cannot underestimate the effects of a yearning for security on the part of so many West Europeans. In the space of thirty years, they had lived through the carnage of two world wars and the twentieth century's worst economic downturn. Reflecting on this issue just before his death, Eucken underscored just how much the problem of *"insecurity* in the special form of prolonged mass unemployment"* dominated

European social and economic policy from 1918 onward.[6] In this light, it is hardly surprising that liberty was not the highest political or economic priority, either in the popular consciousness or at the level of the political elites.

And yet while context may have provided many of the conditions for the emergence of coordinated capitalism, added impetus came from economic ideas and political movements that rose to prominence after World War II. Though differing in many important respects, the paths adopted by most Western European states after 1945 were profoundly influenced by "Keynesian" and "neoliberal" economic policies, and the Christian Democratic and Social Democratic political movements.

Keynes and Keynesianism

The number of economists whose names are indelibly associated with entire economic theories remains relatively small. But even among this select group, John Maynard Keynes features prominently. Part of Keynes's success as an economist was derived from the remarkable advocacy skills that made him an immensely persuasive individual: one who enjoyed instant access to the halls of power in Britain, America, and Europe, and who, as his biographers and contemporaries attest, didn't hesitate to steamroller those disagreeing with him.

These abilities and the circumstances of the 1930s enabled Keynes to take a number of ideas already "in the air" and infuse them with his own views about how Western nations could escape the economic malaise in which they were mired. Even today, Keynes's *General Theory of Employment, Interest and Money* (1936) remains influential in Europe and America, and experienced something of a renaissance following the 2008 financial crisis.

The first thing to know about Keynes is that he was not seeking to "abolish" capitalism. Nor did he seek to end private property and free exchange. Keynes' economic theory did, however, most certainly have a political objective. He wanted the government to manage the economy in ways that promoted and maintained full employment so as to preserve the market from what he regarded as its own inherent instabilities, and to inoculate democratic societies from the siren calls of political extremists.

These objectives were partly shaped by what Keynes thought should be the role of economists in modern democratic societies. Arguments about the purposes of economics and "how to do" economics are not new. One issue in constant dispute in such arguments is "the length of perspective" that economists ought to adopt. Keynes's answer to that question was expressed in one of his most well-known sayings: "[the] *long* run is a misleading guide to affairs. *In the long run* we are all dead." But Keynes didn't stop there. "Economists," he added, "set themselves too easy, too useless a task if in tempestuous seasons they can only tell us that when the storm is long past the ocean is flat again."7

Put another way, Keynes thought that economists (and economics) could only be of practical use if they produced tools that enabled modern societies to address relatively immediate practical problems in relatively quick time. To most people—especially politicians—this sounds very plausible. But it is not, as later chapters illustrate, without its costs.

As Keynes's biographer Robert Skidelsky observes, Keynes's *General Theory* advanced one primary argument that underlay his whole case for government macro-management of the economy: decentralized market economies are inherently unstable and do not automatically gravitate toward full employment.

This position led Keynes to one very important conclusion, whose implications were as much political as economic. If the fluctuations in the market economy caused by ebbs and flows in private-sector investment were to be overcome, governments had to ensure that demand in an economy was maintained at a very high level.

In monetary terms, this meant that the cost of borrowing money (i.e., interest rates) had to be kept low by central banks. Fiscally speaking, it suggested that governments should use their budgets to preserve high levels of total spending in a given economy—either through direct public spending or through government-influenced investment. The amount of government stimulation would vary, Keynes initially indicated, depending on the health of the economy. By 1942, however, Keynes was maintaining that "if two-thirds or three-quarters of total investment is carried out or can be influenced by public or semi-public bodies, a long term programme of a stable character should be capable of reducing the range of fluctuation to much narrower limits than formerly."[8]

Taken as a stand-alone principle, such reasoning provides a rationale for the state taking ever-increasing control of the economy. A government that influences, directly or indirectly, between 66 and 75 percent of investment in an ostensibly market economy is undoubtedly *the* coordinator of the economy.

Keynes was not content to limit the ends of this coordination to maintaining effective demand. Once the employment issue had been solved, Keynes believed, governments should employ the same tools to reduce income inequalities and increase leisure time. Nor did Keynes see any reason to limit such policies to the level of nation-states. Global and regional demand, he thought, also required state stimulation.

Thus we should not be surprised that the Marshall Plan, promoted by the United States after Keynes's death to stimulate Europe's economic recovery, was portrayed by many as an instance of pan-European Keynesianism. One of the Marshall Plan's strongest West European critics, Wilhelm Röpke, argued that the Americans who designed and administered the Marshall Plan were thoroughly imbued with Keynesian and New Deal planning notions and believed that inflationary spending to maintain full employment was necessary and desirable.[9] Consequently, Röpke claimed, Marshall aid had been used to give "almost dogmatic force to the belief in the necessity of the planned guidance of capital use."[10]

Keynes's theories have never had a shortage of critics. Economists such as Hayek and Röpke, for example, argued that Keynes ignored the ability of trade unions to prevent a downward adjustment of wages in response to falling demand. They also underscored the inflationary implications of constantly pump-priming the economy. Others saw Keynes's ideas as a recipe for justifying a gradual government takeover of most of the economy in the name of demand management.

Given Western Europe's extreme economic fragility following World War II, such criticisms were unlikely to receive much of a hearing. Moreover, before and after the war, Keynes's prescriptions were developed, expanded, and invested with supporting mathematical arguments by his disciples. They subsequently became an established orthodoxy in Western Europe and North America.

To governments already inclined to put their faith in planning, the promise of such ideas was irresistible. No longer would governments, politicians, and civil servants play a mere supporting role in economic life. Keynesian ideas provided intellectual authority to the notion that the state *could* indeed coordinate economies toward the realization of very specific, predetermined ends, without degenerating into outright socialism. A form of collusion thus developed between the postwar economics profession and governments pursuing interventionist strategies. State institutions committed to interventionist policies wanted macroeconomic research that added empirical credibility to their proposals. As noted by Robert Skidelsky, the result was government jobs and influence for economists who embraced Keynesian principles and priorities.[11]

The key values in play with the Keynesian way of economic thinking were stability and security. These were to be realized through government planning, through bureaucracies whose *raison d'être* was one of implementing interventionist fiscal and monetary policies in order to manage the economy. While the institutions of private property and free exchange were permitted, market liberties were clearly subordinated to these ends, and to the requirements of *dirigiste* policies. It is arguable, however, that Keynesian economics and its associated institutions aspired to realize a type of liberty in European economic life, liberty in the sense that Franklin Roosevelt employed the term: freedom from want and freedom from fear, especially fear of perpetual economic insecurity.

Neoliberalism: A Different Kind of Market

In postwar continental Western Europe, there was at least one significant competitor in the marketplace of ideas to Keynesian policies. The broad-brush description often given to this body of thought is *neoliberalism*.

In the twenty-first century, neoliberalism is most often employed in Europe and America as a pejorative term. From the standpoint of the history of economic thought, however, neoliberalism is commonly used to describe a group of mainly German economic thinkers uneasy with laissez-faire ideas, but far more market-oriented in their economics and policy prescriptions than Keynes.

Like Keynesian ideas, neoliberal economics emerged several years before the outbreak of World War II. Such ideas were primarily identified with German economists, including Eucken, Röpke, Franz Böhm, Alfred Müller-Armack, and Alexander Rüstow. Among themselves, these thinkers disagreed about many significant questions.[12] They also brought different intellectual emphases to their study of economics. Nonetheless, they had much in common, not least of which was a desire to preserve liberty in the face of the broad trend toward political and economic collectivism.

It is almost impossible to underestimate the impact upon these thinkers of three contextual factors. The first was the steady cartelization of much of the German economy from the 1890s onward. The second was the inflation that destroyed the savings of the German middle class in the 1920s. The third was the rejection of market institutions by much of the German political class—a dismissal that

72

began with Otto von Bismarck, attained unprecedented heights in the war economy adopted between 1914 and 1918, and continued to rear its head during the Weimar Republic, before becoming enmeshed in the Nazis' totalitarian policies of the 1930s and war needs of the 1940s.

These experiences led the German neoliberals to several conclusions. One was the priority of sound money. All of them had witnessed and experienced the political and economic effects of rampant inflation in Germany and Austria in the wake of defeat in 1918. Hence, they viewed any attempt to use monetary policy to promote demand with enormous suspicion. Herein lay the roots of the famed aversion of West Germany's postwar Bundesbank to pump-priming policies.

A second conclusion was that economic liberty was indispensable to political freedom. The neoliberals argued that the breakdown of economic liberty via cartels and protectionism had helped to weaken social and institutional resistance to political authoritarianism.

Third, the German neoliberals were convinced the state had to play a more proactive economic part than allowed under nineteenth-century laissez-faire. They did not believe that the spontaneous interaction of people sufficed to produce a stable and flourishing social order, even against a background of institutions such as secure property rights and rule of law. The pursuit of self-interest, they believed, was not always beneficial, especially when it led to private parties enlisting state power to conspire against others to nullify their economic freedoms.

For the neoliberals, the mistake of laissez-faire advocates was, as Alexander Rüstow put it, their failure to realize that only "so long as the unrelenting market police of a strong and independent state excludes every private formation of monopoly and every obstacle to competition [will] the market economy produce an automatic harmonization of self-interest and public weal." The absence of such an authority "above" the market allowed established businesses to diminish competition through cartels and lobbying for tariffs, subsidies, and regulation. Given these conditions, Rüstow suggested, one could hardly blame Western Europe's working classes for adopting similar strategies through the organizational means of Social Democratic parties and trade union movements.[13]

But while German neoliberalism conceded a wider responsibility for the state, it did not believe in Keynesian-style planning. Interventions, neoliberals argued, should serve to reinforce the workings of market institutions rather than compromise them. A good example was anti-cartel policies. Cartels, according to the neoliberals, had emerged through businesses using the market device of contract to lock potential competitors out of the market. They thought cartels reflected cozy, mutually corrupting relationships between insider business leaders and the political class. The neoliberals subsequently thought the state should act to prevent cartels from emerging to suffocate competition, and even break them up when their existence was confirmed.

Such actions, however, could not be arbitrary. The neoliberals insisted these policies could not depend upon the whims of particular politicians and bureaucrats. Societies, they argued, needed what they called an *economic constitution*. Market economies, the neoliberals held, embodied a distinct order based on the idea of competition. But competition itself was predicated upon certain political and legal decisions that allowed it to emerge. Once competition existed, the legal system had to defend competition's foundations from rent-seeking interest groups. The neoliberals maintained this was consistent with the law's purposes, because law was supposed to serve the common good rather than the sectional interests of any one group—including civil servants. Consumers and citizens, they insisted, should not lose out to the well-organized collusions of industries and unions manipulating laws for their own advantage.[14]

The neoliberals differed among themselves about the precise principles for guiding state action. But the most concise outline may be found in Eucken's writings. His core principles included:

- free competition and a free price system;
- a stable anti-inflationary monetary system (an independent central bank focused on monetary stability);
- open markets and free trade;
- protection of private property;
- freedom to contract (without allowing people to contract in ways that diminish others' freedom to contract);
- liabilities for people's formal commitments and choices (thereby tying risk to responsibility); and
- constancy of economic policy (in the sense of avoiding decisions that create uncertainty).

As economic institutions, all of these principles are characterized by a commitment to *liberty* in the sense of providing a stable framework in which people can make their own free economic choices. *Security*, however, is also implicit to this framework, insofar as it seeks to minimize arbitrary behavior on the state's part. Another operative value is the commitment to *equality before the law*, underscored by efforts to protect market freedoms from being suborned by interest groups, either acting alone or hand-in-glove with the state.

All these commitments are consistent with the emphases of the market economic culture described in the previous chapter. There was, however, another side to the neoliberal program, some of which was inconsistent with market economic culture.

Neoliberalism contained a second set of commitments, which Eucken called "regulative principles." One such regulative principle was the prohibition of the establishment of monopolies.[15] This, Eucken argued, was derived from the insight that an economy controlled by monopolies and cartels effectively undermined the economic liberty of other market participants.[16]

Other regulative principles are, however, harder to reconcile with market values and institutions. One, endorsed by Eucken, was what he called "incomes policy." This entailed redistributive measures (such as progressive taxation) when market outcomes were deemed socially unacceptable. On reflection, it soon becomes apparent that this opens the door for all sorts of government interventions in the economy. Another neoliberal regulative principle concerned the labor market: Eucken accepted the setting of a minimum wage as well as the establishment of trade unions—provided these respected the limits established by market competition.

Such regulative principles would appear to have much in common with corporatist and guild priorities. These include the provision of *security* to employees, through trade unions and mechanisms such as legally mandated minimum wages, and efforts to promote social *stability*, through reducing wealth differentials via redistributive taxation. To many neoliberals, these policies were justified because they would help diminish social tensions that might threaten broader acceptance of the more basic market principles. It is surely undeniable, however, that they create opportunities for more extensive state intervention.

Despite these contradictions, neoliberal ideas were influential in West Germany after World War II. Prominent neoliberals such as Eucken and Röpke helped to make the intellectual case for German politician Ludwig Erhard's liberalizing reforms of 1948. Another instance was the liberalization of much of the French economy in 1958 following the implementation of the Rueff-Pinay Plan, partly named after its major architect, the financial economist and self-described neoliberal Jacques Rueff.

Influence, however, should not be mistaken for dominance. While neoliberalism left a particular imprint on some economic institutions and practices (especially in West Germany), its impact was limited by other factors.

As was the case in the rest of postwar Western Europe, socialist and corporatist ideas were widely pervasive in Germany, and not only among left-wing political movements. In 1951, legislation mandating worker participation in the management of companies of a particular size was passed in West Germany, despite the reservations of many neoliberal economists. This reflected pressures brought to bear on the government by unions, the Social Democrats, and some sections of the Christian Democratic party.

Nor were neoliberals able to resist the rapid implementation of many welfare-state measures. In 1950, West German Chancellor Konrad Adenauer commissioned Röpke to write a defense of his government's economic policies. To Adenauer's surprise, Röpke provided a report that, besides praising Erhard's liberalizing measures, also criticized "a very strong trend" to overly restrict market disciplines in West Germany.[17] Röpke insisted that welfare spending and taxation could not exceed certain levels "without impairing the expansive and regulative aspects of a free market economy." He then ominously added that such spending and regulation was *already* excessive.[18]

In other words, neoliberal ideas in Germany found themselves competing with more *dirigiste* and corporatist streams of economic thought (not to mention Keynesian proposals), and did not always emerge victorious. In part, this reflected the support of some neoliberals, including Müller-Armack, for neo-corporatist policies. But it also testified to the influence of two political movements that had a considerable impact on the emergence of the European social model in postwar Europe: the Christian Democratic movement and social democracy.

Social Democracy: From Marxism to Mixed Economies

To most people today "Social Democrat" invokes visions of a mildly center-left politician interested in promoting greater economic equality and social justice, primarily through a relatively strong welfare state and associated government programs, but within the conditions of a market economy. Social democracy's roots, however, are far more radical.

Socialist and social democratic parties began emerging throughout Europe in the last quarter of the nineteenth century. In continental

Europe, the most powerful intellectual influence on most such parties was Marxism.

In 1891, the German Social Democratic Party embraced what came to be known as the Erfurt Program (named after the town in which it was adopted). Drafted by Marxist theoreticians including Karl Kautsky and August Bebel, many of the Erfurt program's tenets were subsequently adopted by other European socialist parties. The program's two most prominent claims were the Marxist conviction that all societies were characterized by a struggle between classes, driven by their respective economic interests; and the assertion that the end of the bourgeoisie's dominance and the transfer of control of the means of production to the workers would eventually come about through an "inevitable" revolution. Though the Erfurt program did not rule out a seizure of power by the proletariat, it did commit the German Social Democrats to pursuing the betterment of workers' lives through participation in existing political institutions and the progressive implementation of social legislation and welfare policies.[19]

However, a transformation away from the more explicitly Marxist aspects of most Western European Socialist and Social Democratic parties was underway from the 1900s onward. This was partly a result of changing attitudes toward revolutionary tactics. More and more, Socialists and Social Democrats began opting for the "evolutionary" path implied in the Erfurt program. They assumed that the emergence of industrial workers as a numerical majority would eventually bring about a democratic, preferably nonviolent shift from capitalism.

A second moderating factor was that some Western European Socialist parties suddenly had to assume political office in circumstances in which they had the responsibility for maintaining social order in difficult conditions. The German Social Democrats, for instance, were unexpectedly propelled to power following the fall of the Hohenzollern dynasty in November 1918. They were thus squarely faced with having to negotiate an end to the war and returning the economy to a peacetime footing. Almost immediately, the Social Democrats were subject to immense pressure from middle-class centrists, liberals, Catholics, and national conservatives to face down their former comrades on the extreme left who wanted immediate revolutionary transformation. The responsibilities of office consequently meant that Social Democrats found themselves backtracking from the implications of their ideological commitments and behaving more like middle-class politicians inclined toward consensus and compromise.

A third element in the shift toward less revolutionary positions was the relative success enjoyed by Socialist and Social Democratic parties in implementing and expanding a number of welfare-state measures. In France, the Popular Front, which drew support from forces ranging from the moderate Left to the Communist Party, was elected to power in 1936. One of its primary successes was the 1936 Matignon Accords, which resulted in labor laws that established collective bargaining and required businesses to recognize and negotiate with trade union officials. It also mandated a forty-hour workweek, two weeks of paid leave, and raised wages (the biggest increases being for those at the lower end of the pay scale). Six years earlier, across the Channel, a British Labour government had raised unemployment benefits, passed legislation that mandated housing assistance to the very poor, and specifically sought to raise wages and improve working conditions in the coal industry.

Socialist and Social Democratic parties thus discovered the advantages of acceding to power via peaceful democratic means. Through the same mechanisms, they were able to introduce measures that, from their standpoint, helped to realize some of their goals without having to sweep away capitalist institutions.

This complemented another element at work in the "de-radicalization" of much of the European Left's economic positions. Over time, their success in mobilizing electoral support and acquiring seats in legislatures, their often close cooperation with trade unions (with whom they usually shared overlapping membership), and the increasing dominance of their leadership by left-wing intellectuals from middle-class backgrounds led to the growth of powerful party bureaucracies and dedicated cadres of full-time professional political activists.

Thus, while they might still employ fiery Marxist rhetoric in speeches, the incentives for engaging in truly revolutionary activity that would fundamentally upturn the status quo (and perhaps allow more radical elements to take over) became weaker over time. The more Social Democrats and other left-wing parties became acquainted with the halls of power, the more they found themselves dealing pragmatically with captains of industry, professional civil servants, and non-left-wing politicians.

The decisive changes occurred in the two decades after World War II, especially when it was no longer possible to deny the totalitarian character of Communist governments in Eastern Europe. In 1945, the Austrian Social Democrats entered into a grand coalition with the center-right People's Party—a governing arrangement that was to last twenty-one years. The French Socialists abandoned their alliance with the Communists as early as 1947, and participated in French governments alongside Christian Democratic and moderate center-left parties until 1958. By the late 1950s, most Western European social democratic parties were moving toward tactical and increasingly formal alliances with centrist, moderate center-right, and Christian Democratic parties. Some left-wing parties, such as Sweden's Social Democrats (who had rejected radical Marxism as early as 1917) and Britain's Labour Party, even governed in their own right for long periods of time.

The most illustrative symbol of these changes was the German Social Democratic Party's adoption of its Godesberg Program in 1959. It formally rejected Marxist theory and condemned Communist parties and practices. Instead, Godesberg explicitly invoked secular humanism, Greek philosophy, and Christian ethics as providing partial inspiration for Social Democratic principles. Also jettisoned were many traditional socialist commitments such as the state ownership of industry. Given the German Social Democrats' history and the prestige they enjoyed among the West European Left, these changes made a deep impression on other European Socialist and Social Democratic parties.

Undoubtedly, this development owed something to the fact that the Social Democrats had not held office at a federal level in West Germany since the first free national elections of 1949. Many Social Democrats subsequently concluded the party needed to amend its platform to make themselves a viable ruling alternative to the Christian Democrats. Instead of using Marxist language and concepts, they began speaking about the democratization of economic life through co-determination arrangements, subsidies for heavy industry, economic planning through the direction of investment rather than outright nationalization, moderate deficit spending to accelerate employment growth, and wealth redistribution through taxation rather than outright expropriation.

This effort to associate social democracy with a mixture of Keynesian and mildly corporatist policies constituted acknowledgement that the neoliberal reforms implemented by Erhard were a reality that had achieved popular acceptance among the West German population. The Social Democrats also found it difficult to deny that traditional Social Democratic constituencies, like industrial workers, had derived substantial material benefit from the market-driven German economic miracle. At the same time, their new language and policies allowed the Social Democrats to begin articulating arguments and policies not entirely dissimilar to those voiced by the other major force shaping postwar West European political and economic life.

Christian Democracy: Social Markets and Neo-Corporatism

Postwar Western Europe's history and the associated emergence of the European social model cannot be properly grasped without taking Christian Democratic parties into account. Efforts to explain Christian democracy are difficult because of the sheer number of often quite different political, economic, and even theological positions that shaped its development. Compounding the problem is the diversity of political and economic views articulated by self-described Christian Democrats, sometimes within the very same Christian Democratic party. The spectrum ranges from those with strongly pro-market positions to others whose economic views verge on mild socialism.

The roots of European Christian Democratic parties go back to the nineteenth century, and specifically to the Roman Catholic Church's reaction to the Industrial Revolution and modern capitalism's emergence. The church firmly rejected socialism and communism because of the materialism and atheism that are core to these ideologies. Yet while affirming the legitimacy of various market practices and institutions such as free prices, contracts, private property, and free exchange, the church was skeptical of the liberal philosophical positions many people associated with these institutions. In the minds of practicing Catholics, "liberalism" was indelibly also associated with the French Revolution, and the French Revolution meant killing priests and nuns, burning churches, and closing monasteries, convents, and church schools.

The church was also deeply concerned about industrial capitalism's perceived social effects. These included not only the sudden and often very socially disruptive growth of urban centers, but also the depopulation of the countryside, and the gradual disconnection of many who lived in industrial areas from the church's everyday life.

The initial political expressions of what would become European Christian Democratic parties were usually "confessionally

Catholic" groupings: that is, strongly self-identifying with the Catholic Church and Catholic social teaching, and whose membership was almost exclusively Catholic. These were politically isolated from the often quite anti-Catholic liberal parties, the Marxist-influenced socialist movements, and, in religiously mixed countries, Protestant-based political associations. Thus, the German Center Party (forerunner of today's Christian Democratic Union) embraced Catholic aristocrats, Catholic industrialists, Catholic entrepreneurs, Catholic trade unionists, Catholic artisans, and Catholic small businessmen—many of whom advocated very different economic policies. If there was a common intellectual influence, it came from Catholic social teaching, as expressed in papal encyclicals such as *Rerum Novarum* (1891) and *Quadragesimo Anno* (1931), as well as corporatist-solidarist ideas that drew on the writings of German Catholic intellectuals attempting to integrate corporatist and guild values into the conditions of modern economic life.

Just as Social Democratic parties underwent significant changes in the first half of the twentieth century, developments also occurred in the postwar Christian Democratic movements. The first was a breakaway from the old confessional model. Figures such as Adenauer in West Germany brought together Catholics and Protestants under the Christian Democratic banner. In Italy and France, Catholic politicians of the likes of Alcide De Gasperi and Robert Schuman sought to broaden the base of their movements to include those who, while not necessarily religious, recognized Europe's Christian heritage, were skeptical of socialism and resolutely opposed to communism, but who were open to economic policies that would expand the welfare state and reflect particular corporatist emphases. In many instances, these Christian Democratic parties were willing to cooperate with smaller liberal parties (such as the Free Democrats in Germany) and particular left-wing groups (such as the French Socialists).

Though the model varied from country to country, the economic program most associated with postwar European Christian democracy is widely described as the *social market economy*. There is considerable debate about the precise meaning of this expression. Nevertheless, it is possible to identify some of its key elements.

At the heart of the idea of a social market economy are basic neo-liberal commitments to private property, free competition, market-determined prices, and independent central banks. At the same time, most Christian Democratic parties have promoted what might be called "soft corporatist" policies as part of the model. Unlike the "hard corporatist" agendas pursued in Franco's Spain, Mussolini's Italy, Vichy France, and Salazar's Portugal, which focused upon maintaining political control, soft corporatism sought to foster consensus among different economic groups within industries, in order to promote social stability, reduce conflict in the workplace, and facilitate a more equitable sharing of the proceeds of growth.

Soft corporatism manifested itself in postwar Western Europe through institutional formations such as work councils, whose membership was dominated by trade union officials, and whom management was legally bound to consult in many European countries. In other cases, it included worker co-determination arrangements in the management of businesses, whereby employees (again, usually in the form of union representatives) were allocated a set number of seats on company boards. Some countries, like Austria, went so far as to formally co-opt business and trade unions into the setting and implementing of government economic policy. Even today, most EU member states maintain some neo-corporatist arrangements.

Some economic historians have argued that soft corporatism was a way of enabling societies to navigate the unique conditions of a postwar Western Europe, which had suffered terribly from war and which was far behind America when it came to standards of living, industrial capacity, wage levels, and capital accumulation. Through neo-corporatist arrangements, governments were able to secure the "buy-in" of businesses and unions to policies that would help Western Europe overcome these difficulties, especially in terms of unions committing themselves to making wage demands that did not exceed the pace of economic growth.[20]

The effect of neo-corporatist policies was thus to facilitate a political culture that, as the Oxford political philosopher Larry Siedentop notes, "places a high premium on consensus, slowly formed and not easily recast."[21] We will see, however, that the long-term price can be economic stagnation, and an inability to make the difficult choices necessary to escape it.

A number of Christian Democratic parties were sympathetic to the use of planning to accelerate industrialization, or whatever the state identified as a good and necessary goal. This was a prominent part of the Italian Christian Democrats' economic program of the 1950s, as they sought to boost those segments of the economy they considered underdeveloped.

Article 41 of the 1947 Italian constitution (much of which was drafted by Christian Democratic politicians) even made specific provision for such *dirigisme*. Having first stated that "Private-sector economic initiative is freely exercised," Article 41 then insists that "It cannot be conducted in conflict with social usefulness or in such a manner that could damage safety, liberty and human dignity." Article 41 proceeds to state that "The law shall provide for appropriate programs and controls so that public and private-sector economic activity may be oriented and coordinated for social purposes."

It would be difficult to find a more precise summary of contemporary European *dirigisme*. It would be equally hard to find post-1960 European Social Democrats who would substantially disagree with Article 41's formulation.

Another *dirigiste* measure promoted by some Christian Democratic governments was agricultural subsidies to farmers. In certain respects, this reflected a concern for maintaining a domestic food production base. At the same time, we should not discount many Christian Democrats' traditional sympathy with claims that life lived in rural areas and small country towns helps promote closer communities and morally healthier lifestyles that, they held, were harder to sustain in urban areas.

Nor, it should be added, were Christian Democratic parties adverse to generous welfare programs. Over time, Adenauer's Christian Democrats came to vie with the Social Democrats over who could provide the most in terms of state pensions in West Germany. Ironically, it was the economic prosperity of West Germany's liberalized economy that furnished the government with large surpluses throughout the 1950s, and gave many German politicians the means to pay for more generous welfare programs.

The real break occurred in 1957, when Adenauer's government indexed pensions to the earnings of those working. Wage increases thus automatically triggered pension increases. The new policy helped the Christian Democrats and their Bavarian sister party, the Christian Social Union, to achieve an absolute majority in the 1957 Bundestag elections. But it also necessitated tax increases and higher social security contributions from employees. Moreover, once that principle was established, it proved difficult to resist its application to other areas, such as unemployment benefits.[22]

Convergence, Consensus, and Social Contracts

This brief excursion into postwar Christian and social democracy illustrates that by the 1960s, a gradual convergence was well underway between the economic policies and values promoted by the two movements at the center of Western European political power. By 1966, there was sufficient economic ground between Germany's Christian Democrats and Social Democrats that the two parties were able to enter into a "black-red" coalition for three years, after the Christian Democrats' traditional allies, the Free Democrats, were no longer willing to tolerate the tax increases necessitated by increased welfare spending. By contrast, the Social Democrats had no objection to this part of the Christian Democrats' economic policies. Moreover, once the Social Democrats relegated the Christian

Democrats to the opposition benches in 1969, they expanded welfare expenditures even further.

None of this is meant to suggest that differences about economic policies ceased to exist between Western European center-right and center-left political parties. Yet the degree of commonality in economic policies that developed across Western Europe's varied political landscape was remarkable. This helps explain why European nations such as Italy, Belgium, the Netherlands, France, Germany, and Austria have all had governments based upon coalitions formed between Christian Democrats and other center-right groups with Social Democratic, Socialist, and other center-left parties.

This growing convergence in economic policies and beliefs also makes comprehensible how ostensibly center-right European politicians—French presidents Georges Pompidou and Valéry Giscard D'Estaing—could have promoted worker co-determination policies, implemented a national minimum wage, and imposed a capital gains tax. The widespread integration of mildly market-oriented commitments with a high degree of *dirigisme*, and various neo-corporatist and welfare state initiatives—and the accompanying emphasis on developing widespread *consensus* for such policies—was also why so many continental European politicians from the Right and Left were so uncomfortable with Margaret Thatcher, a self-identified "conviction" politician.

Over time, these arrangements have been buttressed by widespread acceptance of the idea that an implicit *social contract* between Europe's citizens and its political classes underlies the European social model. The phrase itself is usually associated with the eighteenth-century French Enlightenment philosopher Jean-Jacques Rousseau and his 1762 book, *Du Contrat Social* [*The Social Contract*], though it first finds full expression in the work of the seventeenth-century English thinker Thomas Hobbes.

In very broad terms, social contract theory is a way of understanding the relationship between governments and the people. It holds that, having agreed upon the need for a government, individuals create a state on the basis of mutual promises. This permits the state to claim that its authority is based on the people's delegation of their rights to pursue their particular interests in their own way.[23]

In raw historical terms, there are no instances of such social contracts being made. They are a political fiction. This does not stop Europeans from invoking the idea to uphold the European social model's political legitimacy. The basic premise of the social contract that implicitly underpins much European economic culture is that citizens give up a considerable degree of economic freedom, not least because this is an indispensable prerequisite to the state's ability to pursue *dirigiste* policies. In return, the state promises to provide people with a strong welfare state and implement a range of redistributionist policies.

Western Europe's commitment to this social contract is not a question of abstract political theory. The language of social contract is used by European politicians, journalists, academics, and citizens from left to right with a frequency that many Americans would find odd. Politically speaking, the effect is to make it harder to challenge key facets of contemporary European economic culture. It also wraps elites and citizens (or, as chapter 5 demonstrates, particular groups of citizens) in a mutually supportive embrace which many are reluctant to abandon, even when the embrace is evidently undermining the foundations of long-term economic prosperity.

Here it is worth noting that prominent center-left American figures are not shy about invoking similar social contract claims and language. In response, for example, to the efforts of a Republican-dominated House of Representatives to significantly cut public spending, President Obama argued in April 2011 that the fiscal agenda advanced by public figures such as Congressman Paul Ryan was "less about reducing the deficit than it is about changing the basic social compact in America."[24] The intent was to absolve the president from the necessity of even discussing the merits of particular details of the House's proposals. Likewise, the Nobel Prize winner and decidedly neo-Keynesian economist Joseph Stiglitz has no hesitation in invoking an interpretation of social contract that bears uncanny resemblance to contemporary European conceptions of this idea, in order to provide his decidedly interventionist economic ideas with a claim to moral and political primacy over alternative proposals.[25]

Back to the Future

From a long-term historical perspective, the convergence of economic and political positions throughout Western Europe toward a broad consensus in favor of the European social model represents a modern integration of the two traditions of European economic culture that have dominated since the Middle Ages. But no matter how sophisticated the knitting, ongoing tensions between market institutions, neo-corporatist commitments, and *dirigiste* attempts at centralized economic coordination have persisted. No amount of political consensus-building, or appeals to fictional social contracts have been able to completely paper them over. Before we illustrate the manifold ways in which this situation explains the deeper economic problems characterizing contemporary Europe, we need to examine the most prominent attempt to realize the European social model at a pan-European level in the postwar era: the unique political and economic experiment known as the European Union.

4

A Very Imperfect Union

*Cinema explains American society. It's like a Western, with good
guys and bad guys, where the weak don't have a place.*

—JACQUES DELORS

If Alexis de Tocqueville is proof of a foreigner's capacity to understand and explain a country better than most of its citizens, then
these words of Jacques Delors—the eighth and perhaps most influential president of the European Commission—testify to how even
highly intelligent and accomplished individuals can fundamentally
misread another nation.

The notion that the American experiment has produced a ruth-
less society in which the less fortunate are ignored is contradicted
by the evidence. By any statistical standard, America is one of the
world's most generous and philanthropic societies. In 2002, 44 percent of American adults volunteered to do something. In raw figures,
that amounted to 83.9 million people.[1] The National Philanthropy

Trust calculates that in an average year, 65 percent of American households make charitable contributions. Of total giving, about 73 percent comes from individuals. In 2011, American giving reached the figure of $298.3 billion dollars.[2]

Vast amounts of this giving goes to private organizations that provide direct assistance to people in distress, from low-income single mothers to those afflicted by disease and disability. These are not the actions of a heartless nation. Delors's comments look even odder when one considers that the amount of American government spending on pensions and health care in 2009 alone was *ten times* the amount of charitable giving.[3]

How, then, are we to comprehend Delors's view of American society as callous and ungenerous, when clearly it is not? It would be easy to dismiss his comments as reflecting a cartoonlike understanding of America. A better explanation may lie in the fact that many West Europeans associate concern for those in need almost exclusively with extensive and ongoing government economic intervention and large welfare states. This is key to grasping many of the policies associated with modern Europe's own grand experiment, the European Union, and its efforts to give expression at a pan-European level to the two sets of values and institutions that characterize European economic culture.

One European's Journey

Delors's personal background testifies to a strong commitment on his part to realizing solidarity in the economy through *dirigiste* means. An economist by training, from a French family with a long history of involvement in Christian Democratic causes, Delors entered political life in 1950, when he became an economic adviser to France's Christian Trade Union Confederation.

Much of Delors's early political career was focused upon the development of social policy. In 1962 he was appointed head of the social affairs division of the center-right French government's

General Planning Commission. Delors subsequently served as chief adviser for social affairs to France's "progressive Gaullist" prime minister Jacques Chaban-Delmas, between 1969 and 1972. During this time, Delors drafted a law requiring French companies to put some of their profits toward their employees' further education.

It was, however, as a member of France's Socialist Party that Delors first became a government minister. Following François Mitterrand's election as the Fifth Republic's first Socialist president, Delors was given ministerial responsibility for finance and the economy. Initially, Delors presided over Mitterrand's implementation of a mixture of decidedly neo-corporatist and left-of-center economic and social policies. These included substantially raising the minimum wage, nationalizing several industries, increasing paid holiday leave, legislating to increase worker participation in management, reducing the working week to 39 hours, and above all, implementing France's "solidarity tax" on wealth— a measure unambiguously redistributive in inspiration and goal.

The comprehensive failure of these policies to reduce unemployment led Delors to press for a reversal of some of them, including reprivatizing erstwhile nationalized industries. Delors thus became publicly associated with a Socialist president's shift away from social democratic economic policies toward more market-friendly positions. This also marked the beginning of Delors's own embrace of aspects of the market tradition in European economic culture.

In 1985, Delors left the French government to take up his appointment as president of the European Commission. From the beginning of his tenure, he worked to integrate the two dimensions of European economic culture at a pan-European level. Delors sought, for instance, to promote greater economic liberalization through the establishment of a single market. This involved increasing the pace for dismantling barriers to trade and exchange within the European Economic Community, and establishing the basis for a single European currency.

But lest one think of Delors as a Thatcherite in disguise, it should be noted that his most significant clash with then Prime Minister Thatcher concerned Delors's equally strong desire to realize what he called, in a 1988 speech to the British Trades Union Congress, "Social Europe." This involved blunting the negative social effects of a competitive market through a range of welfare protections, neo-corporatist protocols, and social policies. Delors's efforts in this area culminated in the late 1980s with the development of a Community Charter of Fundamental Social Rights, which later became the basis for the Social Chapter of the 1992 Treaty of Maastricht—one of the most important documents in the formation of today's EU.

Delors's work to combine market and social-corporatist policies throughout his tenure as European Commission president should not be viewed as simply a reflection of his personal political odyssey. Delors was able to move easily between the "right" and "left" of European politics, because, economically speaking, the differences between Right and Left on such issues had become a matter of degree rather than of kind. To this extent, Delors's mixed-policy predilections were consistent with the picture of European economic culture outlined in previous chapters: a culture that has exerted enormous influence upon the entire modern European integration effort. For, from the beginning, this experiment has sought to combine market, social, and neo-corporatist protocols and institutions through supranational agreements forged by political and bureaucratic elites, which are then implemented "downwards." Here we see just how much the story of postwar European economic integration has been one of an effort to follow this path, and of the struggle to keep these elements together.

Europe, Thy Name Is Bureaucracy

As a political formation, the European Union is a unique, even strange, beast. As of October 2012 it had twenty-seven member states, its own parliament (which meets in two places), two presidents (one for the European Council, and one for the European Commission), a high representative for foreign policy, a commission, a council, a high court, and a central bank. Their activities are supplemented by a court of auditors, an ombudsman, an investment bank, and a Committee of the Regions. The EU even has its own in-house neo-corporatist institution, the European Economic and Social Committee, which purports to represent the views of "civil society, employers, and employees" to the rest of EU officialdom.

There are also no less than *five* different groups of European Union agencies. The first group encompasses community agencies, and includes: the Agency for the Cooperation of Energy Regulators (ACER); the Body of European Regulators for Electronic Communications (BEREC); the Community Plant Variety Office (CPVO); the European Agency for Safety and Health at Work (EU-OSHA); the European Agency for the Management of Operational Cooperation at the External Borders (FRONTEX); the European Asylum Support Office (EASO); the European Aviation Safety Agency (EASA); the European Banking Authority (EBA); the European Centre for Disease Prevention and Control (ECDC); the European Centre for the Development of Vocational Training (Cedefop); the European Chemicals Agency (ECHA); the European Environment Agency (EEA); the European Fisheries Control Agency (EFCA); the European Food Safety Authority (EFSA); the European Foundation for the Improvement of Living and Working Conditions (EUROFOUND); the European GNSS Agency (GSA); the European Institute for Gender Equality (EIGE); the European Insurance and Occupational Pensions Authority (EIOPA); the European Maritime Safety Agency (EMSA); the European Medicines Agency (EMA); the European Monitoring Centre for Drugs and Drug Addiction (EMCDDA); the European Network and Information Security Agency (ENISA); the European Railway Agency (ERA); the European Securities and Markets Authority (ESMA); the European Training Foundation (ETF); the EU Agency for Fundamental

Rights (FRA); the Office for Harmonisation in the Internal Market (OHIM); and the Translation Centre for the Bodies of the EU (CdT). Currently being formed is an agency "for the operational management of large-scale IT systems in the area of freedom, security, and justice."

A second group of agencies is concerned with security and defense issues: the European Defence Agency (EDA); the European Union Institute for Security Studies (EUISS); and the European Union Satellite Centre (EUSC). A third group consists of the EU's crime-fighting organizations: the European Police College (CEPOL); the European Police Office (EUROPOL); and the EU's Judicial Cooperation Unit (EUROJUST).

The fourth group is comprised of "executive agencies." These include the Education, Audiovisual and Culture Executive Agency (EACEA); the European Research Council Executive Agency (ERC Executive Agency); the Executive Agency for Competitiveness and Innovation (EACI); the Executive Agency for Health and Consumers (EAHC); the Research Executive Agency (REA); and the Trans-European Transport Network Executive Agency (TEN-T EA). Lastly, there are EU agencies that coordinate member states' research into peaceful and safe uses of nuclear energy. This work is undertaken by the EURATOM Supply Agency (ESA) and the European Joint Undertaking for ITER and the Development of Fusion Energy.[4]

It would belabor the point to add to this list all the different committees and branches of the European Commission, the departments attached to the European Council, the committees of the European Parliament, the ambassadors and diplomats accredited to the EU by its member states, and the EU's own diplomatic corps. Needless to say, the opportunities for duplication of effort within this bureaucratic labyrinth are tremendous.

But before Americans sigh with relief that they have avoided this, they should recall the alphabet soup of agencies that sprouted up under FDR's New Deal, or the army of bureaucracies created under President Lyndon Johnson's Great Society program. Plenty of these creations are alive and well in America today, eighty years after the Great Depression and fifty years after the 1960s. In March 2011, a U.S. Government Accountability Office report found dozens of overlapping and duplicative programs littered throughout the federal government. These included forty-seven programs for employment training, fifteen programs to oversee food-safety laws, twenty different programs to help the homeless, fifty-six programs designed to increase financial literacy, and fifty-five separate programs for highways.[5]

Within the ranks of the aforementioned European commissions, agencies, committees, and representative bodies, you will find many idealistic and hardworking Europeans committed to realizing the formation of a multinational entity of which there is really no equivalent in the world. Yet you do not need to be a student of bureaucracy to know that these institutions—not to mention the literally hundreds of thousands of laws, rules, regulations, and procedures which they draft, debate, and apply across the entire EU—also provide endless opportunities for empire-building, stifling innovation, obstructing free association, and limiting competition, all in the name of solidarity. In some cases, they constitute a means for businesses and unions to use bureaucratic power against each other, against uncooperative politicians, and perhaps above all, against existing and potential competitors—foreign and domestic.

So how, one might ask, does a multinational entity that many people believe was primarily created to facilitate ease of trade and commerce across European borders end up this way? The answer is that the founders of what would become the EU *always* saw it as far more than an economic liberalization project. They and their successors have *always* regarded it as also embodying specific political and social objectives, many of which are positively corrosive to market values and institutions.

Paris: From Coal to Trade

The idea of a politically united Europe is not new. The long-standing cultural, religious, and economic ties between European nations have inevitably raised the question of whether these links ought to form the basis of closer political integration. Efforts to provide a positive answer to that question received a significant boost from the devastation unleashed by two world wars. This convinced many Western European politicians and civil servants that the development of some type of European political federation was essential if Europe was to avoid yet another continentally destructive war.

In a speech at the University of Zurich on September 19, 1946, Winston Churchill openly called for "a kind of United States of Europe." He viewed this as a gathering of non-Communist Western European nations (from which, interestingly, he excluded Great Britain).[6] Two years after Churchill's speech, several hundred European scholars, trade unionists, clergy, lawyers, and politicians from the Left and Right—including Churchill, soon-to-be German chancellor Konrad Adenauer, a young François Mitterrand, future British prime minister Harold Macmillan, and former French prime ministers Paul Ramadier, Paul Reynaud, and Édouard Daladier—gathered at the Hague in the Netherlands to discuss Europe's future.

Among the resolutions of this Congress of Europe was a declaration that "the time has come when the European nations must transfer and merge some portion of their sovereign rights so as to secure common political and economic action for the integration and proper development of their common resources." The declaration also proclaimed that a united Europe should progressively establish "a democratic social system, the aim of which shall be to free men from all types of slavery and economic insecurity."[7] Significantly, references to promoting greater economic security pervade the declaration. Conversely, expressions such as "economic freedom" are absent.

While the Congress of Europe provided intellectual and political impetus to closer integration of European nations, the first major institutional step forward came with the 1951 Treaty of Paris. This established the European Coal and Steel Community (ECSC) as a common market for steel and coal among its six member states. Not coincidentally, the ECSC's governing arrangements—which included a supranational high authority, a high court, a common assembly, and a special council of ministers which could check the high authority's decisions—closely resembled the institutional framework of today's EU.

To be sure, there were a range of not-always-compatible motivations for a closer union of European nations. Apart from the desire to avoid another European civil war, old-fashioned pursuit of national interest also had a role. For West Germany, the formation of a more economically and politically unified Europe was a path back to international respectability after the moral disaster of National Socialism. A number of French politicians regarded a more united Europe as a means of magnifying France's political influence throughout the continent and the world.

Part of the ECSC's economic objective, as described in the founding declaration of May 9, 1950, issued by French foreign minister Robert Schuman (with the approval of West Germany's Adenauer), was to liberalize Western Europe's coal and steel markets by creating and maintaining an intra-European free market in these products through anti-cartel measures and the elimination of customs duties. These rather neoliberal emphases were, however, accompanied by phrases in the Schuman Declaration maintaining that the proposed ECSC High Authority would oversee realization of the following goals: "the modernization of production and the improvement of its quality"; "the supply of coal and steel on identical terms to the French and German markets, as well as to the markets of other member countries; the development in common of exports to other countries; [and] the equalization and improvement of the living conditions of workers in these industries."[8]

An effort to implement a degree of economic liberalization was thus combined with a desire to achieve specific social and economic goals through *dirigiste* means. This hybrid of objectives was crystallized in the Treaty of Paris. This combined some market liberalization (in the form of abolition of tariffs, subsidies, protectionism, or the use of contracts to block out potential competitors) with the pursuit of social policies (such as equalizing workers' pay and conditions). It also endowed the ECSC with various top-down coordination functions. These included permitting "limited direct intervention" by the High Authority in particular areas, such as setting maximum and minimum prices for certain products in defined circumstances, and implementing procedures for the consulting of employers and workers' associations:[9] in other words, classic social and neo-corporatist ends.

Rome: Liberalization . . . and *Dirigisme*

As industries, coal and steel began to decline in Western Europe after 1950. Yet key players in the ECSC's formation, including Schuman and the French businessman and international civil servant Jean Monnet, had no doubt it should be understood as the first institutional step toward a *politically* united Europe. As the Schuman Declaration bluntly stated:

> By pooling basic production and by instituting a new High
> Authority, whose decisions will bind France, Germany and other
> member countries, this proposal will lead to the realization of the
> first concrete foundation of a European federation indispensable
> to the preservation of peace.[10]

Not everyone in Western Europe was as passionate about political federation. By the mid-1950s, Monnet had become frustrated at the failure of several efforts to forge deeper political union, through devices such as the stillborn European Defense Community, which collapsed in the face of concerns about national sovereignty and fears about reactivating German military forces. Monnet subsequently returned to economic policy as the arena most conducive to facilitating political unification. To further his goals, he founded the Action Committee for the United States of Europe: a confederation mainly of politicians and trade unionists with similar convictions to Monnet's. Their efforts culminated with six nations—France, Belgium, West Germany, the Netherlands, Luxembourg, and Italy—signing the Treaty of Rome in 1957, thereby establishing the European Economic Community.

The Rome treaty and the EEC became, respectively, the legal and institutional means for forging ever closer economic and political unity throughout Western (and eventually Central and Eastern) Europe over the following fifty years. In doing so, they also gave pan-European form to the type of economic culture promoted throughout much of Europe—a slow reduction in barriers to the free movement of goods, capital, people, and services within Europe's borders, but combined with (if not overwhelmed by) numerous *dirigiste*, neo-corporatist and welfare measures.

This much becomes evident from reading the Treaty of Rome itself. For instance, it provided for the progressive dismantling of customs and tariff barriers between member states, but also for the *establishment* of a common customs barrier toward nonmember states.

Some of the most prominent *dirigiste* commitments concerned agriculture, specifically a Common Agricultural Policy, colloquially known as the CAP. Here the treaty's relevant sections referred to objectives such as ensuring "a fair standard of living for the agricultural population," and a Keynesian-like policy of ensuring "a high level of employment." Under the banner of "a common organisation of agricultural markets," the methods permitted to realize these objectives included "common rules concerning competition," "compulsory co-ordination of the various national market organizations," and "minimum prices" for certain products. Needless to say, these contradicted the liberalization efforts applied to other sectors of the economy.

The Treaty of Rome also committed its signatories to embracing social and neo-corporatist policies. As in the case of the ECSC's High Authority, the newly created European Commission was empowered to coordinate the policies of member states regarding employment, labor legislation and working conditions, occupational training, social security, trade union legislation, collective bargaining between employers and workers, and collaboration between national labor administrations. Revealingly, all these measures were to be implemented with a view to "harmonizing" social systems. Another article of the treaty established a European Social Fund (which was to be advised by a committee of civil servants, employers, and trade unionists) to provide various forms of assistance to workers. The European Investment Bank was also created, with the objective of advancing economic development in less developed regions.

Finally, there were the supranational institutions created by the treaty. These included an assembly, a commission, a council, a court of justice, and an economic and social committee. This last entity was given the mandate of representing—corporatist-style— the views of "producers, agriculturists, transport operators, workers, merchants, artisans, [and] the liberal professions."[11]

Early Criticisms

The *dirigiste*, neo-corporatist, limited liberalization, and social policies associated with the Treaty of Rome did not escape criticism from a number of prominent European intellectuals. As early as 1952, Wilhelm Röpke assailed the *dirigiste* tendencies he associated with the Schuman Declaration and the ECSC.[12]

Five years later, in light of Soviet expansionism, Chancellor Adenauer indicated his willingness to compromise West Germany's market-oriented policies in the interests of building a wider European economic unit, Franco-German postwar rapprochement, and West European solidarity.[13] Here Adenauer was opposed by his finance minister, Ludwig Erhard, who—like Röpke—viewed economic projects such as the ECSC and the EEC as backdoor channels for reintroducing *dirigiste* policies into West Germany.

While Erhard lost to Adenauer at the level of government policy, Röpke pressed his anti-EEC case among other German neoliberals. This culminated in a public and much publicized attack on the EEC project by Röpke at a 1957 meeting of prominent German neoliberals,[14] and his pursuit of free-market arguments against the EEC in influential academic journals.[15]

After the EEC's formation, Röpke's critique took on more political tones. Much of the EEC project, he claimed, was driven by a highly centralized vision of political order, of which the growth of highly bureaucratic supranational institutions was just one manifestation.[16] According to Röpke, the intellectual and political context in which the EEC was developing was one of interventionism, *dirigisme*, and Keynesianism. It was therefore sure to embody these characteristics.

By 1964, Röpke had became quite polemical. He claimed, for example, that the EEC's permanent heads were "mostly socialists and ingrained interventionists."[17] Having previously noted how the ECSC had produced large bureaucracies,[18] Röpke argued that these were being surpassed by the European Commission. He labeled the commisssion "an enormous administrative machine"[19] and argued it was subject to considerable interest-group manipulation.

From Röpke's standpoint, the ECSC and EEC fell far short of the neoliberal principles he and other free marketeers thought should be central to any pan-European program. Röpke himself was very much a European in outlook, and was deeply critical of the *dirigiste* tendencies he more generally associated with the rise of nation-states and nationalism. His concerns about the European integration experiment were underpinned by a sense that the same tendencies were likely to be replicated throughout Europe by supra-national institutions. As it turns out, his fears were largely justified.

Maastricht: Resurgent Markets

Maastricht is a small town in the Netherlands, in the southeastern county of Limburg. With a population of just over 100,000 on a continent of several hundred million people, it seems an unlikely setting for one of the most significant events in the formation of today's European Union. Located, however, at a major linguistic crossroads (Dutch, German, French, English, and Limburgish) and populated by university students from across Europe, Maastricht was in many ways an appropriate place for the signing of a treaty that transformed the European Coal and Steel Community, the European Economic Community, and the European Atomic Energy Community into the European Union in 1993.

The formal change in title accorded to this supranational entity underscored the European experiment's now more openly political character. So too did the decision at Maastricht to create an Economic and Monetary Union with a single currency—the euro—by 2002. This latter move was especially important: The right to issue currency has always been understood as an assertion of sovereignty.

Since the signing of the Treaty of Rome, the EEC had made considerable progress toward a common market. The aspiration for an external customs union had been more or less realized more quickly than anticipated. But many nontariff barriers remained within Europe, such as capital controls and restrictions on cross-border competition in services.

At the same time, the EEC's *dirigiste* characteristics had become more pronounced. Not only was the CAP consuming vast amounts of the EEC's budget in the form of subsidies; it had also become a means through which farming lobbies exerted pressure on governments to maintain the barriers and assistance protecting them from competition.

Dirigiste tendencies on the EEC's part were sometimes encouraged by national governments, albeit for different reasons. Just as many American state governments have been content to have the federal government make unpopular decisions, some national governments were happy to allow EEC institutions such as the Court of Justice and the European Commission to assume responsibility for needed, but painful, national economic reforms. Other European nations viewed EEC institutions as the means for implementing more interventionist policies, while avoiding direct association with such measures. Constant squabbling among EEC member states about any number of proposed economic policies created the desire to remove obstacles to faster, top-down decision making that would automatically apply policies to the entire EEC.

By the 1980s, pressures for further liberalization within the EEC had became more intense, not least because, as Eichengreen notes, most of Western Europe was stagnating, while America's and Japan's economies were surging.[20] During these years, the phrase "Eurosclerosis" became commonplace, as Western Europe struggled to deal with growing and persistently high unemployment and began, technologically speaking, falling behind the rest of the developed world.

As president of the European Commission during this period, Jacques Delors capitalized on these concerns. Drawing upon all the political and bureaucratic skills he had developed through forty years of navigating his way through France's Machiavellian political culture, Delors persuaded EEC member states to ratify the Single European Act of 1987—a program designed to eliminate all remaining impediments to the movement of goods, services, capital, and people by 1992.

This was hardly a new objective. It had been integral to the Treaty of Rome. The difference was that several key countries, especially Germany and Britain, were now highly committed to further liberalization. For Germany, it would not only remove a number of regulatory barriers to market penetration by very competitive German industries; it was also a way for Germany to become even more central in a bigger, more united Europe. For Britain, it was a way to accelerate economic liberalization within the EEC against other member states' *dirigiste* instincts.[21]

Maastricht: Resurgent *Dirigisme* and Neo-Corporatism

If these were the only features of the Single European Act, one would wonder why a politician with such strong market instincts as Margaret Thatcher would become progressively opposed to it. Her concerns rested on the fact that, once again, market integration was accompanied by a renewed commitment to social and neo-corporatist policies. These were summarized in what would become known as the Social Chapter of the Maastricht Treaty.

Put together after extensive consultations with the EEC's most explicitly neo-corporatist institition—the Economic and Social Committee—the Social Chapter (more formally known as the Protocol on Social Policy) committed EEC members to realizing quintessential Social Europe goals. These included employer-employee consultation and worker participation in management; "equitable" remuneration; free association in trade unions; collective bargaining; capping the maximum number of working hours per week; minimum pension rights; improvements regarding "the working environment to protect workers' health and safety"; "equality between men and women with regard to labour market opportunities and treatment at work"; and "the integration of persons excluded from the labour market." If that was not enough, the Social Chapter also authorized the Council of the European Community, following consultations, to act directly to promote "social security and social protection of workers"; "protection of workers when their employment contract is terminated"; "representation and collective defence of the interests of workers and employers, including co-determination"; "conditions of employment for third-country nationals legally residing in Community territory"; and to make "financial contributions for promotion of employment and job-creation."[22]

That's quite a list. One effect was to empower national and supranational bureaucracies to pursue the same social policies at the nation-state and pan-European levels. And, despite numerous qualifications appearing in the same text, it's not hard to see how the Social Chapter's provisions could easily be used to significantly blunt the impact of market-oriented policies.

Opposition to the Social Chapter was based on political and economic grounds. Politically, it was viewed as facilitating the centralization of social and labor policy in Brussels. In economic terms, this had the potential to undermine member states' ability to remain competitive, attract capital and investment, and create jobs in what was already becoming an increasingly competitive global economy.

The intensity of British opposition led to the British government securing the right for member states to opt out of the Social Chapter before the Maastricht Treaty was signed in 1992—a right which Britain promptly exercised. Having spent much of the 1980s working to liberalize the British economy and diminish trade union power, Britain's Conservative government was in no mood to see this work overturned by Brussels. Five years later, Tony Blair's newly elected Labour government opted Britain into the Social Chapter.

The intensity of arguments about the Social Chapter highlighted growing tensions within the EU that were becoming increasingly difficult to manage. But the discussion also distracted attention from another market-unfriendly initative associated with Maastricht: the strengthening of the Economic and Social Committee.

Since its foundation in 1958, interest groups frustrated with the committee's attempts to mediate all contacts between the European

Commission and the worlds of commerce and trade unionism had bypassed the committee by simply ignoring it. The drafting of the Social Chapter, however, gave new momentum to its activities. Previous talk of dismantling the committee disappeared. Instead, it emerged intact with an unelected assembly of 344 members, all of whom were nominated by member-state governments for four-year terms. Committee members were further divided (again, in typical corporatist fashion) into groups—employers, workers, and "other interests"—which voted in blocs. To support its work, the committee was equipped with seven sections charged with addressing issues ranging from employment to social affairs.

In practice, it is open to question how much influence has been wielded by the committee since Maastricht, given the maze of officials, commissions, and agencies (not to mention the thousands of civil servants) that make up the EU's bureaucracy. Yet the committee's importance lies not so much in its power but in what it symbolizes, and what it attempts to do.

First, it reflects the *co-option* of different social groups into the EU's internal workings, through a formal bureaucracy. The effect is to cause the representatives of such groups to identify as much with the EU—and its civil servants—as they do with the particular interests they ostensibly represent. Second, it underscores two assumptions that pervade the EU, and which many Americans would find disturbing. One is the implied notion that the state determines what is civil society, and what is not. The other is that while non-state organizations may deal and negotiate with governments and the EU, they should do so primarily through formal institutions established and supervised by the state. Again, the effect is to co-opt—and limit the independence of—non-state associations.

A Fragmented Union

Fifteen years after Maastricht, the EU had been transformed far beyond the faltering economic community of the 1980s. The number of member states expanded as Central, Eastern, and Scandinavian European nations were admitted to membership. The political ends pursued by those involved in the 1948 Congress of Europe seemed to be drawing closer into sight. Two of the most visible features of this impending development were the common currency and the European Central Bank, the latter assuming responsibility for the direction of monetary policy for the seventeen countries that had joined the eurozone by 2011.

Ironically, this deepening of political and economic links had come despite increasing skepticism among many about various aspects of Europe's integration experiment. This was symbolized by the stunning rejection of the 63,000-word, 448-article draft European constitution by popular referenda in the Netherlands and France in 2005. The choice of most European governments to ratify the constitution via legislative vote, rather than seek direct endorsement from their citizenry, highlighted many European politicians' and bureaucrats' growing awareness of the gap between their political objectives and popular sentiment in many countries.

The motivations for the "no" votes varied. Worries about Turkey's possible entry into the EU (partly a proxy for concern about Muslim immigration) were a factor. Other Europeans based their rejection on fears that the EU was becoming a vehicle for economic liberalization. The French socialist Laurent Fabius, for example, insisted the draft constitution had to be modified to "protect West European countries from losing jobs to the East, where labor costs and taxes are lower."[23] The strangeness of a European constitution that would directly discriminate against less wealthy *European* nations was apparently lost on Fabius.

Other Europeans were concerned about the exact opposite: that the EU had become a way to impose Social Europe upon market economies already facing increasing competition from emergent economies such as China and India. The draft constitution contained sixty-five references to the word "market." The word "social," by contrast, appeared more than 125 times.

In other words, the two pillars of the European social model were increasingly unpopular among many Europeans, for different reasons. This frustration was further exacerbated by what many perceived to be the increased bureaucratization of European life. As the historian Dennis Bark observed:

> in the Netherlands as in France, the vote on the constitution reflected a pent-up disgust with rule by haughty "Eurocrats" who never had to face elections or to explain how they came up with the increasingly intrusive regulations that governed everything from the size of condoms to the noise levels of power lawn-mowers.[24]

In the wake of the 2005 scuttling of the draft constitution by the odd coalition of free marketeers, economic nationalists, and those generally fed up with Europe's political and bureaucratic classes, significant fissures broke out among EU member states. The most telling was a loud, hyperbolic argument between Britain, which demanded reform of the CAP (of which France was a primary beneficiary), and France, which wanted to end the rebate enjoyed by Britain from the EU's budget (which had been secured by Thatcher because Britain's smaller farming sector meant it did not receive anywhere near the agricultural subsidies enjoyed by other EU states). It was a decidedly strange case of a British nominally-center-left-sometimes-market-liberalizer-signer-of-the-Social-Chapter prime minister (Tony Blair) lining up against a French nominally-center-right-occasional-market-liberalizer-but-habitual-*dirigiste* president (Jacques Chirac).

The clash illustrated how different emphases in Europe's economic culture had moved European political life beyond the assumptions made about the economic policies traditionally associated with center-left and center-right parties. Equally revealing were the policy contortions adopted by some European governments as they sought to signal reassurances to Market Europe and Social Europe alike.

Following the French electorate's rejection of the proposed constitution, Prime Minister Dominique de Villepin stated that France's government would:

- Partially privatize two publicly owned utilities—Gaz de France and Électricité de France (a somewhat market measure).
- Inject 4.5 billion euros into the French economy to create jobs (a typically Keynesian measure).
- Pass legislation to make hiring new employees a financially worthwhile proposition (a sort-of market measure).
- Abandon President Jacques Chirac's 2002 promise to reduce taxes (a social measure aimed at maintaining the level of French welfare expenditures).
- Obstruct any EU-directed measures of market liberalization that would reduce labor protections or welfare benefits (an unambiguously social measure).

This mélange of policy announcements perfectly summarized the magnifying contradictions in Europe's economic settings. So too did de Villepin's closing comments, in which he simultaneously blamed fifteen years of socialism for France's economic problems while also declaring that market globalization was neither an ideal nor France's destiny.[25]

Social Europe versus Market Europe

It was another European prime minister who identified the nature of some of the fractures developing in European economic culture after the failure of the constitutional referenda. According to Luxembourg's Jean-Claude Juncker, one group was increasingly focused on the idea of a large European free-trade zone; the other concentrated on European integration. The difference, Juncker said, lay in the latter's emphasis on political integration via harmonizing social policy across the EU. The free traders, by contrast, sought to prioritize economic freedom.[26]

The veracity of Juncker's insight was evidenced by the decision of prominent EU market-friendly politicians to press for further liberalization in the early 2000s, and the subsequent push back from Social Europe. In 2005, free-market members of the European Commission advocated implementation of a *directive on services in the internal market* (first proposed in 2004) throughout the EU. In its original draft form, this directive effectively removed administrative barriers to the ability of individuals or companies to offer services outside their country of origin. It was thus squarely based on market principles of freedom of association and movement.

The draft directive provoked a furious response and mass protests from the political Left (ranging from Social Democrats to the hard Left) and trade unions, but also opposition from some Christian Democrats and conservatives, who were convinced it would result in a reduction of wages and benefits, as West Europeans found themselves in competition with immigrants from Central-East Europe (the infamous "Polish plumber") willing to work for lower wages and benefits. And they claimed the directive would encourage "social dumping," as Western European companies took advantage of the directive to move their operations to Central-East Europe's less regulated economies.

The eventual directive approved by the European Commission and the European Parliament in December 2006 reflected the now familiar blending of market and social principles. The directive stressed the principle of free movement, but emphasized that this principle needed to be reconciled with "other competing principles."[27]

This translated into the operations of labor laws being removed from the directive's jurisdiction. Additionally, a range of services were excluded from the directive's free movement provisions. Among others, these included health care, some telecommunications services, transport and port services, financial services, activities of a noneconomic nature provided by the state, some social services, temp agencies, and private security services. These are many of the service areas in which today's Europe continues to underachieve compared to America.[28]

Specific limits were also placed on the freedom to provide services in sectors including water, postal, electricity, and gas (i.e., services often provided by the state). And if that was not enough, the directive allowed member states to restrict service provision on grounds of public security, public health, or environmental concerns.

Today the situation is further complicated by the fact that Europeans working in hundreds of professions (including doctors, lawyers, and engineers) often find it difficult to receive formal recognition of their qualifications if they attempt to work in another EU country. To remove such barriers, in 2011 the European Commission pushed member states to agree to a mutual recognition proposal. While member-state governments generally expressed agreement in principle, quiet opposition from national professional groups concerned about a lowering of standards, or simply opposed to competition from Europeans from other countries, created enormous guild-like opposition to change.[29]

Clearly the market commitment to the free movement of people, goods, and capital, which the EU is supposed to promote, remains highly qualified. As noted in a European Commission report on the single market authored by the Italian economist, technocrat, and eventual prime minister, Mario Monti, the "single market is Europe's original idea and unfinished business" and in some places "is far from being completely in place."[30] The truth, Monti concluded, is that the single market is viewed as essentially "instrumental to several other areas of EU policy making, which do attract greater political interest."[31] And when it gets in the way of other interests in Europe, the market commitment tends to be quietly shoved aside.

Lisbon: The Ascendancy of Social Europe

If anything, more recent formal measures to promote deeper EU integration suggest that the priorities of Market Europe are being increasingly subordinated to those of Social Europe. Prominent EU leaders, including the president of the European Commission, José Manuel Barroso, presented the Treaty of Lisbon as part of an overall strategy to make the EU the world's most competitive economic region. The devil, however, was in the details of the treaty, which took effect in December 2009. Closer inspection would not encourage confidence that Lisbon would help propel the EU in such a direction.

Lisbon's focus was on reorganizing the respective powers of the European Commission, the European Council, and the European Parliament, vis-à-vis each other as well as national governments and parliaments. It also modified voting procedures to reduce the requirements for unanimity on the part of member states, and changed the status of a number of institutions, including the ECB. Finally, Lisbon created positions designed to underscore the EU's sovereignist ambitions, such as a full-time European Council president, and what was called the "European External Action Service"—an EU diplomatic corps.

That Barroso was engaged in wishful thinking about a more market-oriented EU may be found in one prominent section of the Lisbon Treaty: the Charter of Fundamental Rights of the European Union.[32] This text had been "proclaimed" in December 2000 by the European Commission, the European Parliament, and the Council of Ministers. It did not, however, acquire legal sanction until nine years later, with the signing of the Lisbon treaty. The delay perhaps indicates the depth of concerns about the charter's economic implications among market-inclined European opinion.

The charter contains 54 articles that assert a range of rights. These range from the usual freedoms of conscience, speech, religion, and assembly to more idiosyncratic subjects such as the right of EU citizens to access to a European Ombudsman. In economic terms, the charter's preamble states that "it seeks to promote balanced and sustainable development [the solidarist dimension] and ensures free movement of persons, services, goods and capital [the market dimension]."

Any objective study of the charter, however, soon indicates that the solidarist dimension easily trumps market freedoms. Recognizably "market" freedoms are listed in the charter, but are more limited in number and far more subject to extensive qualifications than the various social rights.

Thus, while the charter affirms the protection of private property (Article 17), it also outlines strict limits to the exercise of private property rights. Similarly, the right of freedom of association is affirmed, but includes a specific reference to the right to associate in trade unions (Article 12). Conversely, the freedom to conduct a business is merely "recognized" (Article 16). Freedom to choose one's employment in any member state is also "recognized," as is the right to provide services in any member state (Article 15)—something which, as noted, continues to be quietly impeded by many EU member states.

An entire chapter of the charter—found under the revealing overall title of "Solidarity"—spells out numerous protections and entitlements to be accorded to all EU citizens. These include relatively uncontroversial ideas such as prohibitions on child labor. But they also incorporate the right of workers "or their representatives" (i.e., trade union officials) to be consulted in the operations of an enterprise (Article 27); the right to collective bargaining on the part of workers, employers, or "their respective organizations" (i.e., unions, business associations, and other corporatist entities) (Article 28); the right to access a "free placement service" (presumably provided by the state) (Article 29); the right to social security entitlements and benefits (Article 34); social housing (Article 34); and the right to preventative health care (Article 35).

Finally, the solidarity chapter of the charter insists upon an all-embracive respect of "access to services of general economic interest . . . in order to promote the social and territorial cohesion of the Union" (Article 36). The sheer vagueness of this was presumably designed to cover anything left over.

Needless to say, the charter says nothing about how to pay for the costs of realizing and maintaining these freedoms, rights, protections, and cohesion. To be fair, the charter constantly refers to the fact that these rights must be realized "in accordance with Union law and national laws and practices." That may provide some flexibility at the national level. Nonetheless, that these social and economic claims are given the status of rights in the legally binding charter means they are more than pious aspirations. They have legal teeth, and can be used by any number of interest groups, political parties, and "representative organizations" (i.e., neo-corporatist formations) to pursue various ends in the name of Social Europe.

Security Leads to Insecurity

However strong might be the isolating effects of life as a European politician or civil servant from public sentiment and everyday business and economic realities, these individuals are not oblivious to the growing cynicism and apathy among many Europeans that increasingly shapes their views of the modern European project. One side effect of the humiliating 2005 rejection of the draft EU constitution has been a greater willingness on the part of EU officials to invest effort and resources in trying to explain significant changes to EU citizens.

This itself has proved a revealing process. Public documents designed to explain changes within the EU tend to emphasize issues of economic security and the EU's social goals. Texts designed for mass distribution by the European Commission to mark the signing of the Treaty of Lisbon are a good example. In *Your Guide to the Lisbon Treaty*, the commission goes out of its way to stress that Lisbon was designed to help realize "the sustainable development of Europe based on balanced economic growth and price stability, a highly competitive social market economy, aiming at full employment and social progress, with a high level of protection of the environment."[33]

Such wording reflects a mixture of neoliberal, Christian Democratic, Social Democratic, and Keynesian themes. The "social" emphasis, however, is underscored by statements underlining how the Lisbon treaty would "combat social exclusion and discrimination and promote social justice and protection," "promote economic, social and territorial cohesion, and solidarity among member-states," and commit the EU "to realization of the European Union's values in the wider world and contribute to peace, security, the sustainable development of the earth, solidarity and respect among peoples, free and fair trade, and the eradication of poverty."[34]

Much of this could be dismissed as vague sentimental humanitarianism mixed with a heavy dose of secular utopianism. The employment of such language in a document intended for mass distribution, however, indicates that the EU's political leaders and senior civil servants are acutely conscious of many Europeans' deep wariness of economic liberalization. In fact, the document goes on to stress that the EU's social policy would "take into account the promotion of a high level of employment"[35] and "refrain from any action that would detract from the member-states' role in providing services of general interest such as health, social services, police and security forces, [and] state schools."[36]

The context for these assurances was one of a global recession in the wake of the 2008 financial crisis. As the American economy and global markets faltered, it is hardly surprising the EU sought to sell its own credentials, primarily in terms of security, high employment, and uninterrupted provision of social services.

This tendency may have been accentuated by the eagerness of European countries especially impacted by the crisis to treat the EU as a refuge in difficult economic times, rather than as a platform for accelerated market-driven growth. Ireland rejected ratification of Lisbon in June 2008, throwing the whole process into doubt for the entire EU. Yet less than sixteen months later, in the midst of a housing market meltdown and the implosion of Ireland's banking system, the same Irish citizens dramatically reversed their position. Like a number of peripheral states suddenly facing severe economic difficulties, the hope was that the EU would buttress European countries from the worst effects of the global financial crisis and subsequent recession.

Over the past decade, there has also been a dawning awareness that the European social model's focus upon realizing economic security through *dirigiste*, neo-corporatist, and welfare policies has actually become an acute point of weakness for much of the EU in a competitive global economy. In 2007, Jürgen Stark, a then prominent member of the executive board of the ECB, noted that the level of public spending across the EU (47.6 percent of GDP in 2005) reflected a steady growth throughout Europe of social security spending and outright wealth transfers from the 1960s onward.

Making his point in uncharacteristically direct language for a central banker, Stark then stated:

> This may often reflect the cumulative effect of decades of political economy biases toward higher spending. Many governments are elected on platforms which include commitments to boost investment spending, to increase spending on public transport, or to raise the proportion of GDP spent on health, research and development, education, income re-distribution, etc. Finance ministries are often asked to accommodate these wishes as much as possible even if they do not want to. Believe me, from my own past, I know what I am talking about...[37]

The problem, Stark noted, was that Social Europe could only be maintained through "rather high levels of taxation and public spending." Unfortunately, he added, there were "increasingly signs that such high levels of spending can have detrimental medium- and long-term economic effects especially on growth and fiscal sustainability."[38]

Europe's future in the global marketplace, Stark maintained, meant that it needed a competitive economy that adapted quickly to change. "But," Stark commented (in what now surely seems understated tones), "it is not clear that we can have such an economy while the state continues to absorb almost half of the economy's resources."[39]

Stark is no radical libertarian. In the same paper, he argued there was a significant role for public spending. He also spoke of his desire to see more "efficient spending that attains core social and economic objectives, but [which] leaves us money to adapt to new challenges (such as globalisation and climate change) and maintain a high quality of life."[40] Nevertheless, Stark insisted, Europeans needed to decide whether their economics would become "dinosaurs" in the future. Avoidance of such a fate, he insisted, meant aiming to reduce public spending to something between 30 to 36 percent of GDP—a figure close to that of America's 34.8 percent at the time.[41]

Stark's paper raised serious questions about the effects of public spending. It did not, however, specifically address the related matter of the progressive *decline* in Western Europe's overall economic growth rate: a decline that ominously corresponds to the inexorable rise of Social Europe.

One European head of state, the Czech president Václav Klaus, was unafraid to make the connection. In 2010, he wrote:

> Economic growth in Europe has been slowing down since the 1960s, thanks to the increasingly damaging economic and social system which started dominating Europe at that time. The European *soziale Marktwirtschaft* is an unproductive variant of a welfare state, of state paternalism, of "leisure" society, of high taxes

and low motivation to work. The existence of the euro has not reversed that trend. According to the European Central Bank, the average annual rate of growth in the eurozone countries was 3.4% in the 1970s, 2.4% in the 1980s, 2.2% in the 1990s and only 1.1% from 2001 to 2009 (the decade of the euro). A similar slowdown has not occurred anywhere else in the world.[42]

This did not mean Europe was on the verge of rampant poverty. It did, however, suggest that much of the EU had entered what might be called a period of golden decline.

Taken together, Stark's and Klaus's observations amount to a serious indictment of the economic model that dominated much of Europe for the twentieth century, and the internal contradictions increasingly characterizing European economic culture. The next four chapters illustrate how Europe's economic culture has helped facilitate considerable dysfunctionality in Europe's economies by: (1) establishing insiders and outsiders on the basis of proximity to political power; (2) facilitating fiscally unsustainable welfare states; (3) creating a monetary system that has fallen prey to a dangerous cycle of debt and deficits; and (4) leaving unresolved an ambiguity about economic globalization that is creating new political and economic fractures within the EU.

These developments—and the worrying parallels which exist in America—form the subject matter of part 2 of this book.

II

Continents in Crisis

5

Insiders and Outsiders

Well, maybe people will believe things, but that's why we politicians are here, to put things on the right course.[1]

—GEORGE PAPANDREOU

Whether we like it or not, every society has elites. They attain their positions for many reasons: design, chance, inherited position, family and social connections, merit, hard work, or a combination of such factors. But leaving aside anarchists, few dispute that every society, including free societies, needs some authority to make decisions that bind every member of that community, especially when disagreement exists about the right course of action.

No doubt this was at least partly in the mind of George Papandreou when he uttered the words cited at the opening of this chapter. Papandreou served as Greece's prime minister between October 2009 and November 2011, in the midst of the Greek economy's meltdown. One doesn't need to be a sophisticated student of world affairs to recognize there *are* many occasions when elected officials should chose paths that run counter to majority popular opinion. At the same time, Papandreou's words most likely reflected sentiments common to Europe's more or less professional political class, of which he is an exemplar. Such convictions are based on:

- the assumption that, for all the endless references by Europeans to democracy, political life should be managed directly by professionals such as themselves;
- a self-confidence that they should be in charge; and
- an ingrained belief that the influence upon public policy of those who are not political insiders or civil servants should be strictly limited.

This is a vision of politics and public service, aptly described by the German philosopher Jürgen Habermas as "a kind of post-democratic, bureaucratic rule,"[2] from which Americans have (at least historically) generally recoiled. One characteristic of American society that immediately struck Tocqueville during his travels in the early 1830s was Americans' lack of deference toward government officials and those holding elected office. It was not that Americans thought less of politicians or civil servants than any other group. Rather, they were simply considered people like any other. In France, these same groups were the objects of a particular respect—and yet Tocqueville noted their capacity for relentless self-promotion at the expense of the governed.

The days when European politicians and civil servants were treated deferentially by the citizenry are long past. What has not changed is their status as privileged insiders. Like those in charge of the absolutist-mercantilist regimes of old, they benefit disproportionately from the economic culture prevailing throughout much of contemporary Europe. They are not, however, alone. There are other winners and losers from the European social model: what we might call "insiders" and "outsiders." From this standpoint, there remain significant differences between Europe and America. Yet there are also uncomfortable similarities that are becoming harder to ignore.

Dynasticism, Careerism, *Dirigisme*

George Papandreou was not the first member of his family to be prime minister of Greece. He is the son and grandson of former Greek prime ministers Andreas Papandreou and Giorgios Papandreou. If one was to speak of a modern Greek political dynasty, it would be the Papandreou clan.

Dynastic tendencies, however, are not limited to Greece's Left. Young Papandreou's predecessor as prime minister, the conservative Kostas Karamanlís, has his own pedigree. He is the nephew of Konstantínos G. Karamanlís, who served as prime minister four times, and as the third and fifth president of the Greek Hellenic Republic. Likewise, Papandreou's successor, Antonis Samaras, is the nephew of George Samaras, who was a prominent member of the Greek Parliament for two decades.

Despite modern Europe's break in 1789 with the aristocracy's dominance of politics, family ties permeate every nook and cranny of Europe's political landscape today. Sweden's prime minister, Fredrik Reinfeldt, was until 2012 married to Filippa Reinfeldt, who, like her former husband, is a Moderate Party politician and has served in a variety of government offices. One of France's most prominent Socialist politicians, Martine Aubry, is Jacques Delors's daughter. Former Italian prime minister Massimo D'Alema is the son of Giuseppe D'Alema, a prominent Italian Communist Party politician. The sons of French presidents de Gaulle and Giscard d'Estaing have sat in the French parliament. François Mitterrand's nephew, Frédéric Mitterrand, served as minister of culture under president Nicolas Sarkozy. The latter's son Jean became a councilor in the city of Neuilly-sur-Seine at the tender age of 22. The former partner of current French president François Hollande, Ségolène Royal, was the Socialist Party's candidate for the presidency in 2007. Alexander Graf Lambsdorff, nephew of the former chairman of Germany's Free Democratic Party, Otto Graf Lambsdorff, serves in the European Parliament.

Ireland is a case study in its own right. Literally dozens of family members—sons, daughters, brothers, sisters, grandsons, granddaughters, nephews, nieces, cousins, wives, in-laws—have followed each other into the legislature (often into the same legislative seat) since the Irish Free State's creation in 1922. France's hard-right National Front illustrated just how much it had become a regular part of the political landscape when its leadership passed from Jean-Marie Le Pen to his daughter Marine Le Pen (whose first two husbands were party officials) in January 2011. Eighteen months later, the National Front's dynastic tendencies were confirmed by the election of Jean-Marie's granddaughter, Marion Maréchal-Le Pen, as one of the first two National Front members of France's National Assembly.

In West European country after West European country, these patterns replicate themselves. Of course, similar examples exist in America: the Daleys of Chicago, the Bushes of Texas, the Kennedys of Massachusetts, the Bidens of Delaware, the Quayles of Arizona, and the Cuomos of New York. Thus far, however, those Americans whose family business seems to be politics have struggled to replicate themselves to the extent achieved by their European counterparts.

Another major difference between Europe's and America's political classes is that European political parties are institutions unto themselves, to an extent many Americans find incomprehensible. The Republican and Democratic parties are mass parties with relatively fluid memberships, and (nominally) millions of members, evoking varying degrees of commitment.

By contrast, most European political parties with parliamentary representation are relatively small in terms of membership, yet are a full-time career for many of their members. Such careers might begin with work within the party's youth wing, before election to a minor public office, then work for a party-affiliated organization, eventually entrance to the legislature, perhaps with time spent in a party-linked government-funded think tank (especially if one loses one's seat in an election), before a return to the legislature and/or appointment to a government ministry.

A good example is Tarja Halonen, who served as Finland's first female president, from 2000 to 2012. Her political career began after her graduation from university, when she served as the social affairs and organization secretary of the National Union of Students, between 1969 and 1970. She became a lawyer for the Social Democratic-affiliated Finnish trade union movement, and in 1971 joined the Social Democratic Party (which today has fewer than 55,000 members). In 1974, prime minister Kalevi Sorsa made her his parliamentary secretary. Two years later Halonen was elected to the Helsinki city council, a seat she held until 1996. In 1979 she was elected to the Finnish parliament, serving for twenty-one years. Halonen attained her first ministry in 1987, and held a number of ministerial posts and sat on several parliamentary committees until being elected president in 2000.

In short, from her time in university until her retirement as president, Halonen did *nothing* careerwise except work in politics, perform politically related activity, or hold government office. But her story is not at all untypical of EU politicians, from both the Right and the Left.

The first full-time president of the European Council, Herman Van Rompuy, comes from Belgium's Christian Democratic and Flemish Party, a mildly center-right political movement that arose out of the Christian Democratic tradition and which enjoys strong links to various Belgian neo-corporatist formations and trade unions. Rompuy's political career began when he served as head of his party's youth wing at the age of 26. Apart from a three-year stint in the early 1970s working as a civil servant at Belgium's central bank, and a short time in the 1980s as an academic economist, Rompuy served continuously in party political, legislative, and executive offices, including one year as Belgium's prime minister, before becoming European Council president in 2009.

There is nothing particularly sinister about these career trajectories. Nor is the point to cast aspersions on any particular European politician's commitment to public service. What is disturbing is how much political life is actually (or quickly becomes) a *career* for many Europeans. It suggests that politics in Europe is somewhat of a closed world to those who are not professional politicians, or who have not spent many years effectively training to assume political office. While nonprofessionals can enter political life, and even become head of government (Italy's Silvio Berlusconi is a good example), they tend to be the exception in Europe rather than the rule.

One side effect of this closed world is that it reinforces the conviction among many European politicians that the state *must* have a major role in the economy. This point was illustrated in 2006 by the journalist Gregory Viscusi in an article about the average French politician's knowledge of the world of business.

At the time, Viscusi observed, only thirty of 331 members of France's senate had ever worked in private industry. Apparently deciding they might need to learn something as France's economic growth continued to fall behind other EU nations, some senators decided to venture, Viscusi wrote, "out of their Paris sanctuary in the 17th-century Luxembourg Palace to factories and offices in search of what Finance Minister Thierry Breton calls an 'economic education.'"[3] For many senators, it was a revelation to learn that free markets and genuinely free associations (i.e., those not explicitly linked to or funded by the state) could solve any number of problems better than government planning.

Given the highly *dirigiste* character of European economic culture, this should surprise no one. Why should people who have made politics their life have any particular knowledge of how to create the wealth they are happy to redistribute? It is also predictable that they think about economic life in broad macro terms, with relatively little understanding about what happens at the micro level of the economy. Nor is a *dirigiste* mind-set likely to incline anyone to fully comprehend the nature of entrepreneurship, precisely because entrepreneurship is a classic "bottom-up" activity. If anything, such creativity is likely to be viewed with suspicion, because successful entrepreneurship always involves challenging the economic status quo, and thus requires some adjustment by those who claim to be managing the economy.

The same ingrained *dirigisme* also incentivizes many bright and ambitious young Europeans to invest their energies in forging political careers, rather than entering the private sector. For those seeking well-paid jobs more or less immune to involuntary redundancy, European political life provides numerous safe havens and opportunities: appointments to EU positions; employment with an affiliated trade union or one of the neo-corporatist groups with whom many parties are associated; jobs at party-affiliated think tanks; or joining the army of advisers who swarm through the halls of power at local, regional, national, and European levels.

An American Political Class?

It is not difficult to find American politicians who have spent significant amounts of time involved in nonpolitical activities before entering public office. The former governor of California, the actor Arnold Schwarzenegger, is one example. Much of Schwarzenegger's initial appeal was derived from the fact that he was *not* a career politician. Likewise, the Speaker of the House of Representatives, John Boehner, worked in business for thirteen years before being elected to Congress. The mayor of New York, Michael Bloomberg, spent more than three decades in the financial industry before being elected in 2001. None of these individuals came from "political families" (though Schwarzenegger married a Kennedy).

Nonetheless, America has had—and continues to have—more than its own fair share of career politicians. Since graduating from law school in 1982, New York's governor, Andrew Cuomo, has spent almost his entire post-university life either running for or holding public office at the state and federal level. Apart from short and often very part-time periods as a community organizer, civil rights attorney, and university lecturer, Barack Obama spent most of his prepresidential adult life in politically related activity. Former House Speaker Nancy Pelosi not only hails from a political family of Democrats, but has been involved in the Democratic Party since the 1960s, and has held public office from the 1980s onward. Between graduating from college in 1974 and being elected a Republican senator from Maine in 1996, Susan Collins worked as a congressional and senate legislative assistant, a senate committee staff director, a cabinet member in the state of Maine, and a federal appointee in the Small Business Administration. During that time, Collins spent just two years not working as a political staffer.

To this extent, it is difficult to deny that politics in the United States has developed significant correlations to European political life beyond what is common to modern democracies. Across America, legislatures and executives are full of people who have made a full-time profession out of political office and the exercise of political power.

It is conceivable that this also reflects the emergence of what the political scientist Charles Murray has called America's "new ruling class."

In *Coming Apart: The State of White America, 1960–2010*, Murray presents formidable evidence to suggest that the elites who dominate American political, cultural, and economic life are overwhelmingly drawn from the same type of family background, attend the same first-tier universities, live in the same areas, and increasingly inter-marry—so much so that some members (now in their third genera-tion) know little of life outside their own social circles.[4] From this perspective, they could even be labeled somewhat "provincial."

Part of Murray's argument is that those Americans who come from different backgrounds and, through business success, become part of America's economic "one percent" do not necessarily form part of this ruling class, precisely because they haven't emerged from the same milieu as the elites. For the most part, Murray suggests, such economically upwardly mobile people remain political outsiders.

While the parallels with Europe are obvious, important differences remain between Europe's and America's respective political classes. The political career path in Europe seems to produce people who are remarkably alike in their economic views. They are, after all, working in a context in which the general consensus on economic issues, shared by Europe's mainstream center-left and center-right parties, encourages and incentivizes favorable views of the European social model at the national and European level.

By contrast, America's economic culture, with its stronger emphases on liberty, entrepreneurship, free association, and free competition, makes it possible for politicians with loudly professed pro-market views to be electorally successful. The same culture also makes it harder for those with unabashedly socialist opinions to be elected. Openly socialist politicians such as Vermont senator Bernie Sanders are extremely rare in America. Successfully labeling a poten-tial American politician as a socialist remains a most effective way of ensuring a stillborn political career. Conversely, many center-left and left-wing European politicians wear the socialist label proudly, even if their actual economic views broadly conform to the Euro-pean social model's melding of market, *dirigiste,* and neo-corporatist ideas.

"I Want to Be a Civil Servant"

Dirigisme is not just about top-down political direction of the economy. It also involves bureaucracy. Top-down coordination invariably requires lots of top-down coordinators. While career politicians are among the most prominent insiders created by Europe's economic culture, they pale in comparison to the privileged status enjoyed by the civil service and public-sector workers in most European nations. They are *les intendants* of today's Europe.

A useful illustration of their insider credentials was provided in 2010. Following a range of public-spending cuts in several EU member states, mass strikes and occasional violence broke out at different intervals in countries including France, Greece, Spain, Britain, Portugal, and Italy. Yet at the very height of this wave of unrest, in November 2010, the European Court of Justice confirmed that EU civil servants working in Brussels should receive a pay rise of 3.7 percent. That same month, the European Parliament voted 564–92 in favor of a 6.19 percent increase for its 2011 budget.[5]

Apart from manifesting an apparent lack of solidarity on the part of EU civil servants with their fellow Europeans, who were enduring pay cuts and suffering job losses, it raised questions about just who the EU's civil servants and politicians imagined paid their salaries and benefits. Why did bureaucrats merit pay increases when so many other people's income was headed in the opposite direction? What did this say about the degree to which Europe's politicians and civil servants were in touch with the economic realities then sweeping through the continent?

The impression of detachment was heightened in June 2011 when it was revealed that, after eighteen months of financial turmoil, spending cuts, austerity measures, and several waves of private-sector layoffs, Greece's government had yet to fire a single public-sector worker.[6] Then, after stating—again—its intention to make thirty thousand civil servants redundant, the Greek government fired just one thousand. While it allowed ten thousand to take early retirement (thereby adding to Greece's pension bill), the remaining nineteen thousand stayed in their positions.[7]

In February 2012, as Germany and Greece's creditors began to lose patience with Greek stalling tactics, the Greek government and parliament agreed—in theory—to lay off one hundred and fifty thousand public-sector workers over a three-year period as part of its debt negotiations.[8] This amounted to approximately 20 percent of Greece's total public-sector workforce. The scale of protests and riots in the streets of Athens and other Greek cities by trade unionists of all political stripes, many of whom belonged to the public sector or publicly owned corporations, left no doubt of the anger of Greece's public-sector workers.[9]

For life is good in Europe's public sector. In an October 2010 article about the salaries and benefits earned by EU civil servants, published in *Der Spiegel,* Hans-Jürgen Schlamp pointed out:

> an entry-level interpreter starts out with a base salary of €4,190 a
> month. A senior official can earn as much as €16,000 ($21,459)
> a month. In addition to that, allowances are given for living
> abroad, housing, children, schooling and pre-school. European
> taxpayers in a rough estimate pay around €100 million a year for
> the private EU schools the children of eurocrats attend.[10]

The pension arrangements for EU officials are even more generous. Noting that EU bureaucrats pay nothing into their pension scheme, Schlamp observed that if a civil servant worked sixteen years for the EU, they qualified for a pension of 70 percent of the person's final salary. That worked out to a pension of more than €10,000 per month. In fact, an official need only work for more than five years to become eligible for a pension of almost €5,000 per month. Schlamp concluded by reminding his German readers that "a German worker in the highest wage category could pay the highest contribution to the system throughout their entire life and still wouldn't get that kind of payout."[11]

Britain's National Health Service (NHS) has long served as a model of insider capture: a situation whereby those responsible for the functioning of an organization increasingly pursue their own immediate self-interest, rather than that of their external customers or clients. In 2011, the British social commentator Anthony Daniels (under the pen name Theodore Dalrymple) demonstrated that, in the midst of measureable declines in productivity and quality of health care delivered by Britain's nationalized health care system, "the number of people employed by the NHS rose by a third, with the number of doctors employed by it doubling and overall remuneration for personnel increasing by 50 percent per head" between 1997 and 2007. This pattern of increases in public-sector jobs, salaries, pensions, and benefits in return for little to no productivity gains had been replicated, Daniels illustrated, across all levels of government in Britain. "In Manchester," he noted, "the number of city employees earning more than $85,000 a year rose from 68 to 1,746 between 1997 and 2007."[12]

Across the Channel, a more comical—and disturbing—picture of European bureaucracy emerged in a 2010 book written by a young French civil servant. Entitled *Absolument dé-bor-dée* (*Absolutely Snowed Under*), its subject matter was underlined by a provocative subtitle: *Comment faire les 35 heures en . . . un mois!* (*How to Make 35 Hours Last . . . a Month!*).[13]

Writing under the pseudonym of Zoé Shepard, Aurélie Boullet portrayed her life as an eager, fresh, and highly trained civil servant who had joined the Socialist-led Aquitaine Regional Council's international and European affairs delegation straight from one of France's elite schools for the nation's future leaders. To her shock, Boullet encountered what she called a "five-hour-week" culture in which nepotism was rife and travel expenses routinely abused. Some of her colleagues rarely came to work. Others, she said, competed to see who could take the longest coffee breaks.

It was not a flattering picture of the life enjoyed by France's then 5.2 million civil servants. If only half of Boullet's claims were true, it would still be shocking.

Sadly, there are comparable American examples. In 2010, the state of California was stunned to learn that the city of Bell, a relatively poor town in Los Angeles County of just over forty thousand people, was paying six-figure salaries and generous benefits to senior city bureaucrats.[14] The chief administrator of the city, for example, earned *three times* as much as the CEO of Los Angeles County (which contains over ten million people). Two years later, Americans were appalled by the financial scandal that engulfed the General Services Administration (GSA), involving questionable dealings with contractors and excessive spending on travel, hotels, and entertainment.

There was, however, a crucial difference between these European and American examples. In America, the resulting public outrage about the city of Bell's fiscal mismanagement resulted in dismissals, and eventual criminal charges being laid against public officials and elected council members. Likewise, the head of the GSA and several subordinates were forced to resign, and other officials were put on leave pending investigation. By contrast, media coverage of the French case did not produce demands for resignations, calls for more transparency, or reductions in bureaucrats' salaries (let alone investigations of apparent malfeasance). While *Absolument dé-bor-dée* sold more than one hundred and eighty thousand copies, the whistleblower found herself suspended from France's civil service and embroiled in court battles with the Aquitaine Regional Council.[15]

Given these facts, it is hardly surprising that a 2004 survey of French adults under the age of thirty indicated that more than 70 percent would prefer to work as state employees. Their reasoning included the lifestyle, vacations, salaries, benefits, and more or less permanent job security enjoyed by those in such employment.[16] Such sentiments were most likely reinforced by the kind of austerity measures introduced by the French government in August 2011, as major doubts began to be expressed in financial markets about the state of France's public finances. These austerity policies consisted mostly of tax increases in the form of elevated consumption taxes and higher levies on the wealthiest French citizens' income taxes. From this standpoint, François Hollande's 2012 proposal, to further raise taxes on individuals earning more than one million Euros from the top rate of 41 percent to a marginal rate of 75 percent, merely represented an extension of existing austerity measures. And the 2011 austerity measures did *nothing* to immediately reduce the number of people working in the public sector. France's local government bureaucracies—which, like their British cousins, have grown in recent years in numbers of employees and expenditures—were left virtually untouched.[17]

As if providentially, a U.S. Census Bureau report issued that very same week of August 2011 stated that almost 204,000 local and state government full-time jobs had been eliminated in 2010. Americans, however, should not feel too complacent. First, the eliminations still left American local and state governments employing *16.6 million* people. In other words, the cuts represented a reduction of just 1.2 percent;[18] part-time state and local government employees numbered 4.8 million in 2010. This represented a decrease of just 27,567 positions from 2009.[19]

Second, as Arthur Brooks illustrated in 2010, "the average federal worker earns 77 percent more than the average private-sector worker."[20] If this trend continues, economic incentives alone may start to attract increasing numbers of Americans to a public sector that, by definition, is not focused on wealth creation, and which must be paid for by those working in the private sector. It is possible that such incentives may be negated by growing awareness of the inability of governments—local, state, and federal—to maintain these levels of generosity. Since 2010, America has witnessed an accelerating trend of city governments declaring bankruptcy, most noticeably (and to no one's surprise) in California—Stockton, Mammoth Lakes, San Bernardino—under the weight of unaffordable employee salary and pension commitments. With unions unwilling to make any significant concessions on salaries and benefits, city councils found themselves with little choice but to opt for Chapter 9 bankruptcy—a procedure that allowed independent judges to impose new conditions on all parties concerned, regardless of past agreements.

Fashioning an Elite

One reason for the different reactions of Europeans and Americans to clear instances of public-sector waste, inefficiency, and corruption is historical. As we saw in chapter 2, a key feature of the modern European state's emergence was the development of professional civil services, which were considered essential for facilitating social and economic progress. Consequently, a certain degree of prestige has long been associated in many European countries with being a senior civil servant, at least when compared to activities like trade and commerce.

By contrast, America's own history of bureaucracy is comparatively more recent, and limited. It was not until the New Deal that America experienced its own rapid growth in bureaucracy at the federal level. And no matter how large the bureaucracy, no one would claim that working for federal or state governments in America is viewed as favorably as it is in Europe.

Another crucial difference, however, is that a number of institutional mechanisms exist in Europe for deliberately promoting the development—and maintaining the power and prestige—of political and civil service elites. France exemplifies this phenomenon.

Dominique de Villepin (center-right), Lionel Jospin (Socialist), Jacques Chirac (center-right), Alain Juppé (center-right), Laurent Fabius (Socialist), Édouard Balladur (center-right), Raymond Barre (center-right), Michel Rocard (Socialist), Jacques Chaban-Delmas (center-right), and Michel Debré (center-right) all served as prime minister of France since the 1960s. Whatever their political differences, they share something in common. All are graduates of one of France's *grandes écoles* or *grands établissements*: the elite French state-controlled educational institutions that are quite separate from the university system.

The *grandes écoles* are purposively *designed* to train France's political and bureaucratic elite. Gaining entry is an extremely competitive exercise, because graduates *know* (whatever their politics) that graduating from a *grande école* sets them up for life, as part of the elite who will control the civil service and hold a high percentage of elected positions. They have even acquired an appellation—*les énarques* (after École Nationale d'Administration, or ENA, the most prestigious of France's *grandes écoles)*—which marks them as members of France's most elite insider group.

Although the emphasis on competitive entry into the *grandes écoles* was meant to broaden the social basis of recruitment, Larry Siedentop is not alone in observing that the process has essentially been overtaken by France's upper middle class, often Paris-based elites. Hence, as Siedentop notes, "the French *élite*, for whom political and administrative careers are increasingly bound up together, has become an ever more coherent, self-conscious and relatively small group, well-known to each other and presiding over the destinies of France."[21] It is only a slight exaggeration to claim that *les fonctionnaires*, as they are sometimes called, *are* in effect France's ruling class, regardless of which political party they happen to belong to.

Hamstrung by Bureaucracy

So which Europeans lose out from this situation of political and bureaucratic privilege? One such group of outsiders is those who *pay* for the wages, benefits, and pensions of public-sector employees: i.e., taxpayers. Large amounts of their income are drained into public coffers to cover the cost of the European officialdom that oversees, directs, and deepens the European social model. And when taxes don't yield enough to cover the costs of this public-sector apparatus, government recourse to debt becomes even more likely.

Another set of outsiders created by these circumstances are those who have to navigate their way through EU and national bureaucracies. This can range from farmers having to identify those who predetermine how large their crop size may be to entrepreneurs attempting to obtain the necessary licenses to start a business. The more experienced one is at gaming the bureaucracy, the easier it is. But this is of no help for those who lack the requisite connections, or who may be first-time entrepreneurs.

Alas, there is little evidence of a significant commitment by most of Europe's political class to addressing such problems. This may be partly because so many European politicians have themselves belonged to the civil service at different times, and thus find it difficult to understand how government institutions ostensibly created to resolve problems can themselves quickly become obstacles to economic development. In addition, European economic culture's emphasis on the necessity of extensive state coordination of the economy can easily generate self-reinforcing rationalizations for extensive bureaucratization and endless empire-building.

Time, however, may facilitate some resolution of the issue. As the burden of public-sector pension commitments continues to grow, and most European countries' taxpayer bases shrink due to demographic decline, the capacity of European nation-states and the EU to bear the cost of maintaining their political and civil service apparatuses will steadily diminish.

There is already evidence of this occurring. In 2007, President Sarkozy's government implemented a policy of not replacing one out of every two retiring French civil servants, as part of a general effort to reform the French civil service and reduce costs. Public-sector cooperation with this measure was secured, however, by a formal commitment on the government's part to plow half of the resulting payroll savings into the compensation packages of civil servants. In other words, half of the savings were given back to those working in the civil service, instead of the full savings being passed on to taxpayers or used to reduce debt.

While France's civil service reforms did produce some improvements (such as reductions in hospital and emergency-services waiting times), the man charged with overseeing the reform, François-Daniel Migeon (himself a *grande école* graduate), confessed himself astonished at the degree of sluggishness he encountered. "I didn't," he stated, "expect to encounter inertia of such magnitude—inertia that is due to the scope of the program, the number of workers involved, and the strength of habits anchored for decades or more in the public sector."[22]

Civil services are not, however, the only purveyors of inertia in today's EU. One can have every confidence that attempts to maintain Social Europe—no matter how high the cost—will continue to come from another set of insiders enabled by Europe's economic culture: trade unions.

Declining Numbers, but Not an Endangered Species

Contrary to popular perception in America and Europe, union membership in some West European nations is not high, especially in the private sector. In Britain, only 27.4 percent of all employees were members of unions in 2009. In the private sector, less than 15 percent of employees were unionized, compared to more than 56 percent of public-sector employees.[23] In 2011, the OECD estimated that only 7.6 percent of employees belonged to a union in France, while just 18.5 percent of German employees were unionized.

At the other end of the scale are the Scandinavian countries. On average, more than 67.8 percent of employees belonged to unions in 2011. But without exception, union membership in *all* EU member states has been in decline since the 1990s. By way of comparison, 11.3

percent of American employees were unionized in 2011; American unions were also experiencing an overall decline in membership.[24]

Yet these figures and trends do not mean that trade union power in Europe (or America) has necessarily diminished. This partly reflects the fact that most unionized labor in Europe (and America) is now firmly located in the public sector. The unions are now major financial contributors to most major center-left European political parties, thereby enabling trade unions to considerably influence one side of politics in Europe. By 2010, for example, Britain's Labour Party was receiving 80 percent of its funding from public-sector unions.[25] That the Democratic Party in the United States is also a major beneficiary of public-sector union patronage is hardly a secret.

The increasingly public-sector character of European trade unions comes with advantages not found in the private sector. It is easier, for example, for governments to accede to the demands of public-sector unions for shorter working hours, longer vacations, higher pay, and above all, ever-increasing, generous pension schemes. After all, governments can always raise taxes to pay the bill (unlike the private sector). Likewise, the fact that many basic utilities and vital services are provided by Europe's public sector gives public-sector unions the ability to disproportionately exercise the power to strike beyond their raw numbers—as French citizens discovered in 2010, when garbage across the country remained uncollected for weeks. Needless to say, the same factors contribute to the disproportionate clout of American public-sector unions.

European trade unions do enjoy several advantages that American unions do not. First, European trade unions can—and do—draw upon their claim to represent the values and institutions associated with the guild-corporatist dimension of European economic culture, a factor not as operative in America.

Second, an essentially positive view of trade unions is not confined in Europe to the Social Democratic and broadly left-wing side of politics. To varying degrees, it also forms part of Christian

Democratic and broadly center-right discourse. Strong critiques of the restrictive labor-market practices supported by many European trade unions are not forcibly articulated by most European center-right parties.

Conversely, the center-right party of modern American politics—the Republican Party—does not have a strong pro-union tradition. Nor have Republican politicians been shy about criticizing, and even occasionally confronting, trade unions.

When coupled with Europe's neo-corporatist emphasis on agreement through consensus and the characteristic European fixation with security, the generally positive attitude toward unions has helped them to lobby successfully to limit or block measures that might significantly liberalize labor markets at national and EU levels. It is thus quite difficult to fire unproductive, inefficient, incompetent, or dishonest employees throughout much of Europe. Until 2011, it was actually a violation of Greek law to fire public-sector workers solely on the grounds of incompetence.[26] As the economists Alberto Alesina and Francesco Giavazzi point out:

> Not only does the law impose severe restrictions on firing, but
> even when employers follow the law, judges often step in and
> rule in favor of the workers. In France, for example, judges rule
> routinely against any firing justified by the need to improve
> profitability of the firm. . . . In Italy, when it comes to protecting
> employees against firing, the notoriously slow justice system is
> suddenly very fast and efficient, and many workers are promptly
> reinstated in their jobs.[27]

In April 2012, Italy's prime minister, Mario Monti, sought to change the law that essentially forbade businesses with more than fifteen full-time employees from dismissing staff. Monti's goal was to substitute a situation of jobs for life for some and perpetual insecurity for others with severance provisions for people let go on economic grounds. Under pressure from Italian unions, however, Monti's proposal was watered down. While the new severance provisions remained in place, the new law also upheld the extensive powers enjoyed by courts to investigate whether a company's decision to fire someone was justified. This diminished the potential for reducing the high level of litigation that plagues the Italian labor market.[28] The new labor law also instituted a universal jobless-benefit program, thereby extending a welfare policy that had previously only covered full-time workers to the thousands of Italians subsisting on short-term and often fixed work contracts.

European trade unions have taken full advantage of the manner in which neo-corporatist arrangements have cemented trade union officials into formal institutions of the EU and of most member states. This provides trade unions with influential insider mechanisms through which to advance their sectional interests. In some countries, this extends to legally mandating their representation on company boards through worker codetermination arrangements, and/or requiring companies to engage in consultations with trade unions.

Austria's government, for example, is legally obliged to consult with a "Chamber of Labor" purporting to represent all three million Austrian employees (membership is obligatory). Not surprisingly, the chamber's leadership and staff are dominated by current or former trade union officials. Among its responsibilities are the evaluation of draft legislation from the standpoint of employees' interests (which are simply assumed to be monolithic in character), the proposal of amendments, and participation in implementation of approved laws.

The ability of European unions to use these privileges to slow down or block market liberalization was highlighted by corruption scandals in German business in 2008. One prominent case concerned the Volkswagen corporation. Faced with increasing competition in the global marketplace and the subsequent need to cut labor costs, Volkswagen company officials created a slush fund to buy off employee representatives (through means such as bribes, paid-for shopping sprees, and even visits to prostitutes) to secure their consent for changes in labor conditions.[29]

Punished by Unions

Private enterprise is an obvious loser to the insider status enjoyed by unions in Europe. The extensive labor-market regulation for which unions have successfully lobbied for decades undermines many European businesses' ability to compete in the global economy. In America, the greater ease of hiring and firing allows entrepreneurs to take more and faster risks with new ideas, products, and services. The result is faster and more risk taking in America than in Europe.

There is also considerable evidence suggesting that the prevalence of high labor-force costs and regulations in countries such as Italy, France, and Belgium contributes significantly to their relatively low productivity levels.[30] It discourages otherwise successful enterprises from expanding. Many European businesses consciously choose to stay small because of the heavy regulatory environment and often compulsory unionization legally imposed on many businesses once their employees exceed a certain number (usually forty).[31]

For instance, according to France's 3,200-page *code du travail*, any company inside France that exceeds forty-nine employees is legally obliged to establish no fewer than *three* worker councils. If such businesses decide they need to let go some employees, they are required to present a reorganization plan to all three councils.[32] Is it any wonder that many French businesses simply don't bother expanding their employee base, often inhibiting their capacity to generate more wealth?

But there are less obvious losers from the privileges enjoyed by unions. Trade unions are focused on protecting the interests of those who are already employed. Hence, they have no interest in the well-being of the *unemployed*—whose numbers reached the highest-ever level of 11 percent in the eurozone in April 2012.[33] After all, the unemployed do not pay union dues; moreover, if they could access the labor market more easily, it would be harder for unions to avoid renegotiating the wages and conditions of those with jobs.

Another group negatively impacted by Europe's restrictive labor markets, and the trade union power that limits the ability of governments to reform them, is *young* Europeans.

In May 2011, thousands of young Spaniards began camping out in Madrid's most famous square, Puerta del Sol, to protest the extraordinarily high levels of youth unemployment in Spain (which had reached 51 percent by December 2011),[34] and what they regarded as their dismal economic prospects. By the first half of June, similar protests had occurred in cities such as Lisbon, Paris, Hamburg, Rome, and Vienna. One of the most common complaints of the "indignant ones" (as they called themselves) was their inability, after several years of higher education, to obtain anything other than part-time contracts.[35] At the beginning of 2012, an incredible 40 percent of workers aged nineteen to thirty-nine in most EU countries were on temporary contracts.[36]

No doubt, *los indignados* would have been shocked if they knew that real wages for Spaniards lucky enough to have permanent full-time jobs in 2009 actually *rose* by 3.2 percent, during a year in which the Spanish economy shrank by 3.7 percent and unemployment soared. The reason for this strange development was that many Spanish employees were benefiting from wage-escalation clauses negotiated by unions. These result in price increases that trigger wage increases, regardless of what is happening in the rest of the economy.[37]

More generally, many European companies are overly cautious about hiring people on a full-time, nontemporary basis when they know it is very difficult to fire them. As World Bank economists

Indermit Gill and Martin Raiser note, "Current policies allow 'insiders' to make their jobs incontestable through strict employment protection, while creating considerable work disincentives for 'outsiders'."[38]

The fact that *los indignados'* financial circumstances increasingly made it necessary to live at home with their parents (who, presumably, were among those benefiting from the insiders' almost-impossible-to-fire situation) did not make their situation psychologically easier.[39] How such arrangements of permanent jobs for life (which inhibit young people from acquiring full-time employment) promote solidarity (a phrase endlessly evoked by European trade unions) is eminently difficult to explain. As European Central Bank president Mario Draghi conceded in February 2012, "The European social model has already gone when we see the youth unemployment rates prevailing in some countries."[40]

It is sad to report, however, that *los indignados* were not protesting against overregulation and other labor-market rigidities demanded by unions and conceded by governments. By and large, the indignant ones wanted exactly what unions had helped secure for their parents and grandparents: jobs for life, free health care, state-guaranteed minimal incomes, six weeks of paid annual vacation, early retirement, and generous state pensions. In other words, they *wanted* Social Europe. Far from being revolutionary, they were firm status quonarians.[41]

Since World War II, there has been only one major effort in Europe to effectively diminish the legal privileges of trade unions. The violence and drama associated with the 1984–85 miners' strike in Britain and the subsequent collapse in union power was not simply about resistance to change. The trauma also reflected how rooted much of British society had become in the rather neo-corporatist arrangements that prevailed throughout Britain between 1945 and 1986.

Reluctance to arouse social upheaval helps to explain why many European governments of Left and Right have generally adopted a softly-softly approach to addressing trade union power. In the case of center-left governments, the reality that public-sector unions are among their biggest financial contributors bolsters the general reluctance to adopt confrontational approaches. But the general wariness about addressing the insider status of trade unions and their officials may also owe something to the fact that much of the established business community in Europe *also* enjoys a privileged place in the European marketplace, is *also* sheltered from competition, and *also* derives considerable benefit from the same neo-corporatist structures.

Business Winners

A common premise shared by critics of free markets is that businesses are vigorous defenders of open competition, entrepreneurship, and minimal government. That assumption is often wrong. More than one person has observed that Wall Street gave far more in the way of political donations to Barack Obama (who had not hitherto displayed an especially positive view of markets) than to John McCain (a confirmed free trader) in 2008.

Throughout Western Europe, national governments have not been shy about promoting, favoring, and in many instances protecting established companies through regulation and subsidies. Much of European economic life is consequently characterized by "political markets": situations in which industries lobby politicians and civil servants to regulate existing markets in ways that favor those who already dominate the marketplace. Insider businesses benefit by having potential and real competitors locked out. The political class gains in the form of electoral support, financial backing, and often, jobs in the corporate sector after life in politics has run its course.[42]

Those European businesses that demand protection range from small to large enterprises. Taxi drivers in many European countries benefit from the strict caps on the numbers of licenses issued, thereby blocking and impeding market entry.[43] This, Americans hardly need reminding, is equally true of many American cities. Medieval guilds could not improve on this situation.

Agriculture is another example of a business that benefits from an insider status. In 2006, Alesina and Giavazzi note, *half* of the EU budget was spent on the CAP, even though the agricultural sector accounted for less than 2 percent of the EU's GDP. Interestingly, large sums of CAP money actually go to large agribusinesses, rather than to the dwindling number of small farms and farmers that the CAP was, at least ostensibly, designed partly to protect.[44]

Established businesses in Europe also benefit from the *dirigiste* instincts of many European politicians and civil servants. In this sense, mercantilism is alive and well in Europe. Sometimes benefits occur through the process of governments giving contracts to established national companies in preference to more competitive bids from foreigners or newcomers to the market. But *dirigisme* particularly rears its head when inefficient, uncompetitive, but politically well-connected companies face the prospect of failing.

In 2004, Alstom, a large French manufacturing and technological conglomerate (perhaps most well known for developing the TGV fast train) came close to bankruptcy. A major cause of its insolvency was Alstom's outdated and inefficient power generation and shipbuilding plants.

Instead of allowing Alstom's profitable parts to be sold off and its inefficient plants closed, France's center-right government injected it with 1.84 billion euros in subsidies. Naturally, the move was enthusiastically supported by the relevant trade unions, which were concerned that thousands of plant employees might lose their jobs. Previously, these same trade unions had obstructed updates of plant technology for that very same reason. Two years later, the government sold its share of the company to another French business.

At no stage during these events did anyone ask whether it had been in the employees' best interests to keep them working in outdated and uncompetitive plants, rather than helping them to retrain and find other jobs. Nor did any significant public figure ask whether these policies reflected an unhealthy collusion between the state and large businesses. Few seemed concerned that such policies might encourage European companies to imagine that, as long as they were big enough and employed enough people, governments would bail them out if they got into sufficient trouble.

Similar criticism obviously applies to successive American governments' policies. Agricultural subsidies in the United States go overwhelmingly to large agribusinesses.[45] More generally, government bailouts and subsidies have been received by American businesses with close relationships with federal and state politicians for many years. Throughout 2011, the *Washington Examiner*'s Timothy Carney illustrated in pointed article after pointed article the disturbing links between government assistance and those businesses that enjoy political connections on both sides of the aisle,[46] General Electric being perhaps the biggest target of his criticisms.[47]

The costly rescue of major American car companies in late 2008 reflected a long-term pattern of government assistance to particular failing industries. When the Carter administration chose to save Chrysler in 1980, this conveyed several messages to Detroit-based car manufacturers. First, they could risk producing cars that fewer consumers apparently wanted to buy. Second, they could refrain from confronting the serious inefficiencies introduced into their companies' operations by years of management acquiescence to outlandish demands from the United Auto Workers union (UAW). Why? Because if American car companies again found themselves facing economic oblivion, they had high expectations—based on an established policy precedent—that the federal government would save them. No one should have been surprised to find the CEOs of major American car companies—accompanied by a legion of lobbyists and the ever-present UAW—appearing before Congress in late 2008 requesting assistance in averting bankruptcy.

Again, however, a major difference between Europe and America is the extent to which established businesses have been co-opted into the neo-corporatist arrangements prevailing throughout the EU, which sometimes have acquired institutional expression.

One instance is the formal representation accorded to employers in the European Economic and Social Committee. Another prominent case is the Austrian Economic Chambers (Wirtschaftskammer Österreich). Any Austrian business whose work falls into one of the following areas—craft production, manufacturing, construction, mining, quarrying, commerce, banking, insurance, transport, information technology, telecommunications (including radio and television), or tourism—must be a member of this chamber. Like its employee counterpart, the Wirtschaftskammer Österreich engages in collective bargaining and reviews legislation. The notion that it might be in some companies' interest *not* to be part of this system is considered strange by many Austrians, regardless of their politics.

There are also less formal but equally effective ways that European businesses partake in *dirigiste*-corporatist arrangements. Not all of France's *grande école* graduates spend the rest of their careers working for the state. Many easily move back and forth not only between politics and the civil service, but also the private sector.

A good example is Baudouin Prot, until late 2011 the CEO of BNP Paribas, the largest banking group in France. After graduating from the ENA, Baudouin Prot held a number of civil service positions—deputy prefect of the Franche-Comté region, general inspector of finance, deputy director of energy and raw materials in the Ministry of Industry—before taking this senior banking job in 2003.

Another case is Louis Gallois, CEO of the European Aeronautic Defence and Space Company between 2007 and 2012. Also an ENA graduate, Gallois served in several government positions, worked as a senior political adviser to a Socialist government in the 1980s, and thereafter was employed in a variety of private and state-owned companies. The former CEO of Renault, Louis Schweitzer, worked as an inspector of finance after he graduated from the ENA. He went on to serve as chief of staff to Socialist prime minister Laurent Fabius (yet another ENA alumni) before leaving politics and joining Renault in a senior strategic position.

Similar patterns of movement between the private and public sector may of course be observed outside France and Europe. The point, however, is that the long-term involvement in government *and* private industry by many *grande école* graduates is entirely consistent with France's *dirigiste* ways, and tends to reinforce them through one of the most effective forms of shaping organizations: the selection of personnel.

Given the extent to which many European businesses benefit from these and similar arrangements, it is not obvious why they should favor market liberalization. After all, their success in many instances may have as much (and sometimes more) to do with their ability to capitalize upon their political connections, or familiarity with the regulatory environment, than with any creation of new value in the form of products desired by consumers. Moreover, if market liberalization means you can no longer rely upon governments bailing you out or providing you with subsidies, why would you oppose *dirigisme*? If opening markets means diminishing the regulations that undermine the ability of competitors to offer new products in the marketplace, it is quite logical for insider businesses to invoke the rhetoric, vision, and above all, political blocking power of the European social model to deter significant liberalization.

Worsening the situation is the manner in which the same regulatory and neo-corporatist structures alter the incentives for entrepreneurs in Europe. Instead of creating goods and services at lower comparative costs and then aggressively marketing them, people with entrepreneurial mind-sets are incentivized to do one of two things: (1) leave the EU in search of more hospitable environments; or (2) become "political entrepreneurs." In the latter case, they focus their efforts upon acquiring pieces of established businesses that enjoy high forms of protection. They then apply their entrepreneurial skills to lobbying the political class and influential civil servants to ensure that impediments to competitors remain in place, rather than using the same talents to give economic life to a new idea or insight.[48]

And Business Losers

If established businesses with strong formal and informal links to the political and bureaucratic worlds are truly some of the most prominent insiders created by European economic culture, then who are the outsiders?

When insider businesses concentrate upon maintaining the status quo, instead of thinking about how to outcompete their rivals, the result is often higher prices for lower-quality goods for *consumers.* Business insiders in the EU are very well organized in their ability to resist change. By contrast, consumers—and the taxpayers who ultimately pay for bailouts—are generally less organized, and more diffuse. They are subsequently less able to advance their interests than established companies, who enjoy good and often personal connections in the highly controlled world of European politics.

Another group of outsiders is of entrepreneurs who come from outside the established business world. In some cases, there exist certain market-entry costs that may deter such newcomers from even starting businesses in the first place. In Germany, for instance, entrepreneurs are actually *taxed* on the equity they invest in a start-up.[49]

When it comes to entrepreneurship, EU documents candidly acknowledge that this is an area where America and China enjoy enormous advantages over most EU member states. There are many reasons for this. Official EU reports underscore Europeans' greater risk adverseness and preference for security; Europe's less developed venture-capital industry; Europeans' fear of the uncertainty involved in not having a regular income; the reluctance of European banks to lend capital to young entrepreneurs; the same banks' preference for dealing with established businesses; the stigma attached to business failure throughout Europe; and Europeans' less favorable views of entrepreneurs, when compared to Americans.[50]

Yet when it comes to rectifying this situation, the same reports say relatively little about reducing disincentives and regulatory barriers to entrepreneurship in Europe. Instead, they focus upon how *the state* can promote private entrepreneurship through its own direct action.

In 2005, a European Commission report on entrepreneurship made the commonplace observation that the possibility of market failure can deter people from innovating. It followed, the report stated, that EU member states needed to invest more in *state-directed* research and innovation, because state-backed research allegedly circumvented the market-failure issue. The report then listed the specific objectives that the *commission* (rather than the market) had already decided should be promoted through such research.[51]

It was, one might say, a typically European *dirigiste* approach to facilitating entrepreneurship in ideas and the economy. And it is failing. As a 2011 World Bank report bluntly stated: "This approach does not seem to be working." Europe, the report added, is falling further and further behind America in the areas of research and development.[52]

This is hardly surprising. Efforts to circumvent market failure don't take into account how that failure often illustrates that a new or refined product created by an entrepreneur is perhaps not so new or innovative, or does not actually meet market demand.

More generally, an economic culture with deeply *dirigiste* and neo-corporatist instincts is likely to be quietly distrustful of new entrepreneurs, and entrepreneurship in general. Business entrepreneurs are creative and willing to take risks. They rock the economic boat. They shake things up—including established business practices and existing companies' market share. Where entrepreneurs see opportunity and the workings of creative destruction, *dirigistes* and neo-corporatists see chaos and disorder.

In Tocqueville's America, entrepreneurs were constantly starting new businesses, even moving on to different ventures before the first was even firmly established. Improvisation and a near obsession with economic change were in the air.[53]

Nothing could be more foreign to an EU civil servant with a penchant for planning everything to the last detail; the employment ministry bureaucrat accustomed to weeks of negotiations with his opposite numbers from the chambers of business and labor; the trade union official who expects everyone on the company board to listen for hours to his long list of objections to proposed ventures; or the *énarque* working as a business CEO who, over the years, has grown comfortable with seeing the same old faces in his dealings with senior civil servants and politicians—the only difference being that the seats around the table are occasionally shuffled as the same participants move between the intertwined worlds of business, politics, and the civil service.

Bread and Circuses

Most Europeans and Americans have heard the expression "bread and circuses." Coined by the late first-century Roman poet Juvenal, he used it as a way of expressing his contempt for the people of Rome, who had abandoned thoughtful participation in political life in return for being entertained and fed by rulers who could subsequently count on the *populus'* support for the prevailing system.

While the analogy is not exact, there is a sense in which Europe's economic culture seeks to make as many people as possible an insider—be they a politician, civil servant, trade union official, insider businessman, outsider entrepreneur, consumer, taxpayer, unemployed, young or old. In the long term, it may well turn out to be a fatal flaw in the European social model as we know it. Contemporary Europe's economic malaise—and all it might forebode for America—cannot be fully comprehended until we understand the workings of an increasingly tarnished jewel in the crown of contemporary European economic culture: the modern welfare state.

6

Soft Despotism

After having thus successively taken each member of the community in its powerful grasp and fashioned him at will, the supreme power then extends its arm over the whole community. It covers the surface of society with a network of small complicated rules, minute and uniform, through which the most original minds and the most energetic characters cannot penetrate, to rise above the crowd. The will of man is not shattered, but softened, bent, and guided; men are seldom forced by it to act, but they are constantly restrained from acting. Such a power does not destroy, but it prevents existence; it does not tyrannize, but it compresses, enervates, extinguishes, and stupefies a people, till each nation is reduced to nothing better than a flock of timid and industrious animals, of which the government is the shepherd.

—ALEXIS DE TOCQUEVILLE

In 1880, imperial Germany's Otto von Bismarck, more popularly known as the Iron Chancellor, was a worried man. Having forged a united Germany through a combination of diplomacy and war, Bismarck faced a new problem. This time, it was not foreign powers blocking a grand strategic design. Instead, it was the emergence of a large industrial working class throughout Germany—an urban proletariat which increasingly voted for the Social Democratic party. Though officially banned, the Social Democrats could not, Bismarck knew, be kept out of the legislature forever.

Despite his reputation as a Prussian Junker with all the prejudices of his class, Bismarck's name is associated with the term *realpolitik* for a reason. The growing German working class, he believed, was voting social democratic partly because they were dissatisfied with their economic and social conditions. The pragmatist in Bismarck concluded that he needed to remove the source of this discontent.

To Bismarck, this meant the state needed to go beyond its traditional functions of supplementary provision of poor relief services. Speaking to the German Reichstag in 1884, he proclaimed:

> The real grievance of the worker is the insecurity of his existence; he is not sure that he will always have work, he is not sure that he will always be healthy, and he foresees that he will one day be old and unfit to work. If he falls into poverty, even if only through a prolonged illness, he is then completely helpless, left to his own devices, and society does not currently recognize any real obligation toward him beyond the usual help for the poor, even if he has been working all the time ever so faithfully and diligently. The usual help for the poor, however, leaves a lot to be desired, especially in large cities, where it is very much worse than in the country.[1]

In these words, we find much of the inspiration for the modern European welfare state: the desire to progressively diminish, if not eventually abolish, the economic insecurity that many associated with the rise of capitalism. One hundred and twenty years later,

Europe accounted for an astonishing 58 percent of the entire world economy's spending on social protection.[2]

Unfortunately, some of European economic culture's most negative aspects have manifested themselves through European welfare systems. In this chapter, we see how this aspect of the European social model has become one of the biggest problems facing most European countries, and how some of the same symptoms are present and growing in America.

Tocqueville's Nightmare

From 1881 onward, Bismarck moved to establish the basic legislative foundations of what would become modern welfare states. With the cooperation of the Social Democrats, the Catholic Center Party, and the National Liberal Party, Bismarck implemented three pieces of legislation: a health insurance bill (1883); an accident insurance bill (1884); and an old age and disability insurance bill (1889). Each of these was initially funded by employers and employees. The state, however, increasingly assumed responsibility for these programs. As early as 1891, the German Social Democrats were explicitly calling, as its 1891 Erfurt Program stated, for a "takeover by the Reich government of the entire system of workers' insurance, with decisive participation by the workers in its administration."

By today's standards, Bismarck's initial measures were rather mild. But unlike previous arrangements, these policies did seek to provide *universal* and *systematic* coverage. They also involved a more visible degree of *redistribution* from employers to employees, increasingly through state intervention.

Other European states soon began moving in similar directions. Liberal governments in Britain and Sweden introduced national insurance and pension schemes in the 1910s. In his 2004 book, *The Welfare State We're In*, James Bartholomew demonstrates that the modern British welfare state was well in place, bigger, and more generous before World War II than most people realize. The 1911

National Insurance Act, he notes, not only introduced compulsory insurance for sickness and invalidity, but also—for the first time in the world—for unemployment. The latter quickly escalated from embracing approximately 2.25 million people in 1911 to four million people in 1916, and to two-thirds of the employed workforce in 1920. It did not take long for the rules to be bent such that programs moved from being state-managed insurance schemes, into which people paid contributions, toward systems that made outright state payments to the unemployed and ill, regardless of contributions.[3]

After 1945, the provision of state welfare accelerated across Western Europe. Politicians sought to promote free access to health care, income support, state-provided pensions, and comprehensive social insurance to cover those suffering from disabilities or enduring unemployment. Once again, Britain led the way. Through a slew of legislation—the Family Allowances Act (1945), the National Insurance Act (1946), the National Health Service Act (1946), the Pensions (Increase) Act (1947), and the Landlord and Tenant Act (1949)—the postwar Labour government extended Britain's contemporary welfare state far beyond anything envisaged in 1911.

America was somewhat late to the welfare party. The primary institutions of America's welfare state were not birthed until the 1930s New Deal and the 1960s Great Society programs. Some of the deeper ideological commitments driving these programs are aptly described as derived from modern American liberalism's insistence that the state must provide people with positive rights to certain things such as health and education if they are to enjoy fulfilling lives.[4] But in the day-to-day political sphere, American welfare programs have tended to be justified more on grounds of the apparent failure of markets to resolve particular problems, and rather less by explicit redistributive agendas. America was also characterized by widespread intellectual and popular opposition to many aspects of the welfare state: an opposition less obvious in most of Europe, not least because most center-right European political parties embraced more or less extensive state welfare programs.

None of these policies in Europe, however, resulted in what Bismarck had envisaged: reduced political support for left-wing movements. On the contrary, they grew stronger. By 1912, for instance, the German Social Democrats were the biggest party in the German parliament's lower house, and were busy using their increasing political clout to push for more welfare expenditures. Other Western European center-left parties pursued similar agendas, and many nonsocialist politicians were inclined to meet their demands.

One person who had envisaged something like these developments, and worried about their long-term effects, was Alexis de Tocqueville. Though Tocqueville never used the expression "welfare state," he worried about the potentially corrosive effects upon liberty of democratically elected governments that tried to use their powers to guarantee economic security for as many people as possible. Democracy, Tocqueville argued, was capable of breeding its own form of despotism, albeit of the "soft" variety.

In *Democracy in America*, Tocqueville spoke of "an immense protective power" which took all responsibility for everyone's happiness—just so long as this power remained "sole agent and judge of it." This power, Tocqueville wrote, would "resemble parental authority" but would try to keep people "in perpetual childhood" by relieving people "from all the trouble of thinking and all the cares of living."[5]

In these circumstances, the notion of social contract takes on a particular and not very benign meaning. It becomes a shorthand way of describing a type of Faustian bargain between citizens and the political class: a deal which, eventually, corrupts everyone. Citizens vote for those politicians who promise to use the state to give them what they want. The political class delivers—provided the citizens agree to whatever it is governments deem necessary to provide for everyone's desires. The "softness" of this despotism consists of the people's voluntary surrender of their liberty in return for material ease.

Some may view this as a cynical interpretation of the welfare state's rise in Europe and America. After all, not everyone approached the subject from Bismarck's realpolitik standpoint. Many people of his time (and ours) sincerely believed various forms of social assistance, planned and administered by the state and funded by various compulsory forms of wealth redistribution, would help alleviate economic distress, and pre-empt the market's replacement by outright socialist arrangements. Good intentions, however, cannot disguise the fact that by the last quarter of the twentieth century, even many Social Democrats were conceding that something had gone deeply wrong with European welfare states.

A Welfare State of Mind

To speak of the "welfare state," or even "European welfare states," is somewhat misleading. In one sense, *every function* performed by the state is supposed to serve the people's well-being or welfare. Governments do not, after all, exist for their own sake.

A more precise definition of the welfare state involves attention to the ways in which modern governments have gone beyond traditional responsibilities such as foreign policy, national defense, protecting private property, constructing public works, and administering the legal system. This becomes clearer when we identify the four broad activities associated with state welfare. These are:

- *Social insurance:* legally defined and specified benefits paid by the state to particular categories of people. These are funded by contributions from potential beneficiaries and/or direct taxation. Examples include old-age pensions and social security, health insurance, and unemployment insurance.
- *Labor security policies:* the rules regulating the hiring and firing of individuals by private businesses or the state.

Holding that one of the best forms of economic security is a job, the state establishes high barriers to dismissing people. Labor welfare policies can also include governments creating publicly funded jobs

- *Subsidies:* state supplements to a person or family's income on the basis of criteria such as marital status, number of children, before-tax income, and occupation (e.g., farmers). These are designed to correct perceived inequities. They thus function as a form of wealth redistribution.

- *Services:* specific services provided by the state, sometimes directly and sometimes in partnership with non-state organizations, to all eligible citizens. Socialized medicine is perhaps the best example.

Within these parameters, European welfare states have emphasized different methods, priorities, and principles. Some may be characterized as following a "Scandinavian" model. Here social protection is considered a right, coverage is universal, the system is centrally administered, and general taxation provides the funding. Others adhere to a more "Bismarckian" model. These emphasize employment security, and rely partly upon employer and employee contributions.[6]

Values and Welfare

Some Europeans support their welfare states because, like Bismarck, they consider such systems essential for social stability. This is the stance of many European conservatives. Without large welfare states, it is thought, tensions between the winners and losers from market transactions may well result in widespread conflict.

Other Europeans have invested an element of national pride in developing "their" welfare state. We find this in the commitment of many members of Britain's Conservative Party to the National Health Service as an expression of national decency. Similar sentiments underlie the notion of *folkhemmet* (the people's home) promoted by Sweden's Social Democrats.

Another set of value commitments in European welfare states comes from those with broadly Keynesian outlooks. For them, the welfare state helps to maintain demand, and therefore, higher employment levels. Yet other Europeans view welfare states as vehicles for realizing redistributive justice, equality of opportunity, and greater equity of outcomes. This includes Social Democrats, who see welfare states as a way to equalize economic conditions and posttax and post-transfer incomes without engaging in a full frontal assault on the market economy. But it also embraces some conservatives and center-right Christian Democrats who favor mild redistributions that favor low-income groups or particular occupational categories.

The specific policies associated with European welfare states are sufficiently broad that many different groups finds vindication of their particular priorities in various welfare programs. It helps that many welfare-state measures find echoes in European economic culture's guild-corporatist dimension. It is not for trivial reasons that European politicians invariably employ the language of solidarity and social justice when referring to the welfare state.

Out of Control

Whatever their precise manifestation and underlying value commitments, no one can doubt the sheer economic space occupied by European welfare states, not least in terms of their share of GDP.

Looking at total government spending for EU member states (before the EU expanded to include Central, Eastern, and Baltic Europe in the 1990s), it averaged 29 percent of GDP in 1960. By 1970, this figure had risen to 37 percent. The expansion continued, reaching 47 percent in 1980, and 50 percent in 1990.[7] In America, by comparison, the spending level was 29.9 percent in 2000.[8] Obviously, not all of this government spending was welfare-related. But *most* of the growth in total postwar government spending throughout the EU *has* been in the form of state social spending.[9]

By 2008, the figures across Europe had altered slightly. Some nations—most notably Germany—had reduced the state's share of GDP expenditure from the high 40s to the mid 40s. Others, such as Greece, had increased their spending by the same percentages. Many, including France, Italy, and Portugal, remained stuck at just under or over 50 percent.[10] Overall, however, social spending as a proportion of GDP increased throughout Europe in the 2000s.[11]

These spending increases have been accompanied by declining workforce participation throughout Western Europe. Although today's Europeans work in less physically strenuous conditions, are healthier, and live longer lives than their nineteenth-century ancestors, less than 20 percent of people in countries such as France, Holland, or Belgium work until their midsixties.[12] In the mid-2000s, less than half the labor force in Germany worked until the age of sixty. French men living in 2012 were retiring an average of eight years earlier than their compatriots in the 1960s.[13]

By way of comparison, Western Europeans worked almost a month more than did Americans in the 1950s. In the 1970s, American and West European work hours were essentially the same. By 2011, however, Americans were working a month a year *more* than the French, Swedes, Germans, and Dutch, and much longer than Spaniards, Greeks, Poles, and Hungarians.[14]

Among Western Europeans who do work, the amount of vacation time further diminishes productivity. The economist Michel Godet, a member of France's economic analysis council, calculates that—with national holidays, the legally mandated five weeks of vacation, the compensatory time allowed employees when they exceed the official 35-hour workweek, plus people taking days off in order to "bridge" existing vacation days—the average French worker enjoys *a week off each month* in addition to weekends.[15] The scale of the generosity—or absurdity—of European workers' vacation arrangements was highlighted in June 2012 when the EU's Court of Justice—the same court that confirmed pay increases for EU civil servants in 2010—ruled that workers who become sick during their period of paid annual leave were entitled at some later point in time to a period of leave of the same duration as that of their sick leave.[16]

Before the Sarkozy government raised France's official retirement age to sixty-two, full retirement benefits were offered to French citizens at age sixty (an arrangement partly restored for certain categories of workers by Sarkozy's successor as president, François Hollande, in June 2012), provided that one had worked for thirty-seven and one-half years. That covered the vast majority of French workers.[17] Easy access to disability benefits was another way to retire early in Sweden, Germany, and Britain. Claims for disability payments rose significantly in Britain after disability benefits began to be higher than unemployment payments, from 1973 onward.[18] Prior to 2010, the biggest drop in labor participation in Britain occurred at age sixty—the age when disability benefits could be claimed.[19] In 1994, more than one-third of those aged sixty-four and older in Sweden received full-time disability pensions.[20] These figures suggest that European welfare states had created strong incentives *not* to work.

Attitudes, Politics, and Self-Interest

So why did the welfare state expand so dramatically in Western Europe after the 1960s? One reason was changing *attitudes*.

Numerous commentators[21] have highlighted the widespread sense among Europeans in the postwar years that they needed to make sacrifices and increase productivity if the continent was to have any future. Trade unions were subsequently relatively moderate in their demands. Similarly, many businesses invested much of their profits in facilitating technological catch-up.

By the 1960s, things had changed. Memories of the Depression, the war, and postwar economic hardship had faded. Western Europeans born after World War II began demanding more pay, free (state-provided) education, free (state-provided) health care, more (state-provided) labor security, and more generous state-provided pensions. They also wanted to work less, have longer holidays, and retire earlier.

The willingness of groups (ranging from unions to baby-boomer students) to use means such as strikes to get their way (combined with worries about the radicalization of middle-class students) inclined governments to use welfare programs to buy off discontent. They did so by raising pensions, lowering retirement ages, subsidizing education, and making it harder to fire people. Ironically, this often resulted in people from upper- and middle-income backgrounds benefiting from the welfare state. Even today, free university education in many continental European nations continues to be enjoyed disproportionately by students from families with above-average incomes.[22]

Expectations, however, were only one element of the perfect storm into which Western Europe was stumbling. Politics, regrettably of the more cynical kind, also had an influence.

Once European politicians recognized that the state's ability to spend was one way of building up reliable constituencies of voters, political parties were able to enter into "bidding wars." They attracted the support of various interest groups by making promises in the realms of pensions, retirement age, education subsidies, state-enforced job security, and expanding public-sector workforces. This was paid for with increased taxation and, when that proved inadequate to cover the costs, deficit spending.

On the other side of the table, interest groups that benefited from different welfare programs (pensioners, unions, subsidized businesses, and so forth) used their electoral and financial clout to push politicians into maintaining or extending particular welfare and social programs. In such an atmosphere, politicians who avowed "no favors" or promised to reduce welfare expenditures were at a distinct electoral disadvantage. All the short- and medium-term political incentives lay in the direction of allowing the corrosion to continue.

An additional complication was the internal logic of the welfare state itself. In the 1950s, Wilhelm Röpke pointed out that welfare states are like progressive taxation: once one accepts the basic principle, there is nothing in the welfare state's conception to set a limit to it.[23] If democratic politics become reduced to an exercise in attempting to diminish life's uncertainties by providing security for growing numbers of people, then welfare's continual expansion becomes easily justified. Even someone as apparently committed as Margaret Thatcher was to expanding economic freedom and rolling back the state was unable to stop the welfare state's growth in Britain during her years as prime minister.[24]

The same logic makes any attempt at retraction difficult. The welfare state's growth creates constituencies disinclined to vote for any attempt to reduce welfare.[25] Furthermore, the taxation required to maintain welfare payments progressively undermines the financial position of those who might be expected to support alternative policies.[26] In the conditions of mass democracy, this makes restraining expansions of welfare politically difficult,[27] even when the fact of unsustainability has become well known. As Luxembourg's prime minister, Jean-Claude Juncker, lamented in 2007: "We all know what to do, but we don't know how to get re-elected once we have done it."[28]

Even more insidiously, the same levels of taxation undermine the ability of individuals to take care of themselves and their families, let alone be generous to others—especially those who are not among the superwealthy, but who are by no means poor. The effect is to increase overall reliance on state welfare and weaken private ways of addressing social problems.

Paying the Bill

Wishful thinking aside, welfare states do not pay for themselves. And the costs go beyond the billions of euros expended each year through European welfare programs. As one French economist warned in 2011, "The problem we have is that we can't get people to understand that these privileges are in fact a ball and chain."[29]

The *first* such cost is, ironically enough, a breakdown in solidarity. This sounds counterintuitive. Yet, as Röpke noted in the 1940s, claims such as "the nation pays" disguise the economic reality that, when it comes to the welfare state, "we are *really* asking all our neighbours, and often very rudely, to pay and give us a bit more."[30] Over time, it becomes harder to tell who is giving and who is receiving. In 2009, one German academic went so far as to describe this as having produced a situation that he likened to "fiscal kleptocracy."[31] Solidarity is thus reduced to the welfare state taking money from some and giving it to others.

Not only does this diminish many people's personal knowledge of and contact with those in need; their sense of responsibility for those in genuine need is reduced to paying taxes. In Europe, this is exacerbated by the ingrained *dirigisme* that leads many Europeans to assume that the state is the first port of call in terms of helping those without sufficient material means at their disposal.

Viewed in these terms, the welfare state becomes less a source of social harmony; instead, it begins to generate conflict. The division is between those who perceive themselves to benefit, on balance, from a large welfare state, and those who consider themselves saddled with the welfare state's costs.

A *second* cost of large welfare states is a gradual dulling of productivity. As noted in chapter 4, growth rates in Western European economies have been slowing down since the early 1970s. Welfare states are not the only cause of this. To the extent, however, that welfare systems reduce labor-force participation, they encourage perfectly able and economically productive people to stop working before they need or even want to. In 2010, for example, French employees worked an average of 620 hours a year, compared to 700 in Germany and 870 in America. In the same year, one hour's work in France cost an average of $43; in Germany, the equivalent cost was $36. This gave Germany—and America—an edge in globalized competition over France.[32] Productivity and growth rates are also negatively affected by the higher costs associated with the extensive labor-market regulation throughout Europe prioritizing job security. This undermines businesses' ability to adapt quickly to change.

The *third* cost of European welfare states is the manner in which they create obstacles to reform. If governments choose to address the problem of rising social security costs by raising taxes, they effectively suck more capital out of the economy's wealth-producing sectors. This gradually weakens the state's ability to sustain such spending. On the other hand, cutting welfare spending may be enough to swing a sufficient number of the government's supporters to opposition parties which, in order to get elected, will invariably promise to maintain welfare spending at pre-reform levels.

This factor played a role in the growing strength of a number of nonestablishment right-wing parties in Europe throughout 2010, 2011, and 2012. Such parties draw strongly upon anti-EU sentiment and frustration with mainstream political parties. In some cases, however, they also base their appeal upon explicit commitments to strong welfare states.

Under Marine Le Pen, France's National Front has sought to diminish some of the far-right imagery associated with her father. At the same time, the National Front has become just as insistent as the European and American Left about the need for extensive state-managed welfare systems. Having once been labeled as economic neoliberals, the National Front shifted steadily throughout the 1990s and 2000s toward favoring a large welfare state, as well as protectionism against foreign competition.[33] As Marine Le Pen stated in a June 2011 interview: "For a long time, the National Front upheld the idea that the state always does things more expensively and less well than the private sector . . . . But I'm convinced that's not true. The reason is the inevitable quest for profitability, which is inherent in the private sector."[34]

To the far northeast of France, the True Finns, a political party led by Timo Soini, emerged as one of Finland's largest parliamentary parties in national elections held in April 2011. Undoubtedly, anger with EU bailout proposals for southern European states played a significant role in its rise. The True Finns' economic policies, however, also included state support for particular industries, subsidies to rural areas affected by economic change, and no major changes to state welfare. Such policies, in some observers' view, put the True Finns closer to the Social Democrats than Finland's center-right parties on economic questions. The True Finns, stated Soini, are a "workers party without socialism."[35] To many ears, this sounded like modern 1950s social democracy.

A *fourth* cost of generous welfare states is, of course, high levels of taxation. In 2011, the top statutory personal income-tax rates levied by Western European central governments were as follows: Austria (50 percent), Belgium (53.7 percent), France (46.7 percent), Germany (47.5 percent), Greece (45 percent), Italy (45.6 percent), Netherlands (52 percent), Portugal (50 percent), and the United Kingdom (50 percent). The equivalent figure in the United States was 41.9 percent.

Then there are the further burdens associated with specific taxes used to fund social security. In 2011, almost all European countries exceeded in percentage terms the social security taxes levied in America. Lastly, there are corporate taxes. Here Western European countries actually demand less than the United States. In 2012, the combined corporate-tax rate in America was 39.1 percent. That compared *unfavorably* with every single European country. Only France came even close, at 34.4 percent.[36]

The figures quoted above are the highest rates. When we consider average rates of take-home pay in European countries, the results are even more sobering. In 2011, the OECD reported that "single taxpayers [in Austria] at average earnings take home less than 52% of what they cost to their employer (the 'total labour costs'); taxpayers at higher earnings take home even less than 50%." Belgium's equivalent figures were worse: "single taxpayers at average earnings take home less than 45% of what they cost to their employer . . . taxpayers at high earnings take home even less than 40%." The comparative figures for France were 50 percent and 47 percent, respectively.

The figures for all other Western European countries were not much different. Even in Sweden, which reduced its income-tax rates considerably between 1999 and 2011, high wage earners still took home less than 50 percent of what they cost their employer. By comparison, single taxpayers at average earnings in America took home more than 70 percent of what they cost their employer in 2011.[37]

The usual European rationale for this tax regime is, of course, that it promotes equality in the sense of more equal distributions of wealth. But as one World Bank analysis of European economies stated, it also means that "work incentives are weaker" in Europe.[38] Not only does that further diminish productivity, it also weakens Europeans' capacity to pay for welfare in the first place, without resorting to debt.

A Welfare Cul-de-Sac

However one looks at these numbers, they reflect a major problem for any European politician promoting welfare reform. It is true that generally, taxes have decreased marginally in Western Europe since the 1990s. But public spending as a percentage of GDP hardly changed for most Western European nations between 1990 and

2008. In some instances, it actually increased. This suggests that many Europeans remain quite susceptible to politicians' spending promises and associated appeals to security. They are clearly reluctant to reduce welfare expenditures.

The same figures also indicate that Europe's political class has been trying to have it both ways: offering relatively minor tax reductions (thus pleasing one set of constituencies) while maintaining levels of public spending (thus not overtly alienating another set of constituencies).

Unhappily for America, Europe's story in this area is not exclusively its own. It is also the story of America from the 1980s onward. Average tax rates for all American income earners—except the top one percent—have gradually fallen since the 1980s.[39] But tax cuts have *not* been accompanied by lasting restraint of public expenditures. In 2012, taxes and other revenue covered just two-thirds of federal spending; the balance was made up by borrowing.[40]

There are two ways out of these circumstances. The first involves more short- and medium-term political risk for governments, by cutting public spending, reducing taxes, and beginning to remove impediments to growth. Thus far the track record of such attempts in Europe is mixed.

In 1999, for example, France's Socialist prime minister, Lionel Jospin, tried to reduce public spending from 54 percent of GDP to 51 percent. Almost immediately, France's public-sector unions went on strike. Members of Jospin's own government began expressing strong reservations. Many of the proposed reforms were consequently dropped.

When Jospin's successor, the conservative Jean-Pierre Raffarin, tried to make public- and private-sector employees contribute more to their pension plans, his efforts also failed. Raffarin's successor, Dominique de Villepin, attempted his own reform: a minor liberalization of the labor market by introducing what was called a "first contract." This gave employers more leeway to hire and fire workers for the first two years in their first jobs. Strikes by unions and student sit-ins at universities eventually caused de Villepin's government to water down the reforms.

A second way to try to escape the welfare trap is politically easier, but only temporary, and likely to store up longer-term economic difficulties. It involves a combination of marginal changes to the tax code, maintaining public spending levels, and using debt instruments to cover the ever-growing deficits.

If, however, this goes on long enough, the ability of governments to service their debts (let alone pay them down) becomes increasingly doubtful. In 2011, the financial market analysts Standard & Poor's estimated that without further reforms to state pension programs, German government debt would rise to more than 400 percent of GDP by 2050, Italian government debt to more than 245 percent, French government debt to more than 403 percent, and Spanish government debt to more than 544 percent.[41] Aside from declaring bankruptcy, repudiating debt, or embracing the path of hyperinflation, it was unclear how governments could escape such burdens.

Perhaps the only circuit breaker for this situation is for the fiscal burden to grow so great, and the resentment at paying the bill to become so widespread, that enough Europeans start questioning the perceived benefits of large welfare states to the extent of changing their voting habits. Even then, one still needs European politicians who are, first: willing to take the risk of trying to attract support from such Europeans, and second: able to articulate a positive vision of *why* the welfare state's size ought to be reduced. In economic cultures habituated to generous welfare states, that is an extremely tall order.

Despite the political risks associated with addressing such problems, there is some evidence that governments that embark on significant economic reform have a better than even chance of re-election. In a study of the relationship between budget cutting and electoral results, the economists Alberto Alesina, Dorian Carloni, and Giampaolo Lecce estimated that incumbent governments facing re-election during a period of fiscal consolidation (or within two years after it had been completed) had an election survival rate no worse than the average. In sixty instances in nineteen rich economies where a country had cut its budget deficit by at least 1.5 percent of GDP, they found that the government's chances of losing power were about 40 percent.[42]

So why do European governments hesitate? According to Alesina, Carloni, and Lecce, a likely cause is that they worry about the backlash from particular interest groups affected by cutbacks in welfare, ranging from pensioners to businesses reliant on subsidies. To varying degrees, most European political parties are beholden to different combinations of interest-group supporters. Thus, even if a majority of voters favor reform, this may not be enough to persuade political parties to act.

A Time Bomb

If all these problems associated with European welfare states were not enough, they are likely to be exacerbated by a subject that even Europe's ultracautious, politically correct politicians are increasingly willing to reference: Europe's population problem.

From the 1900s onward, much of the world—and especially Europe—was swept by fears of an overpopulation crisis. Books predicting a new apocalypse of famine, overexploitation of resources, and fierce competition for living space were very much in vogue. One of the most popular was Paul Ehrlich's *The Population Bomb*, published in 1968. Its opening sentences are chilling: "The battle to feed all of humanity is over. In the 1970s hundreds of millions of people will starve to death in spite of any crash programs embarked upon now. At this late date nothing can prevent a substantial increase in the world death rate."[43]

Of course, nothing of the sort happened. Fifty years later, the majority of the world's population has not been decimated by famine. Nor has the world been stripped of natural resources by scavenging hordes.

Instead, by the 1990s, a slew of articles and books with titles such as *L'Hiver Démographique* (*The Demographic Winter*) and *La France ridée* (*France Shriveled Up*) began appearing in European bookshops. To many Europeans' surprise, they highlighted a *drop* of fertility rates in European countries, and outlined the problems likely to follow from this decline.

Changes in Europe's demographic landscape have been underway for a long time. Mortality rates began to drop in Western Europe in the mid-eighteenth century. More babies were surviving the first years of life, and people were living longer lives. Approximately fifty years later, this was followed by the onset of a decline in fertility rates.[44]

After 1945, life expectancy in Western Europe increased dramatically, rising from about sixty-two years in Western Europe in 1950 to almost seventy-nine in 2003. This paralleled a simultaneous fall in infant mortality rates.[45] The causes for these developments were many, but the most prominent included the growing use of antibiotics, better diets, and declining heart-disease rates.[46] These longer life spans, however, were accompanied by falling fertility levels. This meant that by the 1990s, most of Europe was entering a "gray winter."

The replacement level for a population—i.e., what keeps it stable—is a fertility rate of 2.10 children per woman. According to the population division of the United Nations' Department of Economic and Social Affairs, America's fertility rate was 2.07 between 2005 and 2010,[47] having declined from 3.71 between 1955 and 1960.[48]

By contrast, the average fertility rate of European women was 1.53 between 2005 and 2010.[49] The figures for Greece (1.46), Spain (1.41), Portugal (1.36), Italy (1.38), and Germany (1.36) were especially depressing. France (1.97), Britain (1.83), and Sweden (1.90) did marginally better. Ireland alone managed to attain the threshold of

2.10.[50] All these figures represented significant declines from 1955–1960 rates: Greece (2.27), Spain (2.70), Portugal (3.29), Italy (2.29), Germany (2.30), France (2.7), Britain (2.49), Sweden (2.23), and Ireland (3.58).[51] The Great Recession appears to have contributed to further decline. A slight recovery in European fertility rates that began in 1998 came to a shuddering halt in 2008, producing marked reductions in fertility rates in virtually every European country by 2011[52]—a phenomenon matched in the United States.[53]

So what does this mean? According to demographer Nicholas Eberstadt, Western Europe's population "may grow by just three percent over the next two decades, with near-zero growth projected by 2030. Germany and Italy are expected to experience population decline." Eberstadt estimates that Western Europe's median age will rise from forty-two years today to nearly forty-six years by 2030. More worryingly, he adds, this trend toward overall population stagnation would result in Western Europe's over sixty-five population rising by nearly 40 percent, while the manpower pool simultaneously shrinks by twelve million people. These estimates, incidentally, take into account a net inflow of twenty million mostly working-age immigrants.[54]

Looking even further ahead, a 2011 World Bank study estimated that over the next five decades, the European Union will lose almost forty million workers (18 percent of the present labor force) if present population, workforce participation, and immigration trends do not change.[55] When these factors are combined with rigid labor markets and the subsequent disincentives to hire young full-time workers, there is a very real possibility that Europe could face the paradoxical prospect of "impending shortages of young workers and high joblessness among its youth."[56]

How these trends might visually manifest themselves was already apparent in Europe as early as the mid-1990s. Looking at a visibly aging Italy during this period, one French economist observed: "The most extreme case is that of the central province, dense and rich, of

Emilia-Romagna, whose chief city is Bologna and where the number of persons over 60 is twice that of youths younger than 20."[57]

Other figures tell a similar story. In 2008, between 25 to 30 percent of all German women were childless. Germany's population is forecast to shrink by 0.1 percent on an annual basis. Italy will shrink by 0.3 percent annually. The annual workforce shrinkage will be even faster: Germany by 0.5 percent, Spain by 0.8 percent, and Italy by 0.9 percent.[58] In southern Europe, the situation was worsened by the fact that women had low workforce participation rates *and* low fertility, thereby undermining productivity for today and in the future.[59]

Population and Welfare

The economic costs associated with population decline are increasingly acknowledged. In the late 1930s, Keynes argued—to the British Eugenics Society no less!—that population growth helped create demand, and thereby fuel prosperity, while conversely, "declining population will make it immensely more difficult than before to maintain prosperity."[60] In more recent decades, Ettore Gotti Tedeschi, an Italian economist and former head of the *Istituto per le Opere di Religione* (otherwise known as the Vatican Bank), has observed that graying and dwindling European populations imply not only reduced demand, but also higher tax burdens on those who are young and working.[61] The resulting shrinkage of disposable income discourages those of child-bearing years from having more children.

The challenges for European welfare states created by these demographic realities are enormous. The British economist Gabriel Stein presents these in stark terms:

> If the population of the labor force ages, then—other things being equal—so too does the labor force. A contracting labor force means slower output growth. Secondly, an ageing popu-

lation increases the ratio of retirees per member of the labor force—the dependency ratio. This is particularly serious in countries where pensions are primarily funded on a pay-as-you-go basis: this includes most of the countries of continental Europe.[62]

In 1980, every five workers in Southern European nations were supporting one retiree.[63] By current estimates, Italy and Spain (and Germany) will have very high dependency ratios by 2050: every two workers will be supporting one retiree.[64] In the future, those working will have to pay even higher amounts to fund the pension systems, either by way of greater contributions, or through higher taxes.

Stein notes that one way to diminish the impact of these problems is to encourage longer labor-market participation by older people. In present day continental Europe, he cautions, only half (at most) of all men aged 55 and over and less than a third of women of the same age group are working.[65] Unfortunately, Stein argues, increased participation is not likely to occur, given the tightness of labor-market regulation (once you leave European labor markets, it is hard to re-enter) and the tax rates presently levied by these nations (which disincentivizes many older people from working).[66]

Another possibility for reducing the economic drag of aging populations is through increased productivity. But as noted, productivity has on average remained largely stagnant across Europe since the early 1990s.[67] Moreover, population decline makes its own contribution to the productivity problem. The Belgian population researcher Michel Schooyans makes the point that "An aging population tends to put a break on investment of productivity and capacity; nor does it lend itself to creativity. It tends . . . not only to consume savings, but to have recourse to loans whose weight is transferred to the shoulders of the next generation."[68] Stated crudely, fewer people means a smaller pool of human creativity, risk-takers, and potential entrepreneurs, and as the population ages, fewer people working and creating wealth.

America's demographic patterns are such that it may well avoid many of these problems. Between 2010 and 2030, America's population is likely to grow by 20 percent (or by sixty million people). Virtually every age group is set to increase in size during the same period. America is also likely to have a *growing* pool of working-age people, and a slower pace of aging. This, according to Eberstadt, stems from America's ability to more or less maintain its replacement-level fertility rate plus a continuing influx of immigrants.[69] That is good news for America—provided, of course, that it can sustain a replacement-level fertility rate over extended periods of time (fertility rates can change with surprising speed, and often fluctuate), that it continues to admit immigrants, that immigrants settle in the United States and have children of their own, and that new immigrants do not become beholden to political parties using promises of state welfare as a method of creating tame voting constituencies.

Population and Pensions
Why, then, is Europe experiencing falling fertility rates? The reasons are many, and include lower infant mortality rates, higher labor-force participation by women (which translates into more women choosing a full-time career over having and raising children), easier access to contraception, and abortion's legalization.[70]

Few have been willing to openly discuss whether modern European welfare states make their own contribution to the continent's falling fertility. It would be simplistic to attribute the decisive change exclusively to the introduction and expansion of pension schemes. To deny, however, that the welfare state has had any impact seems equally mistaken.

There is considerable empirical evidence for this connection. One 2005 study noted that almost all countries with large pension systems have fertility rates below replacement level.[71] A 2007 analysis of fertility rates, pensions, and a range of other variables in fifty-seven countries indicated that higher social security contributions and other pension taxes had a significant and negative effect on fertility rates.[72]

This connection between declining fertility and generous social security systems is called the "Old-Age Security Motive for Fertility." Viewing the family from a crudely economic standpoint, families functioned for many centuries as a type of pay-as-you-go (PAYGO) social security system. The essence of a PAYGO pension scheme is that it transfers wealth from those working to those who have retired. Each generation pays for the preceding generation and has its own retirement covered by its children.

Before the emergence of social security systems, parents gave birth to children, raised them, and in many instances, provided them with employment. In return, some of those children took responsibility for their parents in their later years. The more children people had, and the better educated and wealthier they were, the easier it was to share the burden of caring for aging parents later.[73] Having children thus functioned as a type of old-age insurance system for each generation.

Large modern public-pension systems—which overwhelmingly follow PAYGO principles—have gradually broken these links of mutual dependency. Once such systems are established, children are no longer so economically necessary for our old age. Instead, the state extracts revenues from everyone who is working in order to provide pensions for those who are retired.

This sounds reasonable—until we realize that state PAYGO pension systems create what economists call a "free-rider" problem. This occurs when people fail to contribute their fair share to the production of a public good, and/or consume excessive amounts of a public good at the expense of others. If large numbers of people engage in such behavior, the public good begins to lack the resources it needs to function over medium to long periods of time.

Hence, when some people choose to have no or few children in a society with large public pension systems, the costs of their state-funded pension is borne by those who have more children. Describing the problem in relatively technical terms, the Finnish economist Oskari Juurikkala writes: "A compulsory nationwide PAYGO pension scheme externalizes the tax-paying capacity of children and distributes it equally to older members of society, regardless of how many children they have, if any."[74] Put bluntly, those with no or few children basically free ride on those with more children.

Population and Politics

The problems associated with declining fertility, aging populations, and Europe's PAYGO pension systems are magnified by the political obstacles that exist to meaningful reform. These impediments flow from an unhappy coinciding of the individual self-interests of the political class, pensioners, and soon-to-be potential pensioners in the conditions of modern democracy.

In the case of soon-to-be pensioners, abandoning PAYGO schemes would mean that many existing contributors—and voters— would have paid significant amounts into the system, only to face the prospect of receiving significantly less than what they had been led to expect. Such people do not have a strong motivation to vote for change. Nor would existing retirees have any economic incentive to support any immediate pension cuts associated with such changes.

Part of the problem is the expectations many European politicians have created about state pension schemes. In the 1950s and 1960s, pensions became more generous throughout Western Europe. At the time, pensioners were relatively few in numbers. The amount of money being put into pension schemes was increasing faster than expenditures. It was easy for politicians of left and right to use more generous pension promises to attract votes.[75]

The situation changes dramatically once the money being taken from taxpayers and placed into PAYGO pension funds is no longer adequate to cover expenditures. And that is precisely what occurs when, as in Europe, fertility rates decline and people are retiring increasingly earlier.

The circumstances are worsened by another problem we have already encountered: the damaging effects of combining democratic political systems with generous welfare benefits. This effectively wears away at something Europeans claim to value: solidarity—this time of the intergenerational variety.

As the British economist Philip Booth writes: "When we set up a state pension scheme, voters can go to the polls and vote themselves pensions at the expense of other voters and potential voters, including people who are not old enough to vote and people who have yet to be born."[76] What many of the young Europeans protesting in Madrid, Lisbon, and Paris in mid-2011 did not appear to appreciate is that they were a distinct numerical minority in European societies. The numbers—and thus the voting power—were increasingly with the old.[77]

The electoral dynamics engendered by such circumstances and developments are not hard to grasp. If large segments of an electorate estimate they can gain from increasing state pensions, then politicians in democratic systems will find it difficult to resist such increases. As the age of European voters rises, they will economically gain by increasing or maintaining the size of the pension system.[78] This increases the already high odds that they will vote to block change. By around 2010, Booth notes, the three main British political parties were effectively competing for older voters by offering any number of special allowances, the wage indexing of state pensions, and special tax concessions.[79]

It is thus entirely possible that the following vicious cycle could develop. As the population ages, we see declines in private and public savings. The pace of economic growth subsequently weakens. A declining economic growth rate makes pensions harder to provide. This necessitates higher taxes, which reduces the income of those who are working. They in turn respond by having fewer children, which makes the problem even worse.[80]

One ray of hope is that some European politicians *are* conscious of the problem, evidenced by attempts throughout Europe to reform pension systems in light of these demographic and economic realities. Long before France's 2010 pension reforms, German politicians had agreed to gradually raise the nation's official retirement age, in 1992, 2001, and 2007 (with this last increase to sixty-seven years of age beginning in 2012, for anyone born in or after 1964). By 2011, a number of senior German government ministers were arguing for increasing the retirement age for *all* EU citizens to sixty-seven.

Most of contemporary Europe's successful pension reforms, like those implemented in Sweden in the 1990s and 2000s, have involved "buying off" older voters.[81] This is based on the political calculation that the incentive of older voters to agitate against change is thereby reduced. In February 2011, for instance, Spain's Socialist government concluded a "social pact" with employers and unions that gradually raises the pension age to sixty-seven. This is not due to take full effect until 2027,[82] by which time a good number of soon-to-be retirees will have begun passing away in large numbers.

America's Dilemma

It hardly need be said that publicly funded social security in the United States is not in good shape. It is no consolation that Western Europe's public spending on pensions per elderly person has long been considerably higher than that of America.[83] The United States federal Social Security program has become the largest government pension scheme in the world in terms of sheer dollars. It is also the single greatest item of expenditure in the federal government's budget.

In 1949, public spending on "human services"—Social Security; Medicare; health expenditures; education, training, employment, and social services; veterans benefits; and the euphemistically named "income security" (i.e., unemployment benefits)—was consuming 4 percent of America's GDP.[84] By 1976, this figure had increased to 11.7 percent.[85] In 2009, it was consuming 15.3 percent of GDP.[86]

A similar pattern may be observed in the federal government's budget. In 1967, spending on "human resources" was consuming 32.6 percent of the budget.[87] By 2009, this figure had increased to 61.3 percent.[88] It is predicted to rise to 67 percent by 2016.[89] And it is not just America's Left that has presided over these developments. In his study of the history of entitlement spending in the United States, Nicholas Eberstadt points out that "the Richard Nixon, Gerald Ford, and George W. Bush administrations presided over especially lavish expansions of the American entitlement state."[90]

To put the welfare dimension of this into perspective, the Heritage Foundation's *2012 Index of Dependence on Government* observed that by 2010, 70.5 percent of total federal government spending was dedicated to welfare programs: an increase from 28.3 percent in 1962, and 48.5 percent in 1990. As the index's authors noted, in human terms this meant that

> Today, more people than ever before—67.3 million Americans, from college students to retirees to welfare beneficiaries—depend on the federal government for housing, food, income, student aid, or other assistance once considered to be the responsibility of individuals, families, neighborhoods, churches, and other civil society institutions.[91]

This situation is even worse once one considers, as argued by Heritage's Robert Rector, that approximately one-third of Americans in 2011 were receiving some type of welfare payment from one or more of the more than eighty means-tested federal government welfare programs—a figure that *excludes* Social Security and Medicare.[92]

And as in Europe, there has been a striking increase in the number of Americans receiving some form of disability payment.

Back in 1960, approximately 455,000 people received monthly federal disability payments. In 50 years, the number had grown to 8.2 million, with an extra 400,000 alone being added to the rolls in 2011.[93] The depth of the problem becomes even more obvious when one considers that, for example, while the American economy generated 1.73 million nonfarm jobs from January 2010 to December 2011, almost half as many workers (790,000) began receiving federal disability payments.[94]

Magnifying the problem is evidence of a shrinking base of those actually paying the taxes that support these arrangements. By 2009, 49.5 percent of Americans filing tax returns paid no income taxes, compared to 14.8 percent in 1984.[95] The 2009 figure is partly explainable by the drop in many people's incomes in the wake of the Great Recession. But even in the more prosperous early and mid-years of the last decade, approximately 40 percent of American households paid *no* federal income tax (though many were subject to payroll tax, which helps fund Social Security and Medicare).[96]

In short, America has well and truly entered its own welfare cul-de-sac. At some point, the party must come to an end. In 2004, the Congressional Budget Office (CBO) reported that, assuming tax levels remained the same, "the Social Security trust funds will become exhausted in 2052." This, the CBO noted, will present the government with an interesting legal dilemma: "On the one hand, trust-fund exhaustion will not affect a beneficiary's right to benefits specified in law. On the other hand, the Social Security Administration will not have the legal authority to pay full benefits."[97] Eight years later, the CBO has predicted that, with present trends, the Social Security Disability Insurance trust fund will be exhausted by 2016.[98]

If poverty in America should have long ago been consigned to history, some Americans might regard the sheer dollar amounts spent on welfare programs as a worthwhile long-term public investment. But Americans have good reason to be dissatisfied with the results of these expenditures. The policy analyst Peter Ferrara calculates that "total welfare spending [in 2008] . . . amounted to $16,800 per person in poverty, 4 times as much as the Census Bureau estimated was necessary to bring all of the poor up to the poverty level, eliminating all poverty in America. That would be $50,400 per poor family of three." The effects in terms of reducing poverty have, however, been abysmal. As Ferrara observes: "Poverty fell sharply after the Depression, before the War on Poverty, declining from 32% in 1950 to 22.4% in 1959 to 12.1% in 1969, soon after the War on Poverty programs became effective. Progress against poverty as measured by the poverty rate then abruptly stopped."[99]

In other words, the American welfare state has *failed* in one of its key objectives, despite the huge resources it consumes. More generally, it is not clear that the United States can avoid similar political and economic challenges to those faced by Europe with regard to the fiscal sustainability of America's welfare state, even absent the demographic challenges facing Europe.

Many Americans believed that the primary message of the 2010 congressional election was that Americans were fed up with successive governments and legislatures running up deficit after deficit, and their associated refusal to seriously restrain public spending. If, however, the results of a 2011 *Wall Street Journal*-NBC News poll indicated what Americans *really* thought about fiscal issues, then much of the country was in denial about what America needed to do if it did not want to go the way of many Western European nations.[100] Though the poll revealed considerable concern about government debt, it also underscored how *unwilling* many Americans were to reduce those welfare programs that, in the long term, are central to America's public debt problems.

Despite the passionate rhetoric from Americans about the need to diminish public spending, the poll suggested that fewer than 25 percent of Americans favored cutbacks to Social Security or Medicare as deficit-reduction measures. As *The Wall Street Journal*'s commentators noted: "Even tea party supporters, by a nearly 2-to-1 margin, declared significant cuts to Social Security 'unacceptable'." Granted, the same poll suggested larger numbers of Americans were willing to lift the retirement age to sixty-nine and means-test social security. But that hardly counts as radical reform.

Why, then, do so many Americans balk at reforms that might reduce welfare spending? One uncomfortable explanation was aptly summarized by *The Washington Post*'s economics correspondent Robert Samuelson, who has long argued that several political dynamics—processes remarkably similar to Europe—are at work in America that make change increasingly difficult. First, these programs come with huge constituencies of voters attached who would likely react negatively to significant cuts.[101] From this perspective, Samuelson maintains, the American Association of Retired Persons (AARP) has become one of America's most powerful and reform-impeding lobbies.[102] Second, any party seeking to raise taxes to cover spending would likewise alienate significant proportions of voters.

Samuelson goes further in identifying the core of the problem, in terms that many Americans may find difficult to hear:

> . . . most Americans don't want to admit that they are current or prospective welfare recipients. They prefer to think that they automatically deserve whatever they've been promised simply because the promises were made. Americans do not want to pose the basic questions, and their political leaders mirror that reluctance. This makes the welfare state immovable and the budget situation intractable.[103]

It might also be called economic Europeanization.

Immigration Matters

However these specific questions are resolved, the good news is that America's demographic trends give it some reason to hope that its social security system will not be as immediately subject to the same specific pressures facing most of Europe. The steady flow of immigrants to America helps mitigate the problem.

Generally speaking, it is a good sign when a country becomes a destination to which people *want* to migrate. The migration of large numbers of Greeks, Spaniards, Portuguese, and Italians to countries such as France, West Germany, Belgium, and Switzerland in the 1950s testified to the recipient countries' better standards of living and more dynamic economies. The same factors help to explain why so many Poles moved to Britain and Ireland in the 1990s and early 2000s.

America has long been a magnet for migrants because it is seen as a land where those who are willing to work hard and take risks can advance socially and economically in ways that are inconceivable in many other parts of the world. In this sense, immigration can be an economic boon *if* a country's economic culture embodies the right settings.

In 2011, a report released by the Kauffman Foundation on entrepreneurship and immigrants in America looked at trends of entrepreneurial start-ups in cross sections of the American population over a fifteen-year period. It indicated that immigrants to America were creating new businesses at unprecedented rates. Immigrants, the report stated, were "more than twice as likely to start businesses each month in 2010 than were the native-born."[104]

This should not be surprising. If the value and institutional settings are right, an influx of immigrants can bring with it highly skilled workers, raw talent, and potential entrepreneurs. The number of immigrants from the Indian subcontinent living and working in Silicon Valley is just one example. Having risked leaving the familiarity of their homeland to work in a country where they often barely know the primary language, immigrants are not slow to take other risks, such as creating new businesses.

Immigrants create competition in relatively free labor markets, not least because many migrants are willing to work longer and for less wages than the native-born. Young working-age immigrants who secure jobs, start businesses, and create wealth are also actual and potential contributors to public and private pension schemes, filling in the demographic gaps that threaten such programs in Western Europe.

Given these facts, one might imagine that immigration would also be a way for Europe to mitigate these welfare-related problems. Here, however, a range of difficulties has emerged, some of which are exacerbated by European welfare states.

Not So Welcome

Over the past twenty years, no regular visitor to Europe can have failed to notice changes in most West European countries' ethnic composition. Whether it is the ubiquitous street vendors from Africa selling fake designer-label handbags in Rome's streets or the *hijab*-wearing women in downtown Amsterdam, Western Europe is now home to millions of legal and illegal immigrants, many of whom do not come from nations or cultures traditionally associated with the West.

In 2005, 12.3 percent (or just over ten million individuals) of Germany's population was immigrant. Comparable figures for Spain, France, and Britain were 10.8 percent, 10.2 percent, and 9 percent, respectively.

The ethnic composition varied. Approximately five million of Germany's migrants were of Turkish background. France's migrants were largely from North Africa and other French-speaking African nations. Many of Britain's migrants came from the Asian subcontinent. A significant portion of Spain's migrants hailed from Latin America. In 2009, just over half of Italy's migrants came from other European nations (mainly eastern and southeastern Europe).[105]

This is not a new situation for Europe. Mass internal migrations occurred inside Europe during and after the two World Wars. Some of these were less than peaceful affairs, and produced a range of problems with which postwar European governments were obliged to cope. Indeed, for all its claims to be an oasis of tolerance and human rights in an often intolerant world, Western Europe has not proved immune to immigration-related problems.

In late 2005, this was vividly manifested by the outbreak of two weeks of rioting and vandalism by young men of predominantly Muslim immigrant backgrounds in the suburbs surrounding the periphery of Paris and other large French cities. This was despite the political class's endless rhetoric about "inclusion," "social cohesion," "solidarity," and "diversity," and policies of multiculturalism—a policy stance increasingly repudiated by European politicians ranging from Britain's Tony Blair to Germany's Angela Merkel.

The warning signs had been there as early as the mid-1990s. During this period, political parties with decidedly skeptical views of immigration began gaining significant percentages of the popular vote at election after election, in countries including France, Belgium, Italy, Austria, and the Netherlands.

On one level, this reflected European angst about the non-assimilation by many immigrants from Muslim countries into mainstream society. But there was an economic dimension to the tension, captured in the words of a spokesman of France's National Front: "If we want to send the Arabs and Asians back to where they came from, it's not because we hate them; it's because they pollute our national identity and *take our jobs.*"[106]

Ironically, many of the first waves of immigrants to countries such as France and Germany in the late 1950s and early 1960s came because of labor shortages in these nations. The operating assumption was that most of these migrants would live and work in Europe on a temporary basis, and eventually go home.

As it turned out, Algerians, Moroccans, and Tunisians (in France) and Turks (in Germany) showed little interest in following this script, especially after they started having children, or brought their immediate (and sometimes extended) families to live with them in

Europe. They were not blind to the vast difference in material standards of living between their host countries and their homelands.

The situation was further complicated by the fact that, by the 1970s, labor shortages in Europe had become a thing of the past. Instead, unemployment had begun to grow. At the same time, as one scholar of immigration in modern Europe observes, "Migrants residing in Europe could continue to sponsor their extended family's immigration and, indeed, relaxation of restrictions on family reunification encouraged further immigration."[107] This change in the complexion of migration from single laborers to families also meant that increasing numbers of immigrants became more concerned about factors such as schooling, health care, and proper housing.[108]

The result was even more fiscal demands on European welfare states. The situation is aggravated by the fact that 66 percent of the two and a half million migrants from North Africa and the Middle East residing in the EU only have a primary education,[109] and disturbingly high numbers of them have gravitated to the welfare system.[110] Conversely, approximately 40 percent of immigrants to America are highly skilled (defined as possessing a tertiary education). Those who are unskilled (mainly from Mexico and Central and South America) typically start working in one or more menial jobs, and then begin working their way up the economic ladder.[111]

Part of the difference between the American and European experiences with immigration and welfare may be explained by what has been the relative ease of accessing state welfare in many Western European countries. But heavy labor-market regulation in Europe has also exerted an influence. The same labor protections that diminish economic opportunities for young native-born Europeans are equally restrictive on young immigrants seeking jobs. These immigrants suffer from additional handicaps, such as lacking the necessary educational qualifications, language skills, and connections to insider groups possessed by many native Europeans. Of the million people who immigrate to Europe each year, less than one in five has more than a high school diploma.[112] All these factors help explain why the labor-market performance of immigrants and their descendants in France, Germany, and Britain has been, on average, worse than that of native populations.[113]

Even more perverse is the manner in which heavy labor regulation and the associated costs of hiring and firing individuals encourages Western European employers to quietly hire immigrants in what effectively amounts to a black market in labor, especially in Southern Europe.[114] Because such immigrants are not officially employed in these jobs, they can be paid less than their native-born counterparts. They can also be let go more easily. Not surprisingly, insider groups such as trade unions regard this as a way of "stealing" "their" jobs, and undercutting the official wage rates negotiated by unions and businesses within the framework of neo-corporatist structures, under the government's benevolent eye.

That many Europeans' objections to immigration often have as much to do with economic questions as worries about ethnicity and identity became apparent during the 2005 referenda debates about the draft European constitution. In France and the Netherlands, there was no shortage of people from the Left and Right who predicted it would lead to Western European labor markets being "overrun" by Europeans from former Communist countries: i.e., individuals whose identity as Europeans is hardly questionable. Four years later, the economic factor came to the fore in Britain, as unemployment rose in the wake of the 2008 recession. Protests occurred in a number of cities, demanding that companies hire British citizens, rather than Eastern Europeans, for "British" jobs. Worker solidarity, it seemed, only extended to those born in the British Isles.

By early 2012, however, evidence was emerging of another immigration trend: a growing exodus of tens of thousands of young EU citizens—primarily young professionals—searching for work in Latin America, North America, Australia, Asia, and non-EU European nations.[115] The odds that many would return to Europe in the near future were dim. Similarly, hundreds of thousands of young immigrants to the EU from developing nations were heading home, no longer confident that Europe offered them the type of employment opportunities enjoyed by earlier migrants.

Such developments are a natural reaction to an economic downturn. But the problem for European welfare states is that the continuation of such trends threatens to diminish even further the number of young Europeans needed to sustain Europe's PAYGO welfare systems over the long term. In raw political terms, it also reduces the number of Europeans who might be inclined to call for change, while strengthening the numerical position of those committed to an unsustainable status quo.

From Welfare Crisis to Currency Crisis

Americans can be somewhat more optimistic than Europeans about their ability to overcome the negative dynamics associated with the welfare state. The welfare reforms introduced by the Clinton administration and the Republican-controlled Congress in the 1990s illustrated that, even after decades of New Deal and Great Society programs, it was possible to change the American welfare state's workings in ways that enhanced economic growth and shifted some incentives back toward the private sector. Contrary to the predictions of those who opposed the reforms, thousands of people were not thrust into poverty. Nor were millions roaming America's streets in search of shelter.

The 2010 congressional elections were correctly interpreted as being, in part, a referendum on the wisdom of expanding government, especially the tremendous growth of the welfare state that was implicit to Obamacare. It is difficult to imagine a single European country where a similar expansion of the scope and size of the welfare state would have generated a similar electoral result. While some Americans are clearly ambiguous about reducing any number of welfare programs, many Americans remain clearly disinclined to *extend* the welfare state.

Unfortunately for those Europeans with a craving for security, time and economic reality have finally caught up with them. By 2009, the need for many European governments to address their debt problems had became apparent to even Europe's more fiscally "relaxed" states, leaving them no choice but to pursue welfare reforms. But to understand how this situation emerged, we need to understand the third dimension of Europe's contemporary challenges: its deficit and currency dilemma.

7

Deficits, Debt, and Deception

I have always found the word "Europe" in the mouths of those politicians who wanted from other powers something they did not dare to demand in their own name.

—OTTO VON BISMARCK

Europe shall be made by the currency or it shall not be made.

—JACQUES RUEFF

Jacques Rueff was perhaps the twentieth century's most influential French economist. A graduate of one of France's *grandes écoles*, the École Polytechnique, a decorated First World War veteran, and passionately pro-American, Rueff entered the French civil service in the early 1920s as a member of the Inspection Générale des Finances: the French state's corps of elite financial advisers. By the 1930s he was a deputy governor of the Banque de France, and a senior economic adviser to successive French governments as they sought to navigate the Depression's stormy waters.

Rueff was, however, more than an economically informed civil servant. He was also a formidable intellectual with a particular interest in monetary theory. Having written several texts on the subject, Rueff emerged in the 1930s as one of the most prominent critics of Keynes's views on monetary policy. For his entire life, Rueff was an unflinching advocate of the gold standard—the system that, in various ways, integrated the world's currencies between 1870 and 1971.

On the subject of Europe's future after the Great War, Rueff was an early supporter of a politically and economically integrated Europe. No one was therefore surprised when he became one of the first judges to sit on the ECSC's Court of Justice upon its inauguration in 1952. As the debates about the proposed common market intensified in the 1950s, Rueff emerged as a strong advocate of supranational European institutions. Whereas his friend and fellow neoliberal Wilhelm Röpke argued that economic integration along free-market lines should occur primarily through unilateral liberalization by individual countries, Rueff did not believe that it was enough to simply end neo-mercantilist and protectionist practices. Supranational institutions, Rueff maintained, would be essential to the spread of market economies throughout the common economic zone. And by institutions, Rueff particularly had in mind the adoption of a Europe-wide currency.

Money has long been a controversial issue inside the EU. Both proponents and opponents of the euro have emphasized that, once a European country adopts the single currency, it has effectively given up control of monetary policy—and thus a degree of sovereignty—within its borders.

This highlights an element that has always underlined the process of European monetary unification: the fact that the single-currency project has only partially been about economics. It is just as much about encouraging the EU's political integration through a *dirigiste* centralizing of key elements of economic policy making in EU institutions. As we shall see, the struggle to achieve such ends in the context of Europe's economic culture—especially the costs associated with maintaining the European social model—explains much of the debt crisis experienced by the EU in the late 2000s and early 2010s. Though there are significant differences between the EU's debt problems and those of the United States, there are several common elements characterizing America's and Europe's respective deficit and debt challenges: most notably, the apparent inability of governments to live within their means and the failure, and at times unwillingness, of large numbers of Americans and Europeans to force them to do so.

Monetary Divisions

From the beginnings of Europe's postwar efforts at building a distinctive economic model, disagreements pervaded Europe's polit ical insiders about money's role in this process. One such division, which emerged in the 1960s, was between the "Monetarists" and the "Economists."

The Economists, primarily associated with the German and Dutch governments and central banks, regarded some form of monetary union as the end result of a convergence of economic conditions among European nations. Only those member-state nations that had realized a particular set of conditions, they held, could be admitted to the monetary union "club." Their views were summarized in 1963 by the head of the German Bundesbank, Karl Blessing, when he stated that monetary union demanded "a common trade policy, a common social and wage policy—a common policy all-around."[1]

The Monetarists, generally to be found in France and Belgium, took a different view. They considered money and monetary policy as tools that governments, and eventually European institutions, could use to *hasten* the process of convergence and integration.

The Economist-Monetarist division was paralleled by another fault line, this time between Keynesians and neoliberals. The Keynesians viewed monetary policy primarily as an instrument for boosting employment and growth via the stimulating effects of easy money policies (a view common enough among Americans with Keynesian inclinations). On the other side were those Europeans with a strict anti-inflationist view of monetary policy.

In practical terms, this translated into a dispute between adherents of neoliberal monetary policy, such as Germany, Austria, and the Netherlands, and nations with more proactive views of central banking's role, especially France and Italy. But this particular division did not always neatly follow national lines. In the 1970s, for example, the German Bundesbank had to withstand political pressures from Social Democratic governments chaffing at the Bundesbank's apparent unwillingness to loosen monetary policy in the face of growing West German unemployment.

And Monetary Dilemmas

Far then from being confined to the arcana of abstract monetary theory, these conflicts about monetary policy reflected disagreements that Europe's politicians, civil servants, and central bankers had to resolve before monetary union could be realized. The first question was, which should come first: economic convergence or monetary union? A second debate concerned the primary monetary policy objective of any European-wide central bank: monetary stability or combating unemployment?

The third dilemma followed logically from any agreement proposing to establish a central bank that would set monetary policy for an integrated European economic area. Would this require fiscal policy—decisions about taxes and spending—to be removed from national governments, and centralized in supranational European institutions?

This last issue is especially important because a common currency clearly implied a centralization of budgetary *and* monetary policy. Even at this early stage, there was awareness that if countries participating in a European-wide common currency were allowed to run their own fiscal policies, there would be little to restrain governments committed to maintaining Social Europe within their borders from running large deficits in order to cover the costs flowing from a fatal nexus of expensive welfare states, large public sectors, unimpressive productivity, heavy labor-market regulation, and demographic decline. Governments knew that if any one country became excessively indebted, other countries participating in a common currency would have to make one of two unpalatable choices. Either they would have to bail out the indebted nation, or witness a gradual collapse of confidence in the currency.

This third European monetary dilemma thus went beyond the merits of technical economic arguments. It raised specifically *political* issues. One was the question of whether Europeans really wanted what figures such as Robert Schuman and Jean Monnet had desired: the effective transfer of considerable economic and political sovereignty from nation-states to a supranational European political community. The other was the extent to which wealthier European countries such as Germany were committed to meeting the expectations associated with the social model, not only within their own borders, but across the entire EU.

Toward the Euro

In October 1970, political union was presented, in what came to be known as the Werner Report, as an inevitable consequence of economic and monetary union. This document was produced by an EEC committee charged with outlining a path to economic and monetary union. The Werner Report foresaw a three-stage approach to monetary union, during which there would be a gradual transfer of monetary *and* fiscal responsibilities from national central banks, national governments, and national legislatures to European Community institutions. These, the report stated, would be supervised by a strengthened and elected European Parliament. Curiously, there was no mention of a European-wide central bank.

Like many other proposals advanced in the 1970s for greater European economic union, the Werner Report was politely ignored by most governments. In the 1980s, however, the drive toward monetary union received fresh momentum. With the support of West German chancellor Helmut Kohl and France's François Mitterrand, the EEC created a committee to chart a path toward monetary union. They also made the politically astute decision to give the chairmanship of this committee (primarily composed of central bankers) to European Commission president (and grand resuscitator of the European project) Jacques Delors.

Issued in 1989, what became known as the Delors Report listed a set of steps toward achieving monetary union. These included the full integration of financial markets, complete liberalization of capital controls, the unalterable fixing of exchange rates, and an irreversible conversion of currencies. The other major recommendation was for what would become the European System of Central Banks (ESCB), to be independent of national governments and other European-wide institutions, and whose prime objective would be price stability.

The ESCB thus amounted to the replication of a type of Bundesbank at the European level, imbued, like the Bundesbank, with neoliberal rather than Keynesian objectives. As the financial journalist David Marsh observed, a considerable body of opinion within the French finance ministry was opposed to granting independence to such a bank—including, ironically enough, a certain Jean-Claude Trichet (later the second president of the ECB, and staunch defender of the ECB's autonomy).[2] Even today, plenty of European politicians adamantly oppose this independence.

Three years later, the path to, and conditions for, monetary union and entry into the single European currency—the euro—were spelled out at Maastricht. The convergence criteria for countries seeking admission were fourfold.

The first was an inflation rate no more than 1.5 percentage points higher than the average of the three best-performing (lowest-inflation) EU member states. A second was a nominal long-term interest rate no more than 2 percentage points higher than the three lowest-inflation member states. The third was that applicant nations had to join the exchange-rate mechanism under the European Monetary System for two consecutive years, and not devalue their currency during this time.

The fourth—and what later turned out to be fateful—criterion concerned *public finances*. This had two components.

One was that the ratio of an applicant country's gross government debt to GDP should not exceed 60 percent at the end of the preceding fiscal year. Some wiggle room was, however, permitted. If this goal could not be met because of "special" conditions, then the ratio had to have fallen "sufficiently" and be moving toward realizing the objective.

The other public-finance requirement concerned the ratio of annual government deficit as a proportion of GDP. This, Maastricht stated, should not exceed 3 percent at the end of the preceding fiscal year. But yet again, wiggle room was allowed. If this goal was not attained, the applicant country was required to reach a level "close to" 3 percent. The treaty further specified that exceptional and temporary excesses might be granted for extraordinary cases.[3]

These criteria were formalized more closely in what became known as the Stability and Growth Pact (SGP). Adopted in 1997, its purpose was to enforce fiscal discipline throughout the EU. It sought to ensure that, once admitted to the eurozone, countries did not embark on fiscally profligate policies. German politicians were especially insistent upon these conditions. They were desperate to reassure a wary German electorate that adopting the euro did not mean Germany was sacrificing its strict anti-inflationary policies on the altar of European unification.

The euro's formation was thus based on significant political compromises. National governments only gave up *part* of their economic sovereignty: i.e., their ability to conduct *monetary* policy in the interests of their respective nations. But they did not lose their *fiscal* powers. The great unknown was whether this pattern of monetary centralization and continuing fiscal decentralization could sustain itself *after* countries entered the currency union.

Another compromise was the manner in which those sections of Maastricht addressing these currency issues reflected a merging of market principles and *dirigiste* instincts. Article 125 of Maastricht, for example, insisted that neither the EU nor a member state was liable for or could assume "the commitments of central governments, regional, local or other public authorities, other bodies governed by public law, or public undertakings of any member state, without prejudice to mutual financial guarantees for the joint execution of a specific project."

Germans thus rested easy, believing they would not end up paying for excessive spending by countries with extravagant spending records. This confidence was further cemented by Article 123 of Maastricht (and confirmed by Article 123 of the Treaty of Lisbon). This forbade national central banks and the envisaged ECB from granting "overdraft facilities" to "Union institutions, bodies, offices or agencies, central governments, regional, local or other public authorities, other bodies governed by public law, or public undertakings of member states."[4] It also prohibited the purchase of debt instruments from the same institutions by the ECB or national central banks. In other words, there was to be no "monetizing" of the debts of member states or EU institutions via the ECB or national central banks choosing to print money.

Yet, as Christopher Caldwell observed, if these "no-bailouts" and "no-printing-money-to-wash-away-debt" articles were meant to be effective, there would have been no need for the SGP.[5] Fiscally irresponsible countries would simply have been left to be disciplined by financial markets. These would respond to questionable debt levels by either calling in debts or raising interest rates significantly.

In this light, the SGP acquires a *dirigiste*-like character inasmuch as it sought to *forestall* potential market responses to reckless government spending. As it turned out, these structures proved utterly ineffective in the face of some EU governments' failure to exercise fiscal restraint, as they expanded the breadth and depth of the European social model within their borders.

Dirigisme, Deficits, and Euro-Fudging

By the time the euro formally entered into circulation in 2002, the Economists appeared to have won the decades-old battle. Monetary union seemed to be *following* a process of convergence of fiscal conditions. Yet this was only partly true. The *prospect* of monetary union was also clearly being used to encourage prospective members toward predetermined fiscal conditions. Monetarists could happily endorse this as a partial realization of their *dirigiste* strategy.

But almost from the very beginning of the euro as a day-to-day reality of European economic life, several European member states employed what might be described as "creative accounting" to meet the conditions specified by Maastricht and the SGP. Several *dirigiste*-inclined governments with strong commitments to Social Europe moved different parts of their finances into "off-budget" arrangements, such as pseudo-private but essentially state-owned corporations. This allowed them to technically reduce their spending and get close to the Maastricht convergence criteria, while actually maintaining and even boosting their social spending.

One country—infamously—simply *lied* about its fiscal position. In 2004, Greece's finance minister at the time, George Alogoskoufis, confessed: "It has been proven that Greece's budget deficit never fell below 3 percent since 1999"[6]—a clear violation of the SGP.

This fudging at the national level was matched by EU-level fudging. A number of countries that did not come close to meeting specific Maastricht criteria were given generous waivers, thereby negating the convergence criteria's entire purpose. In the end, most applicant countries were admitted to the euro despite having debt levels exceeding 60 percent. Italy and Belgium, for example, were permitted entry despite having debt ratios of over 120 percent.

The fact of such subterfuge was public knowledge. Instead, however, of insisting that eurozone members should abide by SGP criteria, many EU politicians sought to discredit the criteria. Within half a year of the euro's entry into circulation, the then president of the European Commission, Romano Prodi, famously labeled the SGP as the "Stupidity Pact." It was, he proclaimed, "too rigid," and should not be enforced "dogmatically" without consideration of circumstances.

The other context for these remarks was the growing awareness that many member states had no intention of playing by the rules once officially admitted to the euro. The rules concerning limits on government deficit spending, for example, meant that many spending programs associated with Social Europe would require significant trimming—something many EU states silently declined to do.

The two countries that had pushed the most for adherence to the SGP (France and Germany) discredited it, for all intents and purposes, by breaching its provisions in 2002. The Netherlands and Greece followed suit in 2003. Italy joined this somewhat disreputable club in 2004. By 2005, five of the then twelve euro-area countries had or were planning deficits above 3 percent. Seven of them had debt-to-GDP ratios above the 60 percent reference value, with two having debt ratios above 100 percent of GDP.

Unpacking the Pact

It was to prevent precisely such behavior that the EU had established disciplinary measures for fiscally lax eurozone members. Such nations were supposed to be subjected, as one member of the ECB's executive board said at the time, "to excessive deficit procedures."[7]

This turned out to be a toothless tiger. Under pressure from France and Germany, the European Commission proved reluctant to enforce the SGP's disciplinary measures. Moreover, in October 2005, when then EU Commissioner for Economic and Monetary Affairs Joaquín Almunia accused a number of member-state governments of mimicking the corporate sector in finding ways to circumvent the SGP's criteria,[8] few governments seemed to care. By 2006, Germany's public debt was 66.8 percent of GDP. Greece's was well over 100 percent.

No one was consequently surprised when the European Council suspended the SGP in 2005 and sought to create a new pact. It maintained the previous rules about debt and deficits, but added a long list of exceptions for particular types of spending that would not be included when determining debt and deficit figures. The excluded spending included expenditures on research, defense, education, aid, and (as if that was not enough) anything spent to further "the unification of Europe." Leaving aside the fact that some of these items constituted major spending elements of any national government's budget, the fifth exemption could be used as a catchall justification for whatever a national government decided would further advance European unification.

Perhaps the most disturbing feature of these measures was the manner in which they simply ignored certain fiscal realities. An inter-European agreement could certainly declare that spending for education and defense no longer counted when assessing whether a country was adhering to the pact. But no agreement could disguise the *reality* that spending on education and defense *did* count when anyone—including lenders—tried to assess a country's *true* surplus or *actual* deficit. No amount of wishful thinking could change these facts. As one Portuguese politician commented in late 2010, "The state has for many years been removing from the budget a series of activities, which has made a large part of our numbers fictitious." He went on to estimate that Portugal's *true* total public debt stood as high as 112 percent of GDP, instead of the 82 percent claimed by the government.[9]

In April 2011, Portugal became the third EU member state, after Greece and Ireland, to request a bailout from the EU and the International Monetary Fund. Evidently, no amount of "off-balance sheet budgeting" could disguise the reality of years of excessive public spending fueled by debt. There was, as *The Wall Street Journal* observed at the time, something troubling about the fact that the country in which the Lisbon agenda had been agreed upon by EU member states as the future path for Europe had just effectively declared itself financially insolvent.[10]

Muddling Through, Euro-Style

While the European Commission continued to act throughout most of the 2000s as if violating the SGP was a serious matter, Alberto Alesina and Francesco Giavazzi summarized matters perfectly when they observed that "countries in Europe can do just about anything they please with deficits."[11]

In 2006, for instance, Portugal began implementing a grand plan of public investments through infrastructure improvements. It was financed by deficit spending that would not have been permitted under the old provisions of Maastricht and the SGP.

The new conditions also meant Greece no longer had to lie so blatantly about its levels of deficit spending. Instead, Greece could now openly use its deficit spending to cover the ever-growing costs of Greece's low economic productivity and extravagant welfare state. Greece embarked on an orgy of financial indulgence, borrowing money to pay for increased unemployment benefits, patronage politics of Left and Right, and, of course, growing private-sector and public-sector wages increases. Between 2000 and 2005, public payroll expenses (the salaries and pensions of public-sector workers) rose from consuming 38 percent of Greek state revenue in 2000 to 55 percent in 2009.[12]

Nor apparently did the EU's other less competitive "Club Med" economies—Portugal, Italy, and Spain—believe there to be any good reason to prevent wage increases from exceeding productivity increases. They also idly watched while debt and asset bubbles in their countries were inflated by easy credit. As Robert Samuelson noted, "Interest rates suited to Germany and France were too low for 'periphery' countries (Greece, Ireland, Portugal and Spain)".[13] Common central bank interest rates for all eurozone members were, however, integral to the very concept of a single currency.

One way to address these conundrums would have been for the EU to declare that eurozone members who failed to observe fiscal discipline would be left to their own devices if financial markets started raising interest rates or investing less in these countries. Legal grounds for such a stance existed in those articles of Maastricht forbidding bailouts of eurozone member states by the EU or any other member state, or the printing of money by central banks to obviate debt.

To make such a statement, however, would have raised questions about the euro's long-term durability. It would have also reminded Europeans that deficit spending was not a long-term solution to the costs associated with the European social model. Nor would this message have been palatable to those many insiders who benefit directly from the expensive policies associated with Social Europe.

Cows versus PIGS

Not long after the revision of the fiscal discipline requirements associated with eurozone membership, a little-known fact about euro notes began to be increasingly noted. The designs on the 500, 200, 100, 50, 20, 10, and 5 notes appear to be of European artifacts or architecture. Closer inspection reveals, however, that they are not in fact images of any *actual* European building, bridge, or historical site.

For more than one person, this symbolized the air of fiscal and monetary unreality they associated with the euro. By 2009, however, the consequences of apparently chronic fiscal indiscipline of countries using euro currency were becoming all too real to ignore.

For businesspeople, the benefits of a common currency covering several geographically close economies are obvious. At the most basic level, the need to change money when traveling to another country disappears. Parties to a contract from different states or countries have more certainty about the likely cost of purchased goods and services. Those receiving payment need no longer fear that the value of promised payment will gradually oscillate downwards if, over time, the value of French francs declined vis-à-vis German marks.

Greater certainty about a currency's worth also depends upon paying attention to fiscal conditions prevailing within the region in which the currency circulates. From 2007 onward, it was becoming apparent that a number of "peripheral" economies—Portugal, Ireland, Greece, and Spain—had engaged in excessive borrowing, thanks in part to the low interest rates associated with the euro. For the PIGS, the euro itself had effectively served as an incentive to financially irresponsible behavior. The PIGS' unspoken assumption was that their eurozone membership diminished their risks because, Samuelson observed, they believed that "[w]eak countries would be protected by the strong."[14]

In Spain's and Ireland's cases, the subsequent inflow of easy capital helped fuel housing bubbles. When these started imploding in 2007, unemployment rates in both countries grew. This increased the costs incumbent on their already expensive welfare states. The housing bubble's collapse in Ireland raised such profound questions about its banks' solvency that the Irish government eventually guaranteed all the banks' debts—only to find its own solvency consequently thrown into question. The bailer-out was now searching for a bailout.

Throughout late 2009, confidence in the PIGS began to collapse. Investors and lenders become more attentive to just how much debt these countries had taken on. Like all debt, the financial liabilities of European governments required regular and consistent servicing. In a recession, that meant that less money was available for investment and spending. The result was further economic deceleration. As confidence in the PIGS' capacity to service their debts declined, lenders increased their interest rates. This signaled an increasing lack of confidence, which in turn ignited its own vicious cycle of rising interest rates and further declines in confidence.

In a pre-euro world, options for addressing these situations would have been for national central banks to expand the money supply or devalue the currency. But this choice was no longer available to eurozone members. Monetary policy was in the hands of the ECB. Upon entering the eurozone, Samuelson noted, Greece and other vulnerable debtors had effectively forfeited such safety valves.[15]

Suddenly the question of government debt started to become *the* topic of European public-policy discussion. Magazines such as *The Economist* began dwelling at length upon the long-term fiscal challenges created by policies associated with Social Europe that European countries faced. They also noted that commitment to a common currency implied that the "cows" (Europe's wealthier nations) would have to bail out the PIGS. It soon became apparent, however, that there were limits to the cows' willingness—especially the German super-cow—to do so. For many hardworking Germans, the prospect of bailing out notoriously fiscally ill-disciplined countries such as Greece was deeply distasteful. As the German tabloid *Bild* put it in 2010: "Will we finally have to pay for all of Europe?"[16] Little did its editors know that by June 2012, Greece, Portugal, Ireland, Cyprus, and Spain would have received some form of bailout.

Truth, Lies, and Euros

With the PIGS' fiscal situation becoming worse, the European Commission, the ECB, and EU member states entered a prolonged period of searching for solutions. Concerns about the political implications of bailouts—not to mention their legality—were swept aside in February 2010 when European Council President Van Rompuy proclaimed that the EU would bail out any eurozone country unable to extradite itself from its fiscal woes.[17] Quite how that was to be squared with Maastricht's no-bailout articles remained unclear. Immediate expediency, it seemed, was more important than rule of law.

In early May 2010, the European Union established a €440 billion bailout fund called the European Financial Stability Facility (EFSF), to stabilize financial markets and rescue not only the holders of Greek government debt, but also, implicitly (as chancellor Angela Merkel later confirmed[18]), the holders of *any* EU government debts that seemed shaky. While the plan stressed it would adhere to all EU rules concerning bailouts, it failed to specify how.

Almost one year later, the pretense of avoiding bailouts was abandoned when the EU's political leaders approved, in March 2011, the creation of a European Stability Mechanism (ESM) to replace the EFSF. This new bailout fund is scheduled to begin operating in late October of 2012. As part of the new arrangements, the EU's member states and the European Parliament agreed to amend the relevant European treaty clauses forbidding bailouts.

Significantly, such plans and actions—and even talk of setting up a European Monetary Fund—were justified by a number of European politicians using "social" language. "France," declared Nicolas Sarkozy after a meeting with Greece's George Papandreou, "is by the side of Greece in the most resolute fashion . . . The euro is our currency. It implies solidarity. There can be no doubt on the expression of this solidarity."[19] Accountability for one's actions—a classic market principle—was not, it seems, so important.

This disinterest in transparency was manifest in other governments' failure to be forthright with their own populations (let alone their fellow Europeans) about the scale of their debts. In June 2011, for instance, newly elected Spanish regional and local governments discovered evidence of concealed debts run up by their predecessors. This contradicted claims by Spain's then finance minister, Elena Salgado, that Spain's regions had no hidden debts on their accounts.

Spain's business community had long complained about local governments pressuring private companies to do business with them "off the books," and to delay sending them bills—the latter being a practice that Portugal's finance ministry admitted it had been using as a means for decreasing, for accounting purposes, the size of government debt.[20] One reason for such sleight of hand is that the Spanish and Portuguese governments knew that the greater their *real* overall public debt, the higher would be the interest rates demanded by financial markets, and the more stringent the conditions attached to any bailout they might need.

Further compounding the difficulties with these proposals was widespread failure—once again—to acknowledge certain economic realities. There was a real question, for instance, about whether some member states were even capable of meeting their obligations to secure the debts of other member states under the ESM.

Italy had agreed, for example, to guarantee 18 percent of the ESM. But as the *Financial Times* journalist Wolfgang Münchau bluntly stated: "Do we really believe that Italy—a country with public-sector debts of 120 percent of gross domestic product—is in a position to find tens of billions for the bailout of another member-state?"[21] By August 2011, Italy itself was struggling to ward off the perception that the state of its public finances would transform the PIGS into the PIIGS.

Another problem with the various financial mechanisms created by the EU to address member-state debt problems was their arguably counterproductive effects. In the short term, they sought to help already indebted nations like Greece and Portugal by guaranteeing more loans to these nations. That, however, only brought these countries the breathing space to enact austerity measures. It did nothing to push these nations into combining internal reform with long-term debt restructuring.[22] Moreover, it encouraged them to see the EU as a perpetual bailout mechanism that the taxpayers of wealthy nations such as Germany, the Netherlands, and Austria were apparently supposed to fund on a perpetual basis. Indeed, in an agreement to bail out—once again—Greece, reached by EU heads of government in July 2011, eurozone members effectively committed themselves to paying for the financing of eurozone countries that took bailouts for as long as such nations took to recover access to private lenders.[23]

In the long term, protecting governments from the consequences of their failed economic policies by socializing their losses is unlikely to deter many European governments from future fiscal irresponsibility. As *The Economist* commented in May 2010:

> . . . keeping up the pressure on countries with big deficits may
> prove difficult with a safety net in place. After all, the rescue
> package is, in effect, an attempt by policymakers to convince
> investors that eurozone sovereign debts are collectively insured:
> the debts of one are guaranteed by all. The idea that the €440
> billion scheme will be retired after three years is hard to believe:
> it is difficult to withdraw a guarantee once it has been given.[24]

But the more long-term damage of these arrangements may have been to the ECB's independence. Ever since its foundation in 1998, the ECB has been a whipping boy for European politicians from both the Left and Right. They argue that the ECB's legally mandated priority[25] of maintaining price stability has kept European productivity and economic growth rates far below those of America. In March 2012, for instance, the Socialist candidate for the French presidency, François Hollande, called for expanding the ECB's mandate to allow it to directly facilitate growth.[26] By April that same year, Hollande and his opponent Nicolas Sarkozy were both arguing that the ECB should adopt something like the Federal Reserve's dual mandate of price stability and keeping unemployment low through stimulating growth.[27]

In reality, these problems have little to do with monetary policy, and everything to do with the European social model. Blaming the ECB is a way for many European politicians to avoid acknowledging the growth-killing effects of the endless quest for economic security through welfare states and neo-corporatist and *dirigiste* policies.

Thanks to Europe's debt and deficit problems, however, European skeptics of central bank independence have made inroads into the ECB's prized autonomy. In May 2010, the economist John Taylor pointed out that part of the 2010 bailout deal involved the ECB buying "the debt of the countries with troublesome debt burdens, just days after it said it would not engage in such purchases."[28] It was hard to reconcile with Article 123 of the Treaty of Lisbon, which prohibits such actions.

The shock of the ECB's decision to buy the government debt of some weaker economies was such that it provoked a rare public criticism of the decision by Germany's then central bank president Axel Weber in the German financial newspaper *Börsen-Zeitung*.[29] Weber's complaint was not simply about monetization of the debt. He was equally concerned that a key German—and neoliberal—principle of an independent central bank had been compromised, and might become a precedent for further compromises.

No doubt the ECB might argue that its particular role in the EU's implementation of its very own TARP schemes for bankrupt governments in 2010 and 2011 was in the interests of long-term monetary stability. Yet the more the ECB involved itself directly in supporting European governments' fiscal policies, the less independent it appeared. Summing up the problem, *The Economist* stated: "The central bank's credibility relies in part on a reputation for living up to its pledges and partly on its disdain for political expediency. On both counts, then, [the ECB] has lost something"[30]—so much so that Germany's then representative on the ECB board, Jürgen Stark, resigned in 2011 in protest against the ECB's secondary-market purchases of sovereign bonds.[31] Such actions, he believed, had undermined the ECB's autonomy by succumbing to political pressure to bolster the capacity of EU governments to pay their bills.

When in Doubt, Centralize

Given these developments, it was not long before many European politicians started claiming that the eurozone crisis indicated that the time for European-wide economic governance had arrived. There were, however, disputes about what was meant by "fiscal coordination."

Neoliberals, especially in Germany, viewed it as the establishment and enforcement of rules that limited and punished a lack of fiscal discipline by eurozone members, such as stripping violating members of their voting rights on the European Council. Others interpreted European economic governance as a call to create *dirigiste* institutions that would oversee the implementation of common fiscal policies across the eurozone.

In June 2011, for example, ECB president Jean-Claude Trichet proposed "a ministry of finance of the Union" that would exercise "surveillance" of "fiscal policies and competitiveness policies," carry out "all the typical responsibilities of the executive branches as regards the union's integrated financial sector," and represent the EU in international financial institutions.[32] Something similar had previously been proposed by Nicolas Sarkozy in late 2008, when he suggesting creating a council consisting of heads of state and government to negotiate and decide fiscal policy issues.

By 2011, Sarkozy was referring to the various bailout strategies as the path toward a European Monetary Fund, and eventually a European "economic government."[33] Later that year, similar arguments were made by Germany's finance minister, Wolfgang Schäuble. He insisted that the EU treaty needed to be changed, so as to provide the European Commission with enforcement powers for budgetary matters similar to those that the commission already possessed in the realm of competition policy.[34]

For France and most southern EU countries, European economic governance implied a European-wide harmonization of policies regarding welfare, wages (including a minimum European wage), taxes, and greater redistribution of resources and capital from richer European nations to less wealthy EU states. In other words, it concerned the full-blooded enforcement of the European social model via EU institutions across Europe.

Though there were real clashes here between economic philosophies, they had one thing in common: a top-down focus. One concerned the top-down application and enforcement of European-wide rules. The other involved centralized fiscal institutions and the coordinated implementation of classic European social policies across the EU. This may explain why, in February 2011, France and Germany were able to propose what they called the "competitiveness pact," which combined elements of both.

This plan involved harmonizing tax policies, having Brussels exercise oversight over wage bargaining, raising the retirement age to sixty-seven across the EU, and implementing constitutional "breaks" upon government deficits. Other measures included ending the practice of keeping parts of government spending "off budget," and allowing governments to effectively look at each other's accounts in detail.

In return for these moves toward European-wide economic governance, Merkel and Sarkozy proposed that the EU—meaning Germany—would rescue the financially troubled peripheral euro-zone countries, not least by increasing the amount of euros in the EFSF.

Despite the offer of what essentially amounted to an EU-wide redistribution of wealth (which pleased France), to funnel money from richer, more solvent nations to poorer, insolvent countries in return for agreements on spending cuts (which pleased Germany), these proposals triggered immediate resistance from other EU member states. Not surprisingly, most of the objections flowed from concerns about what the "competitiveness pact" would mean for key policies and expectations associated with the European social model.

Spain, for example, eventually proved willing to introduce a constitutional balanced-budget amendment[35] (despite considerable public protest against such a move),[36] but joined Belgium and Portugal in rejecting the notion of jettisoning the social practice of indexing wages to inflation—not least because of pressure from public-sector unions. Austria, which had one of the EU's earliest retirement ages, claimed that raising the pension age to sixty-seven across the EU was "impossible."[37] Other nations, such as Britain and Sweden, saw such measures as opening the door to EU-wide economic government that would diminish their international competitiveness in the name of growth-killing "harmonizations" required by priorities associated with Social Europe.[38]

Given such opposition, few were surprised that, within a month, the competitiveness pact had been watered down to a "pact for the euro." Though this did identify some broad areas for EU coordination, such as aligning wages with productivity increases, the new pact insisted that the precise policy mix remained "the responsibility of each country."[39]

Intractability: Attitudes, Expectations, and Reform

Throughout 2011 and 2012, observers lost count of the number of times that EU government leaders produced "agreements" or "fiscal pacts" designed to "fundamentally resolve" Europe's debt crisis, only to see their credibility dissolve after the fine print was closely examined. In early March 2012, twenty-five of twenty-seven EU government leaders signed yet another fiscal pact (called the Treaty on Stability, Coordination and Governance in the Economic and Monetary Union). This required eurozone members to balance their budgets, cap what were called "structural budget deficits" at 0.5 percent of GDP, and inscribe this rule into their national laws or constitutions—or else face fines from EU judges.

While this sounds like a revolution in the way European governments had hitherto treated public debt, careful reading of the new eleven-page pact made it clear there was plenty of room for governments to wiggle their way through and out of—the stringency of the terms. As one journalist commented at the time: "A 'structural' budget balance allows for deficits to rise *automatically* in hard economic times, through higher social spending and lower tax revenues."[40] The agreement also allows eurozone members to deviate temporarily from the established guidelines in cases of severe economic downturns or "unusual events"[41]—the precise meaning of which was left vague and undefined. The important question of whether the debts of state-owned enterprises counted in the deficit calculations (not to mention what constituted a state-owned enterprise) was also left unaddressed.

There remained a lingering question of whether some European governments would actually adhere to proposals for fiscal discipline. There were, after all, *already* rules in place prior to the 2012 treaty to limit the size of public debt and government deficits in eurozone states. Indeed, within hours of the 2012 pact being agreed upon by EU leaders, Spain and the Netherlands announced that they might well miss EU-designated budget-deficit targets that *already* exceeded the levels specified in the 2012 treaty.[42] More generally, why some governments would suddenly decide to obey new rules after disobeying the old rules for so long was unclear. Germany was so distrustful that Greece would do what was needed that at one point it actually proposed (in the very same month that the new treaty was agreed upon) that an EU commissioner be given supervisory responsibility for Greece's budget.[43] In the words of one aide to Chancellor Merkel, "Even when the Greek Parliament passes laws, nothing changes."[44]

All this makes it very likely that fudging will continue. "Temporary" and "provisional" funds to rescue fiscally crippled economies may turn out to be not so temporary. Expressions like "financial stability arrangements" will be used to describe the workings of what many European leaders profess to be against: i.e., bailouts. For all the talk about stripping voting rights from fiscally irresponsible countries, or imposing fines on wayward governments, it is hard to imagine many nations, especially core countries such as France or Germany, humbly accepting such punishments.

The problem with all proposals that seek to resolve Europe's fiscal troubles by kicking the problem upstairs to an EU level is the assumption that a more serious, less-subject-to-popular-pressures approach will be taken to revenue raising and public spending. There is, however, no reason to believe that government leaders who pursue fiscally irresponsible policies at the domestic level will suddenly change their behavior in pan-European settings—especially if they remain committed to the European social model. Similarly, if European governments are willing to ignore and gradually dispense with fiscal conditions specified in intergovernmental treaties, such as Maastricht and agreements like the SGP, then the chances that they would meekly abide by the rulings of a European finance ministry during economic downturns seem rather small.

More fundamentally, we need to recognize that the apparently intractable character of these fiscal issues is partly driven by the problematic dynamic at work between democratic political mechanisms, an economic culture that does not incentivize fiscal responsibility, and the underlying attitudes of politicians and citizens at the heart of this culture. However irresponsible many European states' spending, it *did* reflect the choices of democratically elected governments. These *had* in turn reflected the wishes of insider groups and many European citizens who, for their own reasons, had consistently prioritized Social Europe's requirements over fiscal prudence. As observed, the capacity of fiscal and monetary rules written into constitutions, treaties, or pacts to blunt the force of such bottom-up demands is limited.

Throughout 2011, the Greek parliament passed reforms diminishing regulations that applied to many professions in the economy's service sector. But as two *Wall Street Journal* journalists demonstrated one year later, "despite the change in the law, the change never became reality. Many professions remain under the control of professional guilds that uphold old turf rules, fix prices and restrict opportunities for newcomers." Even more fundamentally, one Greek economics professor claimed, "There has been no change in mind set. There is still no sense in the community that things really have to change."[45]

Tocqueville argued that when seeking to understand a community's particular character, factors such as geography, rules, and law were important. He insisted, however, that the most important factor were people's *mœurs*: their moral-cultural habits. Changing policies and structures is important. But if Tocqueville was right in suggesting that the force of democracy is well nigh irresistible, then addressing fiscal irresponsibility in Western Europe requires significant *attitudinal* change on the part of not just Europe's elites, but also its citizens. The same maxim is applicable to America as it wrestles with similar issues.

Deficits and Dollars: American-Style

Since the beginning of the 2000s, the subjects of debt and deficits have weighed heavily on Americans' minds. After 2009 the concerns amplified, as public opinion and political rhetoric became increasingly focused on the size of the deficits being incurred by the federal and state governments, not to mention the tax dollars being spent on servicing deficits.

The raw facts are as follows. Deficits have been the *norm* for the federal government since 1931, the notable exceptions being surpluses for three years of the Truman administration, two years of the Eisenhower administration, and three years of the Clinton administration.[46]

On August 31, 2012, the total public debt of the United States was $16.015 trillion.[47] The annual federal deficit picture is equally uninspiring. In August 2011, for example, the Congressional Budget Office released figures which projected that the federal government's 2011 deficit would amount to almost $1.3 trillion.[48] At the beginning of 2012, the CBO predicted that the federal deficit would once again exceed $1 trillion.[49] Six months later, the CBO sounded a veritable debt alarm. It projected that "the federal debt will reach roughly 70 percent of gross domestic product, the highest percentage since shortly after World War II" by the end of 2012. If current tax and spending policies remained in place, the CBO added, America would realize a national debt-to-GDP ratio of 93 percent by 2022, and an incredible 199 percent of GDP by 2035.[50]

A subsequent CBO update in August 2012 confirmed that America had ended fiscal year 2012 (which ends on September 30) with a federal budget deficit of $1.1 trillion, "marking the fourth year in a row with a deficit of more than $1 trillion." The CBO added that the end of the 2012 fiscal year would see federal debt held by the public reaching 73 percent of GDP, "the highest level since 1950 and about twice the share that it measured at the end of 2007, before the financial crisis and recent recession."[51]

In itself, debt is not inherently problematic. For example, debt is the normal way many people acquire the capital they need to jump-start a new business. Even governments occasionally must run deficits in order to fulfill what Adam Smith thought were legitimate functions of government in the economy, such as building public infrastructure.

That said, both Europe and America have grave reasons to worry about both public debt and government deficits. One such cause for concern is what appears to be the negative effect of public debt on overall growth.

In one study that examined data on forty-four countries over approximately two hundred years, the economists Carmen Reinhart and Kenneth Rogoff found considerable evidence indicating that developed nations with gross public debt levels that exceed 90 percent of GDP find that their medium growth rates fall by one percent, while average growth declines by an even greater proportion.[52]

A similar finding was made in a 2010 IMF Working Paper, which suggested that a 10 percentage point increase in public debt ratios correlates with a slowdown in annual real GDP growth of 0.15 in advanced economies.[53] That does not seem much, until one realizes that growth rates in America were projected to be less than 1.1 percent in 2013.[54]

Likewise, the economists Mehmet Caner, Thomas Grennes, and Fritzi Koehler-Geib concluded in a separate analysis that if "debt explosions move debt ratios above the threshold and keep them there for decades," then "economic growth is likely to suffer."[55] In 2011, three Bank for International Settlements economists argued that once government debt is in the range of 80 to 100 percent of GDP, the impact upon growth is decidedly negative.[56]

So how did the federal government get into its own situation of excessive indebtedness? In raw fiscal and political terms, the size of the federal deficit in America reflects the federal government's willingness—with many American citizens' apparent acquiescence—over a period of decades to take on obligations not adequately covered by revenues. These include long-term military commitments, particular programs such as the lending policies of Fannie Mae and Freddie Mac, the bailout of specific industries, and deficit-fueled stimulus packages.

Above all, as chapter 6 illustrated, deficits have enabled the federal government to pay for growing welfare expenditures without commensurately increasing the tax burden—again, with the implied consent of many American citizens. Deficits have thus allowed American lawmakers and citizens to square, albeit temporarily, a circle: that of keeping taxes and spending at levels that seek to strike a balance between not killing the goose that lays the golden egg, and fulfilling spending promises to the electorate as a whole and key constituencies in particular. Deficits fill the gaps not covered by tax revenues.

To this extent, the parallels between European and American fiscal policies are worrying. This was dramatically underscored in August 2011, when the wave of downgrades by international credit-ratings agencies that had begun sweeping through European nations in 2010 finally embraced America, when Standard & Poor's removed the United States government from its list of risk-free borrowers for the first time, citing concerns about America's political capacity to bring the federal deficit under control. The immediate financial fallout was relatively mild. But the symbolism of the downgrade was lost on no one.

Debt Divergences

For all these similarities, important differences remain between America's and Europe's respective debt situations. The first is political.

By 2010, no one could doubt the widespread concern of millions of American citizens about the size of government deficits. Such concerns were far less obvious among European citizens. This created significant bottom-up political pressures on American leaders to do something. By contrast, Europe's political classes were forced to address their nations' debt problems primarily because of pressures exerted by international financial markets, and particular EU nations such as Germany.

The second difference is monetary. America is not engaged in a grand monetary experiment equivalent to that of the EU, which, as observed, created enormous incentives for some EU member states to behave in fiscally irresponsible ways.

Third, unlike the EU, America's fiscal arrangements are more centralized. America enjoys a combined taxing and borrowing authority. Conversely, the EU's fiscal arrangements are more accurately described as a "deficit-control agreement."[57] It is true that each of America's fifty states has its own budget, and that each levies often quite varying levels and types of taxes. To that extent, America enjoys some degree of budget flexibility and decentralization. Nevertheless, federal taxes and spending constitute the largest share of America's taxation and government expenditures.[58]

The federal government is thus able to indirectly exert a "smoothing" fiscal effect throughout the American economy in ways that EU institutions cannot. At any one time, different states and regions in America are likely to be growing, while others will be less economically dynamic. In booming states, there are more revenues from federal taxes and fewer calls on public welfare. Conversely, there are more welfare payments from the federal government and less tax revenue to collect in stagnant states of the Union. To the extent that EU-wide fiscal policies exist—primarily in the form of (a) EU funds that address imbalances between different EU regions and (b) the newly created bailout mechanisms for dealing with severe and emergency debt situations—they are far less attuned to automatically adjusting to regional ups and downs over long periods of time.

The downside of America's arrangements is that they create their own form of incentives for Greek-like economic behavior. Fiscally responsible states in America indirectly pick up the tab for those states not doing as well, or whose governments simply behave in a fiscally irresponsible manner. That, some might say, is one of the costs of belonging to the United States. It also means that years of irresponsibility by, for example, New York and California end up being indirectly covered by Texas and Utah.

In some instances, direct federal help to states in financial difficulty actually deflects states in trouble from making painful but fiscally responsible choices. Portions of the 2009 stimulus package the federal government injected into the economy enabled several state governments to refrain from implementing public spending cuts they had hitherto been planning to stave off effective insolvency.[59]

A fourth, more tangential difference between America's and Europe's respective debt issues concerns the greater mobility of Americans within America's sovereign boundaries. Americans are more willing to leave states enduring economic downturns and move to more prosperous parts of the country. In fact, Americans are *three times* more mobile within their own borders than Europeans in the EU.[60]

Unfortunately, as illustrated by the journalist Paul Hannon, "a troubling feature of the EU is that labor mobility is very low; even when they are unemployed and have little prospect of getting a decent job any time soon, many Europeans stay where they are."[61] "In 2010," Hannon wrote, "only 3.2% of those working in the 17 members of the euro zone were citizens of another EU member nation." Before the 2008 recession, the equivalent figure was an even lower 2.9 percent.[62]

Language differences play a role here.[63] Inadequate knowledge of German, for example, may deter some Portuguese from moving to Germany or Austria. Thus, while Europeans may live within the same currency zone, they often cannot adjust as flexibly to their country's straightened circumstances by moving to a more prosperous economic region. They are more inclined to stay in their home country and collect welfare payments, thereby increasing the burden on an already overextended welfare state, and magnifying the likelihood of the government taking on more debt to cover welfare costs. Indeed, there are many instances in Europe where what one World Bank analysis described as "generous unemployment benefits" in one European country may further disincline people from seeking jobs in other European nations where welfare payments may be lower.[64]

Europe and the World

When the euro entered into circulation in 2002, it was described by its supporters as symbolizing a "post-nation state" era. In a speech that same year, the ECB's first president, the Dutch Labour politician and central banker Willem Duisenberg, described the euro as "the first currency that has not only severed its link to gold, but also its link to the nation-state." He then suggested that the euro reflected the realization of solidarity among Europeans, and represented an expansion of the social contract throughout Europe.[65] Nonetheless, with words apparently designed to reassure the market side of European economic culture, Duisenberg also stressed the ECB's primary commitment to the goal of monetary stability.

Such remarks make it all the more remarkable that ongoing disputes about the conduct of monetary and fiscal policy have only underscored the depth of political fractures between many EU member states. Divisions between fiscally "conservative" and fiscally "progressive" nations, anti-inflationist and monetary-expansionist countries, and core and peripheral EU member states have become increasingly evident.

These fractures highlight the disparity between the EU's aspiration to present itself as a unified economic player on the international stage, and the less congenial economic realities that continue to play themselves out within the EU. Such differences are not only relevant to the question of whether the EU will eventually become the political entity envisaged by figures such as Schuman and Monnet. They also affect the EU's ability to compete in the global marketplace with America and newly emergent economic powers around the world. As the next chapter illustrates, European economic culture and the social model put the EU at a distinct disadvantage.

8

Globalization: The Last Frontier

If the signal we give to our children is "Protect yourself—hide under the table because there is globalization, resist it"—then we are nothing.

—JOSÉ MANUEL BARROSO

When the Portuguese president of the European Commission uttered these words in a 2005 interview with the *London Times*, he was reacting to rising angst about globalization in a number of Western European countries. His remarks followed protests from Spain and France against proposals to cut EU farm subsidies and successful lobbying by other member states to have the European Commission raise tariff barriers against imports of Chinese textiles.[1]

Few subjects divide or worry Europeans as much as globalization. What, they ask, does globalization mean for the EU in a world in which nations such as China, Brazil, and India are emerging as global competitors alongside already established rivals like Japan and America? Is globalization an opportunity for the EU? Or does it confirm that Europe's global stature is in inexorable decline? And what does globalization mean for the European social model? Differing responses to such questions are now deepening existing fractures between and within European countries.

Opposition to different dimensions of globalization apparently makes for a range of strange bedfellows in Europe. Commitments to protectionism are shared by France's hard-right National Front and Germany's radical-left Die Linke. Similarly odd alliances manifest themselves in America. Skepticism about free trade, for example, places the very conservative Pat Buchanan in the same economic camp as the very liberal Nancy Pelosi.

In some respects, Europeans have been grappling with the challenges of globalization for longer than anyone else. The period of seaborne European exploration that began in the late fifteenth century was a manifestation of globalization, albeit one marked by mercantilist practices. A second age of globalization was partly driven by protectionism's decline throughout nineteenth century Europe, ending when Europeans went to war with each other in 1914. The subsequent disintegration of what had been a relatively globalized world economy was concretized by the economically nationalist policies that became the norm throughout Europe through the 1930s. Since 1945, European economic integration has been portrayed as one instance of the workings of the most recent phase of globalization within one continental region.

In more recent decades, economic globalization has deepened its impact upon Europe. The EU has become China's primary export destination. Throughout the EU's debt crisis, China continued to buy up large amounts of European sovereign debt.[2] But these developments are hardly unique to the EU. In January 2011, China was the largest holder of U.S. Treasuries.[3] America has been one of China's major export markets for more than a decade.

These circumstances represent a sea change in the world's geo-economic settings. In 1900, China was the plaything of the European powers, and of Japan and America. India was the jewel in the crown of the British Empire. The world today could not be more different.

Neither Europe nor America can avoid asking how they should react to this reversal. Some Americans believe the United States can only retain its global preeminence by withdrawing into a type of "bloc economy"—a North American bloc characterized by import barriers against other economic groupings including the EU and a Chinese-dominated East Asia.[4]

Taking such a path is not inconceivable. While some speak of globalization as inevitable, history tells us a different story. If enough governments chose to do so, they could seriously impede global economic integration. War is only the most violent way. Less apparent measures are also available to squelch globalization.

In modern Europe's case, the outcome of its internal debate about globalization will partly depend upon which side of its economic culture—market or social—dominates the EU's engagement with a rapidly changing and, above all, relentlessly competitive global economy. Will the EU be a way for European nations to secure the most economic advantages from globalization? Or will it be a means for Europeans to isolate themselves? Whatever Europe decides, it has lessons for America.

The Case for Global Economic Liberalization

Any discussion of Europe's reaction to a globalized economy requires clarification about what is meant by globalization. Though economic liberalization is a very visible aspect of globalization, it also embraces other dimensions. These include:

- the emergence of planetary dimensions to business, finance, trade, technological, and information flows.

- the diminution of many hitherto common political and economic barriers, such as tariffs.
- the proliferation of transnational organizations and movements, both of a private (e.g., multinational corporations) and public (e.g., international judicial bodies) nature.
- the diminishing—though not extinction—of the decision-making abilities and sovereignty of nation-state governments in favor of some of these transnational bodies.
- an increasing degree of cultural mixing and homogenization.
- the unparalleled expansion of personal relationships beyond the level of the family, local communities, regions, and nations.

Globalization thus involves economic, social, cultural, and political transnational integrations. The process is driven by bottom-up market pressures, and also by top-down government choices. A European firm's decision to start exporting goods to foreign markets is one instance of bottom-up economic globalization. A choice by the U.S. Congress to unilaterally remove tariffs on most imports into America would be a case of top-down global economic integration.

The most concise economic justification for global market liberalization is still the case for free trade set out in Adam Smith's *The Wealth of Nations*. Smith challenged the then reigning mercantilist orthodoxy that one country could only become richer at other nations' expense. "The modern maxims of foreign commerce," Smith wrote, "by aiming at the impoverishment of all our neighbors, so far as they are capable of producing their intended effect, tend to render that very commerce insignificant and contemptible." Observing the conflict between the eighteenth century's two great European powers, France and Britain, Smith commented: "If those two countries . . . were to consider their real interest, without either mercantile jealously or national animosity, the commerce of France might be more advantageous to Great Britain . . . and for that same reason that of Great Britain to France."[5]

Smith's point was simple yet revolutionary: free trade would, in the long run, mutually enrich everyone. First, free trade encouraged an ever-increasing depth and sophistication of the division of labor. This facilitated technological development and the ability to grow ever-increasing amounts of wealth. Second, trade liberalization created an ever-widening space for individuals, businesses, and nations to discover and even change their respective comparative advantages. "If a foreign country," Smith wrote, "can supply us with a commodity cheaper than we ourselves can make it, better buy it of them with some part of the produce of our own industry employed in a way in which we have some advantage."[6] Individuals, businesses, and countries in a global free market would be thus encouraged to focus on doing what they did best. They would not be incentivized by protectionism into developing industries that, in the long run, cannot compete in the marketplace, no matter how high the tariffs.

Among the economic benefits flowing from the opening and integration of markets across the globe would be lower prices, an increased availability of goods from which to choose, and considerable incentives to use technology to produce more and better-quality goods at more competitive prices. Consumers thus stand to benefit considerably.

It would be naïve to deny that economic globalization involves trade-offs. To choose openness to the world economy means to opt for long-term growth and greater adaptability, but also to risk greater economic turbulence, and thus political turmoil. By contrast, to reject economic liberalization is to choose stability, but also likely long-term economic stagnation, which may produce profound political instability.

There are also losers from the process of globalization. They include those who have worked in particular industries all their lives, and are not especially able to retrain when their industry becomes uncompetitive. Less deserving of sympathy are the insider groups created by the European social model, another potential set of losers. In a globalizing world economy, they are discovering that the benefits associated with their insider status cannot always protect them from the effects of increasing competition.

This has not prevented European insiders from using bottom-up and top-down methods to try to maintain their privileges. European trade union officials, for example, may politically agitate from below for high tariffs on imports of Chinese shoes. This can be complemented by a European Commission top-down choice to impose barriers on imports of Chinese shoes into EU member states. The rationale for the tariffs flows directly from classic guild-corporatist priorities: the need to protect the continued employment of presently employed European shoemakers, and to ensure that European shoe-manufacturing companies do not go out of business as they struggle to compete against non-European businesses.

Though economic liberalization's effects are central to many disputes about globalization, not everything on our list of features associated with globalization facilitates economic liberalization. There is no reason to assume, for instance, that some of the transnational institutions that emerge as a result of cross-border political and legal integration will automatically promote economic liberalization. Indeed, tensions between global economic integration and the establishment of supranational EU institutions have been central to the European integration experiment since the 1950s.

Free Trade or Bloc Economy?
Much discussion of European integration during the 1950s focused upon how to progressively remove trade barriers between European nations. By the late 1980s, more attention was being devoted to trade relations between a politically integrated Europe and non-ECC/EU nations.

The latter subject was already on many Europeans' minds in the 1950s. The context was a debate about the different objectives and organizational forms assumed by the EEC in 1958, and by a parallel organization—the European Free Trade Association (EFTA)—created two years later, following the signing of the 1960 Stockholm Convention by seven non-EEC countries.

EFTA's emergence owed something to the politics of the time. Britain's major part in EFTA's formation reflected its ambiguous view of the entire EEC project, and uncertainty about what form would be taken by the British Empire as it transitioned into the British Commonwealth of Nations. Other EFTA signatories were conscious that the EEC's original six members were also all NATO members. Of the seven original signatories of the 1960 Stockholm Convention—Austria, Denmark, Norway, Portugal, Sweden, Switzerland, and Britain—three were officially neutral during the Cold War. In a Cold War context, EFTA seemed less geopolitically aligned than the EEC.

As their respective names suggest, the EEC and EFTA had different focuses. The EEC was founded with a spirit and organizational structure designed to increasing political integration. EFTA had no such political agenda. Though an EFTA council and secretariat were created following the Stockholm Convention's ratification, these were never envisaged as supra-European institutions that would subsume elements of member states' sovereignty. It was a *free trade* association: nothing more, nothing less.

For some time, agriculture and maritime trade were excluded from EFTA's provisions. But these arrangements were also liberalized, as was the movement of persons and capital between EFTA nations. Nor did EFTA involve its member states signing up to particular social policies. Though some of its early members, such as Austria, internally pursued neo-corporatist goals, EFTA was never concerned with efforts to spread such models among its members.

235

EFTA's prominence as a global economic player has diminished over time. Another neutral country, Finland, joined as an associate member in 1961, as did Iceland in 1970. In 1973, however, Britain and Denmark left EFTA to join the EEC (easy exit being one benefit of EFTA's decidedly nonpolitical orientation). Liechtenstein's entry into EFTA in 1991 did not compensate for the loss of Austria, Finland, and Sweden in 1995. By 2010, only Iceland, Norway, Switzerland, and Liechtenstein remained as members, and Iceland had begun the process of applying for EU entry.

EFTA's disinterest in political integration was not the only difference between it and the EEC. Once again, it was Wilhelm Röpke (himself a resident of EFTA-member Switzerland since 1937) who highlighted a key contrast.

Just as the nineteenth-century global economy had emerged without any supranational organization masterminding its appearance,[7] Röpke held that the development of open market economies in Europe should come via *unilateral* and open liberalization at the national level, rather than what he called the regionalist "closed economic integration" characteristic of the EEC. By the latter, Röpke meant a gradual opening of markets between EEC nations, supervised by supranational EEC authorities, which simultaneously maintained barriers between EEC member states and non-EEC countries. EFTA, by contrast, left each member state free to make its own decisions about trade relations with non-EFTA states.

Thus, despite the EEC's claims to be a free-trade facilitator, Röpke insisted this was only half true. A regionally limited free market, he conceded, might be a politically expedient first step toward a liberalized international economy. But, Röpke noted, "there is a conflict between liberal principles and regionalism, for regionalism does not make sense unless it creates some kind of preferential arrangement."[8]

Abolishing trade barriers between EEC members, Röpke pointed out, was quite different from one nation's unilateral abolition of tariffs against imports from *any* country.[9] The benefits of dismantling regional trade barriers within the EEC, he held, would be offset by the long-term disadvantages accruing from the EEC's protectionist barriers against goods, capital, and people from non-EEC countries.[10] In Röpke's view, there was every reason to assume the EEC's common external tariffs would be higher than those previously maintained by individual countries. This, he predicted, would be the price of membership demanded by the EEC's stronger, more protectionist-inclined nations—most notably France.[11]

Lower Tariffs, Higher Complexity, Successful Lobbying

As it turned out, Röpke was wrong about the EEC's external tariffs. Over time, the tariff rates applied to goods entering the EEC/EU has dropped from the levels maintained by most European nations before the EEC's formation. Most of these European-wide reductions in tariffs have flowed from Europe's adherence to tariff-reducing measures evolving from the trade discussions associated with the General Agreement on Trade and Tariffs (GATT), now the World Trade Organization (WTO).

Social Europe has fought back against these measures. Evidence for this may be found in the details of the EU's tariff system. Low tariffs typically signify openness to the competitive pressures created by globalization. There are, however, other ways in which *dirigistes* can obstruct competition. In its own 2010 commentary on the current Doha Round of WTO trade negotiations, the EU noted that the benefits of tariff reductions can be undermined by "obstacles to trade generated by a too complex and non-transparent regulatory system."[12]

Close inspection of the EU's tariff schema reveals a baffling degree of complexity. Some of this reflects factors such as the preferential status given to countries with former colonial ties to particular EU member states. It is nonetheless difficult to avoid concluding that ongoing adjustments to the EU's tariff barriers reflect pressures exerted by insiders seeking to protect their privileged positions.

A good example is the EU's Commission Regulation 861/2010. This outlines tariff levels applied to imports into the EU, and entered into force on January 1, 2011.[13] The document is more than 870 pages long. The further one digs into the text, the more one realizes that navigating this commission regulation would tax the most experienced trade negotiator, let alone anyone seeking to export goods to the EU. It is riddled with references to other EU regulations, council directives, and commission decisions. Regulation 861/2010 even goes into immense detail about *how* particular goods are to be presented to customs officials.

But it is when we examine the regulation's "Schedule of Tariff Duties" that we begin to realize how much the EU's formal commitments to free trade have been diluted by successful insider lobbying. This schedule spells out the precise tariff provisions applied to goods ranging from elementals such as iron and steel to more exotic products such as tanning equipment, dental waxes, and riding crops.

The specific duty to be paid, for example, on "Liquorice extract containing more than 10 percent by weight of sucrose but not containing other added substances" is 13.4 percent.[14] The reasons for this particular formula are not obvious. Different tariffs are applied to citrus-based non-orange, non-grape fruit juices with added sugar; and to citrus-based non-orange, non-grape fruit juices without added sugar. In these and many other instances, the sheer detail and specificities that distinguish one tariff rate from another most likely reflect successful lobbying by particular European businesses for preferential treatment.

Hence, while Röpke may have been wrong in predicting that European common external tariffs would exceed those hitherto maintained by pre-EEC Western European states, he was surely right to argue that transferring the setting of tariffs from the nation-state to a pan-European level did not address the issue that it is protectionism itself which is the problem. European businesses know that if they can successfully lobby the European Commission and enough EU member states, they can secure protection from non-EU competitors for their service or product across the entire EU.

Here we should recall that a single or common European market is not the same as an open market. German juice producers, for instance, can't lobby for protection against French juice producers. But all European juice producers can—and apparently do—lobby for protection against non-European juices produced more competitively and sold at lower costs. As a result, *all* European consumers end up paying higher prices for juice products.

Unfortunately for America, its tariff situation is not much better. America often presents itself as a free-trade country, yet its own tariff system is as Byzantine in its complexity as that of the EU. As pointed out by the trade analyst Daniel Griswold:

> The official Harmonized Tariff Schedule of the United States
> rivals the U.S. income tax code for random complexity. It
> fills 2,959 pages, encompasses 99 chapters and features 10,253
> tariff lines. Each tariff line is designated by an eight-digit tariff
> code and accompanied by three different tariff rates . . . Like the
> federal tax code, the tariff schedule has devolved into a mish-
> mash of disconnected duties with varying rates that defy any
> rational explanation. The rates are arbitrary, discriminatory, and
> distortionary.[15]

The only thing that provides a semblance of rationality for this schema, Griswold concludes, is successful lobbying by American businesses.

Leaving aside the negative effect on consumers, all of Europe's and America's tariffs have the insidious effect of making Europe and America slower to adapt to changes in the global marketplace. They lull Europeans and Americans into a sense of complacency, and dull their awareness that they may be losing their comparative advantage in different industries.

For Europeans, however, the tariff issue touches on a larger question. In light of globalization, is the EU's primary economic purpose one of helping to make Europe a truly global competitor? Or is the economic point of the EU to keep globalization from undermining the European social model? In its own way, this debate reflects a growing conflict between the two strands of economic culture within Europe itself.

Corporatism's Crack-Up

In a December 2010 article entitled "Europe in the New Global Game," European Council President Van Rompuy argued that the previous twelve months had seen the EU put its "own house in order, practically, economically and financially." Even at the time, this was a highly questionable assertion. In retrospect, it appears absurd. The year 2010 will surely be remembered for the financial turmoil that rocked the EU and raised questions about the euro's long-term viability. As if to demonstrate further detachment from reality, Van Rompuy then stated that one of Europe's advantages, as it adjusted to the new global economic realities, was its "social systems."[16]

As we have seen, Europe's social systems are under considerable internal strain from the remorseless deterioration associated with unaffordable welfare states, population decline, low productivity levels, and the preferential treatment of politically connected insiders. Viewing such systems as bolstering, rather than hindering, the EU's capacity to cope with continuing globalization will strike some as another instance of wishful thinking by an archetypal EU insider.

It is more likely that the pressures released by globalization will make many features of Social Europe increasingly untenable. This is particularly true of those Western European labor markets structured along neo-corporatist lines.

In his study of post-1945 European economies, Barry Eichengreen observed that neo-corporatist structures may have helped many Western European countries, shattered by war and characterized by sharp ideological divisions, to sidestep these fractures in addressing pressing problems of reconstruction and development. The whole point of such institutions was to hardwire protocols for extensive, often legally mandated consultations between management, workers, trade unions, and employer associations into the entire economy.

In a globalizing age, the utility of this approach is harder to see. The opening of economies across the world provides European businesses with the opportunity to circumvent inflexible European labor markets, and thereby reduce their costs and keep their prices low. European consumers will be among the beneficiaries. The downside for Europeans is that the people being employed are less likely to be Europeans.

For example, employer associations, trade unions, and governments can negotiate wages in France as much as they want. But if labor is less expensive in Korea, many European companies may decide it is much simpler, less time-consuming, and in the long run more cost-effective to cut out the middleman of neo-corporatist officialdom and build new factories outside Seoul, rather than in Normandy, and employ Koreans, rather than Normans.

Another anticorporatist dynamic unleashed by globalization is the manner in which it facilitates transparency. With the intensification of market competition across the world, European businesses that fail to perform are more likely to find themselves gradually priced out of a globalized market. In such circumstances, neither unions nor businesses can avoid accountability by arguing to their members and shareholders that they have a "higher" responsibility to the national interest, or no option but to abide by arrangements already negotiated by business, union, and government leaders.

One way for European societies to address the economic problems created by neo-corporatist structures is simply to abandon such institutions. To a certain extent, this is already occurring.

Many Europeans have, for instance, simply exited vital cogs of neo-corporatist arrangements like trade unions with mass memberships. The viability of neo-corporatist protocols is heavily dependent upon unions being able to claim they represent the majority of workers in their industry; declining membership diminishes their ability to make such assertions.

And there is also evidence that some Europeans not only understand the growing redundancy of neo-corporatist arrangements in a globally competitive environment, but are actually willing to weaken them. In 2002, the rate of GDP growth in the Netherlands—hitherto one of those European countries most committed to neo-corporatist structures—dropped below that of the eurozone average for the first time. Two years later, its Christian Democrat-led government chose to reject a deal on pension reform presented to it by Dutch unions and employers. The government then took the unprecedented step of outlining its own reform, and attempted to push it through the Dutch parliament. As if to drive home the point that things had changed, the government simultaneously decided to scrap tax breaks for early retirement and reduce unemployment and disability benefits. In doing so, the government simply ignored what the Dutch call the *polder* model of consensus-building and collaboration between employers and unions.[17]

The reaction to this approach was swift, most notably in the form of demonstrations and strikes on a scale the Netherlands had not witnessed for decades. In the end, both public protests and unrest from within the Christian Democrats' own ranks about the government's apparent lack of concern for corporatist-negotiated solidarity forced the government to modify some of its proposals.

The significance of these events lies less in the actual reforms than in what was revealed about a changing Netherlands. First, the 2004 struggle indicated that some segments of Dutch opinion—the Dutch being nothing if not practical people—had concluded that neo-corporatist processes were becoming an unaffordable luxury in a competitive global economy. Also worth noting was the degree of resistance that the government's attempt to bypass neo-corporatist protocols aroused from across the Dutch political spectrum. It was a classic instance of market priorities, magnified by the economic pressures of globalization, coming into conflict with Social Europe. The end result was an untidy compromise that in retrospect may have introduced sufficient reforms to allow the Netherlands to weather the vicissitudes of the 2008 recession better than most other EU member states.

Goodbye to *Dirigisme?*

Other aspects of the European social model have shown considerable resilience in the face of globalization pressures. A good example is the CAP. As noted in chapter 4, the Treaty of Rome addressed the treatment of agriculture in great detail. It identified the "objectives of the common agricultural policy" as:

- Ensuring a fair standard of living for the agricultural community, in particular by increasing the individual earnings of persons engaged in agriculture.
- Stabilizing markets through price controls and subsidies.
- Assuring the availability of supplies.
- Ensuring that supplies reach consumers at reasonable prices.

A closer approximation of guild-like concerns in the modern era is difficult to imagine. Consumers are literally last on the list of priorities. The entire emphasis is upon stability, equal outcomes, and planning. It is little wonder that Röpke described the EEC's agricultural policies as a "quasi-autarchic system" that actively discriminated "against agricultural imports from third countries".[18]

The CAP's entire history reflects how these foundational principles and organizational methods have hardly altered since 1958. Most people associate the CAP with subsidies to European farmers. Unfortunately, subsidies are only part of the *dirigiste* apparatus established to realize the CAP's goals. This includes quotas designed to restrict food imports into the EU, and the imposition of import levies upon specific agricultural imports into the EU. The purpose is to raise the price of such goods set by the global market to a pre-determined EU price (called "the maximum desirable price"). If these methods were not *dirigiste* enough, the CAP also allows for the setting of an "internal intervention price." This means that once the internal EU market price for an agricultural product falls below the "intervention level," the EU buys up enough goods to raise the price to the intervention level.

These measures have not been able to stave off the pressures of global competition. The exodus of Europeans from rural areas has continued unabated for decades. Despite all the protections in place, many forms of agriculture have not proved to be among Europe's comparative advantages. Recognition of this helps explain why, under the Uruguay Round Agreement of the GATT, the EU committed itself to reducing import tariffs for agricultural products by an average of 36 percent over a six-year period. The last tariff reductions occurred in 2000.

Rather than concluding that the CAP has failed to realize its goals, however, there is increasing discussion in Europe of using the CAP to promote "environmentally-sensitive farming," or to address subjects ranging from climate change to the promotion of biodiversity. In short, while globalization and the CAP's own failures have rendered it obsolete, the resistance within Europe to abandoning a classic *dirigiste* approach to one economic sector remains considerable.

Similar observations can be made about America's own agricultural policies. "Price supports" (as they are euphemistically called) for agriculture have existed in America since the 1920s, when more or less permanent price subsidies for farmers were legislated into being. By the 1940s and 1950s, the federal government was exerting significant control over agricultural commodity prices. It even paid farmers to leave land unused in order to prevent what was called "overproduction"—a policy that was not terminated until 1996.

Like the EU, agricultural policy in America has partly been driven by the desire to keep rural areas populated and family farms in existence. Again, neither objective has been realized. Small- and medium-sized American farms have largely been replaced by larger agribusinesses. Some estimates put the number of Americans working full time and living on a farm today at only 2 percent of the population.[19] Another parallel to the EU is the shift of American agricultural policy in the late 2000s toward encouraging via subsidies—"green" policies like renewable energy and the production of ethanol-based fuels.

Economic Nationalism and Tax "Harmonization"

Dirigisme at the EU level as a way of resisting globalization has been accompanied by a resurgence at the national level of economically nationalist policies and sentiments throughout Europe. In a genuinely world economy, nationality and national boundaries should count for little when questions about companies' ownership and management emerge. Yet this has not stopped some European countries from trying to prevent cross-border mergers of companies, or even their acquisition by non-EU businesses.

In the mid-2000s, for instance, France announced a range of measures—aptly described as *neo-Colbertiste*—designed to protect particular industries that the government deemed "strategic" (energy, aviation, biotechnology, and the like) from being acquired by foreign companies. Such policies were explained as "promoting the national interest."

In practice, such policies involved preventing the restructuring of companies that typically follows takeovers. Such reorganizations can mean painful adjustments, including layoffs of line workers and management, in the search for efficiencies. *Neo-Colbertisme* seeks to circumvent, if not block, such changes. One argument often used to justify these policies was that France needed "national champions" that could compete in the global marketplace. This begged the question: Why would true "champions" need protection from competition?

Another instance of ingrained European resistance to globalization concerns the issue of EU tax harmonization. In a globalized economy, countries compete to attract investors from around the world. One means of doing so is through tax competition, especially corporate-tax competition. This involves governments using the prospect of lower corporate-tax rates to incentivize companies into shifting their headquarters (and sometimes significant operational elements) to new locations. This is one reason why Switzerland— a non-EU member—is home to so many corporate headquarters. Even within Switzerland, the different cantons compete among themselves to offer optimal tax rates—and not just for companies, but for individuals as well.

The reaction of many EU nations to tax competition reflects how torn Europe is about globalization. Corporate-tax rates across the EU have dropped steadily over the past twenty years.[20] This is nor only the result of competition from non-EU states such as Switzerland, but also internal competition *among* EU member states. Nonetheless, European governments (especially those in Western Europe) do not hesitate to invoke the language of solidarity to complain about countries that structure their tax regimes in even more competitive ways.

Ireland, for instance, has some of the lowest corporate-tax rates in Europe. This has attracted much criticism from other EU countries. In early 2011, German chancellor Angela Merkel made the extraordinary claim that Ireland's financial crisis had been partially fueled by its 12.5 percent corporate-tax rate.[21] Merkel added that, while EU countries should be allowed to set their own corporate taxes, member states should agree to limit them to a certain range. Tax competition in Europe, it seems, is acceptable, provided it is not *too* competitive. Such comments are especially curious in light of Germany's own steady reduction of its corporate-tax rates, from 51.6 percent in 2000 to 29.8 percent by 2010.[22] The question to be asked is why *any* country in a globally competitive environment should not be free to set whatever tax rates it so chooses.

Despite this resistance to the forces unleashed by global competition, there are cases of European countries liberalizing their economic settings in order to cope with globalization. The reforms introduced in Britain during the Thatcher years are well known. Britain's economic culture is, however, widely perceived as somewhat different to what we find in continental Western Europe. Hence, it is worth looking at more recent and less well-known Western European reform stories involving considerable adjustments to the prevailing economic culture: stories with lessons for an America grappling with similar problems.

Deutschland über Europa

One of the dominant objectives of intra-European politics following World War II was to ensure that Europe's future would be one that contained a European Germany, rather than being a German-dominated Europe. By 2012, many were wondering if one long-term consequence of Europe's prolonged economic problems would be Germany's ascendancy, not only as the EU's economic locomotive but also as its political engine.

In the 1990s, few would have imagined such a scenario being possible. For Germany, this period was marked by the immense economic challenge of integrating the former East Germany into a West German economy already exhibiting signs of sclerosis. The cost was enormous, and involved Germany taking out considerable loans to finance the process. At the same time, productivity levels fell and unemployment rose—not all of which could be explained by East

Germany's chronically high unemployment. Living standards also failed to keep track with the growth being experienced in the rest of Western Europe throughout this period.

Then there were the demands of globalization. When Eastern European countries physically close to Germany began adopting more friendly economic environments (especially concerning taxes), Germany started losing businesses and employment to nations such as Slovakia and Poland. Once Austria began adopting similar tax policies, it became even harder for Germany not to follow suit.

In the early 2000s, Germany chose to respond to these pressures with policies of qualified liberalization rather than *neo-Colbertisme*. In a speech to the German parliament in March 2003, Chancellor Gerhard Schröder, the leader of Germany's Social Democrat-Green coalition government, outlined a set of liberalizing reforms of the German economy known as Agenda 2010. Its focus was on tax reform, social security reform, and measures to improve Germany's international competitiveness.

In practical terms, Agenda 2010 resulted in the gradual implementation of considerable income- and corporate-tax cuts. It also included introducing more flexibility into the labor market, raising the official retirement age, and changes to medical benefits, pensions, and unemployment payments.

This latter reform was especially important. No longer could unemployed Germans simply refuse jobs when they were offered: to do so could possibly result in a loss of unemployment benefits. Large numbers of Germans subsequently calculated that they would be better off working rather than taking unemployment benefits, the eligibility for which had become more stringent. By 2012, Germany was being referred to as the "jobs miracle," unemployment having fallen to 5.5 percent in December 2011. This was the lowest unemployment rate since German reunification in 1990.[23] The contrast with Southern Europe was vivid.

Agenda 2010 should not be characterized as a radical liberalization of the German economy. Several measures concerned streamlining particular welfare structures, rather than their reduction or abolition. Many neo-corporatist policies—such as worker codetermination arrangements—remained in place. And many Germans reacted negatively to the reforms. Spurred by an upward rise in unemployment after the reforms began to be implemented, as employers started restructuring their workforces and outsourcing both factories and employment to Eastern Europe and Asia, Germany's trade unions put up considerable opposition to the changes. Throughout 2004, there were mass demonstrations in several German cities against the reforms.

Politically, the reforms resulted in Schröder's Social Democrats hemorrhaging members to parties further to the left; Schröder's government eventually lost office, in 2005. The Social Democrats fared well enough in the election that the Christian Democrats had to take them on as partners in a grand "black-red" coalition. But the new chancellor, Angela Merkel, found herself facing a greater presence of explicitly left-wing parliamentarians insisting upon a return to a more expansive welfare state.

This continuing wariness about globalization on the part of many Germans helps to explain why German trade unions managed to secure the government's agreement to the implementation of new and higher minimum wage levels for temporary work agencies in March 2011. This was designed to discourage such firms from hiring migrant workers from Central-East Europe, whose primary competitive advantage was their willingness to work for less than their German counterparts. Not coincidentally, these measures were implemented just before the expiration in May 2011 of several other barriers to these workers entering Germany's (and Austria's) labor markets, such as work permits and quotas.[24]

Despite such instances of obstruction of further economic liberalization, Agenda 2010 certainly helped to turn around Germany's previously dismal economic performance. But just as important was the embrace of the advantages of globalization by large, medium, and small German companies.

Many German companies began, for example, to move parts of their operations abroad to capitalize on lower labor costs. This had the effect of putting management in a better position in its negotiations with German unions. Lifting their eyes beyond the German and EU markets, German companies also focused on producing goods and services that people in emerging economies—most notably China—wanted to buy, and then selling them at competitive prices. By 2008, German exports to non-European markets were easily outstripping exports to EU member states.[25] The strategy also resulted in the growth of Germany's share of EU exports.[26]

By way of comparison, France experienced a decline in its share of European merchandise, from 15.7 percent to 13.1 percent, during the same decade. This was accompanied by a growing increase in the costs of France's social policies. Between 2002 and 2005, France's minimum wage increased by 17 percent. France also maintained the 35-hour week (which was only reformed at the edges by Sarkozy's government) implemented by Jacques Delors's daughter, Martine Aubry, in February 2000. Even more ominously, the social costs borne by French employers amounted to €50.3 for every €100 paid to each employee. The comparable rate in Germany was €28.[27]

Of course, there were some unique dimensions to Germany's success. A primary motor of German economic growth, *The Economist* noted in early 2011, was "the legion of mainly small and medium-sized firms, typically family-owned and highly-specialized, that build products that dominate obscure branches of industry."[28]

Yet while these were important contributions, the willingness of German companies to embrace the opportunities provided by economic globalization, rather than using the state to try to resist, King Canute-style, the pressures of competition, was a critical element in Germany's reemergence as the EU's economic heavyweight. When combined with the Agenda 2010 reforms, the long-term economic results included greater wage stability (at a time when wages in much of Europe were spiraling upwards), increased productivity, and eventually, falling unemployment throughout Germany. Greater international competitiveness also resulted, especially vis-à-vis other EU states. Spain, for instance, found that its competitiveness deteriorated by 33 percent against Germany between 1999 and 2009.[29]

A Swedish Miracle

A similar story of the benefits of reducing the expectations and structures of Social Europe in the face of globalization is apparent from another non-British story of reform over the past twenty years: the once religiously Social Democratic Sweden.

Faced with growing economic stagnation under the pressure of maintaining one of the world's most generous (not to mention famous) welfare states, Sweden implemented a number of rather unsocial democratic policy measures in the late 1980s and early 1990s. This included diminishing both its marginal tax rates and the levels of state ownership of many companies. Another change involved allowing private retirement schemes—a reform accompanied by a reduction to the state's contributions to pensions.

These reforms, however, proved insufficient. In the early 2000s Sweden found itself in a situation whereby, according to former employment minister Sven Otto Littorin, "1 out of every 5 people who were of working age was either outside of the regular labor market or working less than he or she would like to."[30] This, Littorin added, was compounded by the fact that up to 12 percent of

Sweden's labor force was on early retirement or disability pensions. Further complicating matters was the fact that Sweden's tax structure made it more financially beneficial for many people to stay on unemployment benefits instead of entering the labor market.[31] More than one in five Swedes of working age, observed James Bartholomew, was receiving some type of benefit.[32]

But with the election of a four-party non-Social Democratic coalition government in 2006, Sweden's reform agenda was resumed. Property taxes were scaled back; income-tax credits were introduced allowing more middle- and lower-income people to keep more of their incomes; inheritance tax was simply abolished. The sale of once state-owned businesses (including the mighty steel industry) accelerated. Private health providers were allowed to enter the health-care market, thereby introducing an element of competition into what had been one of the world's most socialized medical systems. Particular transportation industries such as taxis and trains were deregulated. Centralized state control of education was weakened by the introduction of voucher schemes, and a shifting of responsibility from the central government to municipalities.[33] Even farm prices were now determined by market supply and demand. Finally, the government reformed unemployment benefits so that the longer most people stayed on benefits, the less they received.[34]

The results of reform are clear. Unemployment levels fell from the 10 percent of the mid-1990s. Budgetwise, Sweden started running surpluses instead of deficits. The country's gross public debt declined, from a 1994 figure of 78 percent to 35 percent in 2010. Sweden also weathered the Great Recession far better than most other EU states; its 2010 growth rate was 5.5 percent. By comparison, America's was 2.7 percent.

The lesson for Europeans and Americans, according to Littorin, is "that a combination of fiscal stringency by reducing unemployment benefits and having policies in place to make it worthwhile for people to work does the trick."[35] As in Germany's case, the willingness of Swedish companies to expand and grow in the global economy magnified the impact of these changes. Names such as IKEA (furniture), Ericsson (technology), SCA (paper products), and Volvo (cars) became increasingly prominent fixtures of their respective markets—not just in Europe, but throughout the world.

It Must Get Worse So It Can Get Better

Naturally, there was resistance in Sweden to many of these changes. Nor is the Swedish story perfect. Between 1980 and 2010, Swedish government spending still averaged 59 percent of GDP.[36] Approximately one-third of working Swedes today are civil servants. And some of the benefits of tax reform have been blunted by Sweden's embrace of carbon taxes since the early 1990s.

Nevertheless, the Swedish and German stories provide many insights into Europe's possibilities in light of globalization.

The first is that, despite Social Europe's resilience in most Western European economies, liberalization is not impossible. A second, less encouraging insight is that both countries had to endure significant periods of economic stagnation before some sections of their respective political classes proved willing to implement liberalizing reforms.

Third, and equally discouraging, there are plainly political limits to the pace and extent of reform. While Germany and Sweden have become more market-oriented in their economic settings, many of the values and institutions associated with the European social model's guild-corporatist side remain prominent features of their respective economic cultures.

For example, high unemployment persists among immigrants and the young in Sweden (25.9 percent among 15- to 25-year-olds in 2011), not least, as Bartholomew notes, because of "the high minimum wage imposed on the various industries by the still-powerful unions. Those who cannot command a good wage are not allowed to work for a lower one."[37] Moreover, from 2006 onward, the four-party coalition government was careful to present the reforms as essential if Sweden's welfare state (which remains generous even by European standards) was to be maintained in light of demographic and financial pressures. In short, Sweden's "liberalizers" worked within the contours of European economic culture, and avoided challenging it.

The fourth, perhaps most depressing point is that those European countries that chose to embrace economic reform and pursue greater integration into global markets were, until 2010, a distinct minority. That it took a sovereign debt and currency crisis on the scale of the 2010 financial rollercoaster to push many European governments toward implementing some reforms tells us something about the strength of European economic culture's nonmarket side. As long as these societies could afford to pay for all the costs associated with Social Europe, they were willing to do so.

Perhaps, some might say, this does not matter: what matters is that the economic and financial crisis that began in 2008 has forced European governments to begin changing their ways. The flaw with this line of reasoning is that, without fundamental change at the level of values and institutions, it is likely that much of Europe will slowly drift in the opposite direction, once the crisis has been surmounted. This occurred in Germany within fifteen years of its famous 1948 neoliberal reforms.

The dilemma facing all these countries—and America—is that economic prosperity helps generate the conditions for future stagnation. Markets create new and greater amounts of wealth. This gives countries the luxury—for a time—of maintaining large welfare states if they choose to do so. Affluence also distracts attention from re-encroaching regulation. Likewise, economic success give companies the option of simply acquiescing to excessive demands made by trade unions. Finally, market-generated wealth provides governments with the tax revenues they need to maintain large public sectors at the EU and member-state level.

In societies whose economies are more firmly rooted in market-oriented cultures, these tendencies may be less likely to transpire. Given the settings of European economic culture, however, regression is an ever-present possibility. To imagine that a country like Greece will wholeheartedly shun the attitudes, expectations, and accompanying institutions that have pervaded its economy for at least the last fifty years will strike many as wishful thinking.

America, Globalization, and Europeanization

In February 2011, many Americans were shocked to read that the New York Stock Exchange—a world-renowned symbol of America capitalism—was in the advanced stage of negotiating a merger with Deutsche Börse, the operator of the Frankfurt Stock Exchange. At the time, it was proposed that Deutsche Börse shareholders would enjoy 60 percent ownership of the new entity. Just one year later, the deal was vetoed by the European Commission.

The failed merger symbolized the continuing spread of the cross-border mergers and acquisitions associated with globalization in a world increasingly anxious about the realities created by ever-integrating global markets. Such anxiousness is not absent from America; many Americans have distinctly negative views about the steady globalization of the world's economies. The cases of America's tariff and agricultural policies illustrate how desires to ward off the impact of international economic liberalization have shaped several policy choices that, in scope and design, are not so different from those made by Europeans.

Obviously, there are clear differences between the American and European experience of globalization. The vacuum created by the drawdown of Western European political power around the globe after World War II was filled by a period of unprecedented American expansionism. Financially, this was symbolized by countries tying their currencies to the U.S. dollar following the United Nations' Bretton Woods conference of July 1944—a linkage further deepened in August 1971, when America abolished the dollar's convertibility into gold, thereby establishing the U.S. dollar as the world's fiat money reserve currency.

With Communism's collapse in the former U.S.S.R. and Eastern Europe, however, America has gradually found itself having to address the many challenges flowing from the increased breakdown of many barriers to economic liberalization. The circumstances have been complicated by the conscious decisions of large nations such as China and India to move away from centrally planned economies. America has consequently been faced with the same choice that confronts Europe: either to embrace economic liberalization with all its trade-offs, or assume that it is big enough to shield itself from the competitive pressures that globalization unleashes.

Thus far, America's response to economic globalization has oscillated between openness and defensiveness. China's rise as an economic power is seen as an opportunity by some American business leaders to penetrate new markets. Other Americans express angst about how much of the United States' sovereign debt is owned by China.

In the 1990s, the North American Free Trade Agreement (NAFTA) resulted in considerable liberalization of trade between America, Canada, and Mexico. Its passage through the U.S. House of Representatives in November 1993 by a vote of 234–200 split both major parties. NAFTA's supporters included 132 Republican and 102 Democratic congressmen. Among NAFTA's most prominent supporters was President Bill Clinton. Before his 1992 election, however, Clinton had expressed his admiration for Japan's emphasis on industrial policy, and his reservations about free trade's potential effects on American employment.

Clinton's successor, President George W. Bush, described himself as a free trader, and pushed for the ratification of free-trade agreements with many countries. Yet Bush also supported the temporary imposition of 8 to 30 percent tariffs on a range of steel imports for a five-year period beginning in 2002. They were eventually withdrawn in 2003, under pressure from the EU and the WTO. At the time, Bush argued that the tariffs were necessary to "give the industry a chance to adjust to the surge in foreign imports and to give relief to the workers and communities that depend on steel for their jobs and livelihoods."[38] That sounds suspiciously like an effort to "manage" the impact of globalization. The language is almost identical to what one would expect from many EU politicians.

Whatever their views about tariffs, few observers doubted that one of Bush's motives for raising steel tariffs was American domestic politics. The American steel industry's downsizing in the face of global competition during the 1990s negatively impacted employment in swing states such as Pennsylvania. Likewise, it was no coincidence that President Barrack Obama's decision in 2009 to raise tariffs on tire imports from China was praised by Thea Lee, the AFL-CIO's chief economist, as a positive step forward in the struggle to preserve American manufacturing jobs.[39] The same union, incidentally, joined a number of other unions (as well as many prominent conservatives) in opposing George W. Bush's proposed immigration reforms in 2007. This unlikely coalition shared a concern about what an influx of foreign workers would mean for those Americans already holding manufacturing jobs.[40]

But Not Yet Europe

America's internal wrestling about the impact of economic globalization, and its subsequent policy inconsistencies, are not dissimilar to what we find in Europe. But it also fits into a more general pattern detailed in previous chapters: one which suggests that America's economic culture has become more akin to Europe's than many Americans care to admit.

That said, there remains considerable resistance in America to the prospect of Europeanization. Though the welfare state is large in America, many Americans are not as casually inclined as some

Europeans to accept its size or its workings. Moral, political, and economic critiques of state welfare programs resonate with many Americans in ways not so apparent in Europe. Even reducing the welfare state's size is seen by many Americans as a positive good in itself, rather than an unfortunate economic necessity. Nor has America more or less exclusively channeled "concern for neighbor" into state welfare programs.

Another manifestation of "un-European" economic culture in America is the widespread concern, among some politicians and some large segments of the citizenry, with the size and growth of state expenditures, deficit spending, and public debt. In Europe, such concerns are certainly articulated by some members of the political class. But with some notable exceptions (like Germany), evidence of *popular* discontent with the fiscal burden associated with the European social model is harder to find. By contrast, American politicians are deeply conscious of public concern about these matters, even if American public opinion expresses contradictory impulses about how to address them.

Also still relatively absent from America are the type of neo-corporatist protocols that are legally hardwired into most European economies. While the degree of European-like collusion between different interest groups and governments in America is worrying, the weakness of neo-corporatist protocols in the United States limits the bureaucratization of American economic life, and helps America maintain more flexible labor markets compared to those of most European countries.

Above all, it is the strength and persistence of private entrepreneurship that continues to differentiate America's economic culture from that of Europe's. America remains far ahead—and, in some areas, continues to pull ahead—of most of Europe when it comes to private innovation (including European nations that are strong on innovation, such as Germany). The elements that fuel such innovation, such as robust intellectual property rights, ease in obtaining patents, competition, and venture capital, continue to be far stronger in America than in most of Europe. Moreover, it is young firms that are driving innovative growth in America, whereas most innovation in Europe occurs in old, established companies.[41] Young innovators in America are responsible for 35 percent of total research and development of America's leading innovators. The equivalent figure in Europe is a meager 7 percent. [42]

This suggests that America has a bright entrepreneurial future. As a World Bank report stated, Europe "has few companies that match the dynamism of Apple, Amazon, Google, Facebook, or Microsoft."[43] So while political entrepreneurship is alive and well in America, so too is the habit of private risk-taking to create and market new ideas, products, and services. That this persists in spite of some of the highest corporate-tax rates in the world demonstrates how deeply this impulse runs in American economic life. No doubt it is helped by the fact that America remains, at least by way of comparison, a relatively economically free nation, being ranked tenth in the world (with Switzerland and Ireland the only European countries ahead of it), according to the Heritage Foundation's *2012 Index of Economic Freedom*.[44]

Unfortunately, there is some evidence that America's advantage here may be eroding. Having listed America as the world's most innovative economy in 2009, the *Global Innovation Index 2012* identified America as having fallen to tenth place in 2012, behind three non-EU states (Switzerland, Singapore, Hong Kong) and six EU nations (United Kingdom, Ireland, Netherlands, Sweden, Finland, and Denmark).[45]

Overall, however, it is arguable that the claim that America is in some type of irreversible economic decline is much exaggerated. In 2011, the international economist Charles Wolf argued that some basic economic measurements indicated that the American story of economic success is far from over. Looking at what he called some "crude economic indicators," Wolf pointed out that:

In absolute terms, the U.S. enjoyed an incline this past decade. Between 2000 and 2010, U.S. GDP increased 21% in constant dollars, despite the shattering setbacks of the Great Recession in 2008–09 and the bursting of the dot-com bubble in 2001. In 2010, U.S. military spending ($697 billion) was 55% higher than in 2000. And in 2010, the U.S. population was 310 million, an increase of 10% since 2000. The notion that demography is destiny may be a stretch, but demographics are important when, as in the U.S., population increase—due to higher birth and immigration rates than other developed countries—cushions the impact of an aging population.[46]

But Wolf then asked what these same numbers suggested when compared to other countries. Here the results were less encouraging. Although America's GDP grew substantially in real terms during the decade, it actually declined by 19 percent relative to the G-20 major economies as a group. America's decline relative to China, Wolf added, was even larger.

These measurements tell us something. But as Wolf cautioned, there are also things they do not tell us. They do not tell us about the "effects of culture, property rights, law and political freedom in the near and long terms" in shaping countries' economic future. In that sense, Wolf wrote, "the numbers ignore more than they convey."[47] In other words, economic culture may be harder to measure. That, however, does not reduce its relevance to America's economic future.

Each of the detailed Europeanization trends in American economic culture noted in this chapter and addressed in the previous three chapters represents a serious long-term problem. In some cases, they are becoming worse. Between January 2008 and January 2011, there was a marked growth in the amount of regulation in America—the pace being almost 40 percent more than the annual rate of increase between 1992 and 2008. Similarly, between 2008 and 2011 the number of people working in federal government regulatory agencies rose by 16 percent—a total of more than 276,000 people—at a time when private-sector employment was falling.[48] In this light, it is little wonder that the economist and Nobel laureate Robert E. Lucas asked (in his 2011 Milliman Lecture at the University of Washington) whether the United States was now "imitating European policies on labor markets, welfare, and taxes."[49]

Nor is there any guarantee that some of the barriers impeding economic Europeanization in America will not, at some point, begin eroding. If the same types of political and economic trends that have manifested themselves throughout much of Europe gain additional traction in America, we should not assume they can be easily resisted. If, at some point, the economic incentives shift enough Americans—and not even necessarily a majority—decisively toward political entrepreneurship, acquiring a public-sector job, favoring further expansions of the welfare state, or supporting protectionism, the subsequent political dynamics could override existing institutional and value formations in America's economic settings.

But why, it might be asked, should America and Americans simply wait for that to happen? As our concluding chapter demonstrates, proactive steps can be taken to resist decline, particularly at the level of the attitudes that are so influential in shaping economic culture.

III

The Choice

9

How America Can Have
a Non-European Future

I am not among those who fear the people. They, and not the rich, are our dependence for continued freedom. And to preserve their independence, we must not let our rulers load us with perpetual debt. We must make our election between economy and liberty, or profusion and servitude.

—THOMAS JEFFERSON

Thomas Jefferson knew a thing or two about debt. When his father-in-law, John Wayles, died in 1773, Jefferson found himself inheriting Wayles's considerable liabilities. Like many American farmers of his time, Jefferson discovered that many of those who owed him money were irregular in their payments. In later life, Jefferson found himself accumulating more debt, as a consequence of a major financial panic in 1819. As if that were not enough, even Jefferson's admirers readily concede that he lived far beyond his means for most of his life. The result was that Thomas Jefferson died owing other people a great deal of money—so much so that his heirs had to sell off much of Jefferson's estate, including his beloved Monticello.

Whatever the vicissitudes of his own finances, the remarks cited above underscored the conviction by America's third president that debts incurred by government can grow to the point whereby they begin to suffocate freedom, particularly people's economic liberty. Jefferson may, however, have underestimated the degree to which subtle and not so subtle forms of collusion between legislators and citizens allow these and similar situations to emerge in free societies and undermine the foundations of economic prosperity.

Not everything about America's and Europe's economic problems can be attributed to this dynamic. It does, however, explain much of the European social model's dysfunctionality, why moves toward more market-oriented values and institutions encounter such resistance in Europe, and why America finds it so hard to address many of the problems that disfigure its still relatively market-oriented economic culture.

In Europe's case, a further complication is emerging in the form of a further decline in many Europeans' already low opinion of market institutions and culture. Though more Europeans may be willing to concede that there are problems associated with their social model, Europeans are not noticeably enthusiastic about the market alternative. But in this regard, American attitudes also leave much to be desired. And this *matters* because, as this final chapter argues, attitudinal change is essential if America is to avoid a European-like fate.

Loving, Hating, Tolerating Markets

In April 2011, the international polling firm GlobeScan released survey results of different countries' attitudes toward the market economy. In response to the statement "The free market system and free market economy is the best system on which to base the future of the world," only 19 percent of those surveyed in Britain in 2010 firmly agreed. Though the numbers were higher in Spain (24 percent) and Italy (21 percent), they were lower in France (6 percent). Of those Europeans surveyed, Germans expressed the highest approval levels (30 percent).

Before this is considered evidence of the European social model's cultural triumph, some qualifications should be made. If we add the percentages of those who "somewhat" agreed with the statement about the market economy, the numbers rise significantly.

In Germany, for example, a total of 68 percent of Germans "agreed" or "somewhat agreed" with the statement. The equivalent figures for Britain and Spain were 55 percent and 52 percent. In France, conversely, a total of 57 percent of French respondents "disagreed" or "strongly disagreed" that free markets are the way of the future. A mere 31 percent had a favorable or somewhat favorable view of free markets. Back in 2002, the equivalent "favorable" figure in France had been 42 percent.

The real shock was to be found in American reactions to the same statement. In 2002, 80 percent of Americans surveyed expressed a strongly or somewhat favorable view of free markets. Eight years later, the figure had fallen to *59 percent*. Among lower-income Americans (defined as those earning less than $20,000 a year), the trend was worse. In 2009, 79 percent of this group expressed favorable views of the market; just one year later, the figure had fallen to less than 45 percent.[1]

No doubt these apparent shifts in American and European opinion owed much to the 2008 financial crisis, and subsequent recession. Nevertheless, as Douglass North and Edmund Phelps insist, if attitudes are central to economic culture, then the struggle to prevent America from slouching further down the path of economic Europeanization faces significant challenges.

In Europe's case, it is difficult to see how some European nations can break away from their current trajectories of creeping economic stagnation and minimal growth. While a number of countries have introduced meaningful market reforms, the long-term future for the EU looks bleak, not least because of the absence of any fundamental attitudinal change. As the Czech president Václav Klaus charged in a remarkably blunt 2011 lecture:

> It seems that Europeans are not interested in capitalism and free markets and do not understand that their current behavior undermines the very institutions that made their past success possible. They are eager to defend their non-economic free-doms—the easiness, looseness, laxity and permissiveness of modern or post-modern society—but when it comes to their economic freedoms, they are quite indifferent.[2]

It may well be that Europe will move in the direction of one set of countries adopting more market-oriented policies at a domestic level, while paying to prop up those EU nations unable or unwilling to shift in the same direction. The sustainability of such arrangements would depend on the willingness of German, Austrian, British, Swedish, Dutch, and Finnish taxpayers to foot the bill indefinitely. By mid-2011, economic growth patterns across the EU—characterized by a sharp division between "northern" countries moving ahead and "southern" countries falling further and further behind—provided some evidence that such an economic split was indeed developing.[3]

Politically speaking, however, there was much to suggest that the willingness of "northerners" to carry the "south" was not unlimited.[4] The increasingly loud insistence by German government officials and legislators through 2012 that Greece *must* meet its reform commitments, instead of continually failing to fulfill its promises, was perhaps the most visible evidence of declining intra-European solidarity.

Our focus here is not upon detailing the policies that America should adopt to avoid economic Europeanization. Legions of scholars, think tanks, and policy makers are engaged in this important work—so much so that it is easy to lose sight of the bigger picture and deeper underlying causes. Instead, our attention is upon identifying the *attitudes* and *principles*—or ways of thinking—that America must get right if its economic culture is not to slide further in a European direction.

The ways of thinking outlined below are more than mere guidelines for the refurbishment of a robust market culture in America. They presume a particular vision of *society* that would, in many respects, make more moral-cultural demands upon Americans than what many are presently accustomed to. Not only do they require Americans to be more entrepreneurial, experimental, open to failure, and competitive; the attitudes to be discussed also imply that people—rather than the state—need to be more involved in addressing social problems through the type of mediating associations and institutions that Tocqueville identified as a distinct part of the American experiment.

The Two S's: Smith and Subsidiarity

Historically speaking, market economic cultures have never translated into anarcho-capitalist societies. Revitalizing market economic culture in America is thus not a question of abolishing the state, but rather a matter of limiting its role. One way to think clearly about how to realize this end is to ask what functions can *only* be performed by the government.

This was one of Adam Smith's starting points for identifying legitimate government economic functions. Though often caricatured as an eighteenth-century Ayn Rand, Smith thought long and hard about the government's appropriate economic role. Smith's view was that the government's general responsibilities concerned the conduct of foreign policy, the organization of national defense, the administration of justice, and the provision of public works. Each of these responsibilities has an economic dimension, especially the last two. In other areas and in particular circumstances, Smith was willing to contemplate limited economic interventions. But these were plainly the exception rather than the rule.

The Smithian principle might therefore be summarized as asking whether the government is the *only* organization that can perform a given economic role. If there is a viable nongovernmental alternative to meeting a given economic need, the normal Smithian position is that the state should not intervene.

For many Europeans and some Americans, Smith's vision suggests an excessively small government. That perhaps underscores how habituated we have become to the state's involvement in so many spheres of life. Moreover, when we consider the functions as identified by Smith, we realize that activities such as the administration of justice (understood as the application of the rule of law through courts, and maintenance of public order through the police) for all three hundred and ten million Americans are not at all small undertakings. The adjudication of contract disputes alone requires a far-reaching state presence throughout the economy. Nor can the responsibility for building and maintaining public works be dismissed as a minor activity.

Regrettably, it is not at all evident that American government institutions are performing even these basic functions especially well. In his 2009 book *Bold Endeavors: How Our Government Built America, and Why It Must Rebuild Now*, the diplomat, banker, and longtime Democratic Party supporter Felix Rohatyn detailed the dilapidated state of much of America's infrastructure.[5] Given, however, the present scale of demands on America's public purse, there are only three ways that government can pay the costs of fulfilling its traditional responsibilities in this area: raising taxes; taking on more debt; or reducing government expenditures in those areas that fall outside the core economic competencies of the state identified by Smith.

This being the case, some might ask: What would happen to the state's work in areas such as welfare and education if America was to recalibrate the government's economic role along broadly Smithian lines? Does a vibrant market economic culture mean that those who cannot help themselves, or who face significant hardship, would simply be cut adrift?

Such questions reflect valid concerns. Yet they also downplay certain points often missed during debates about the state's economic functions. One is that what are initially regarded as temporary expansions of government to help those in genuine need easily morph into more or less permanent fixtures that displace private actors. The same questions often also assume that the state must be the primary actor in addressing social and economic problems and meeting particular needs.

It follows that we need some type of principle to regulate the depth and breadth of government economic interventions that take the state beyond Smithian restraints, and also to provide a mechanism for determining when such temporary or exceptional interventions need to be wound back or ceased altogether. Here America may wish to look to what is called *the principle of subsidiarity*.

Ironically enough, this principle is regularly invoked by EU politicians and in European legislation. Many Europeans understand subsidiarity as a way of dividing up government functions between local, regional, national, and EU levels, according to the criteria that the level of *government* closest to social and economic problems should address them. This conception of subsidiarity appears, for instance, in Article 5 of the Consolidated Version of the Treaty on European Union.

This is at best an idiosyncratic understanding of subsidiarity. It maintains focus on government intervention as the solution to many problems, while ignoring a critical insight expressed in the subsidiarity principle: that most social and economic problems are more appropriately addressed by *non-state* forms of human association.

The roots of the idea of subsidiarity go back to the medieval theologian Saint Thomas Aquinas. He insisted that "it is contrary to the proper character of the state's government to impede people from acting according to their responsibilities—except in emergencies."[6] A similar (but fuller and more recent) definition of subsidiarity was articulated by Pope John Paul II in the following terms:

> in exceptional circumstances the State can also exercise *a substitute function,* when social sectors or business systems are too weak or are just getting under way, and are not equal to the task at hand. Such supplementary interventions . . . must be as brief as possible, so as to avoid removing permanently from society and business systems the functions which are properly theirs, and so as to avoid enlarging excessively the sphere of State intervention to the detriment of both economic and civil freedom . . . Malfunctions and defects in the Social Assistance State are the result of an inadequate understanding of the tasks proper to the State. Here again *the principle of subsidiarity* must be respected: a community of a higher order should not interfere in the internal life of a community of a lower order, depriving the latter of its functions, but rather should support it in case of need and help to co-ordinate its activity with the activities of the rest of society.[7]

On this basis, we can make a number of points about subsidiarity. First, its conception of communities is not confined to political or government organizations. Subsidiarity encompasses the relationships between *all* associations and communities—political and nonpolitical. This indicates that subsidiarity has two purposes. One is to inhibit the state from permanently supplanting non-state forms of association. The second is to limit government intervention, outside its core functions, to those cases in which nonpolitical forms of community closer to a given difficulty have proved temporarily incapable of addressing that problem.

Subsidiarity, for example, suggests that it is reasonable for courts of law to adjudicate contractual disputes when private parties are unable to resolve their disagreement. But subsidiarity also indicates that it is unreasonable for the government to be the first port of call when a family has a problem child. Why? Because in normal circumstances, the function of child-raising is best performed by families—not civil servants. Subsidiarity thus tells us that when a family proves incapable of addressing particular problems associated with child-raising, nongovernmental actors such as churches should usually be the first to render assistance. When no other group can provide appropriate forms of help, governments may then need to act—at least until the problem is resolved, at which point the state should bow out, to prevent the permanent displacement of families from their proper functions.

Adam Smith himself provided an example of what might be called subsidiarity at work in his treatment of education. He specifically rejected the idea of nationalizing education or making it free to all. Smith also made several references to the superiority of private education as compared to then existing public schools. Yet Smith thought education was so important for society's well-being that he was willing to allow government intervention in those instances where "it can never be of the interest of any individual or small number of individuals to erect and maintain a school." Smith was additionally open to governments legally enforcing particular educational standards, and subsidizing school buildings and the private fees payable by poor parents.[8]

In short, Smith was willing to permit the state to intervene to *assist* private associations in their efforts to realize this good end, but *only* to the extent such assistance was necessary to help civil society to do so. Smith thus maintained an abiding concern for preserving liberty, despite what he considered to be a pressing need for government to fill gaps left by civil society and the market. Such an approach is light-years away from the top-down policies beloved of European governments.

Obviously, people of good will can reasonably disagree about the precise point when the state has no option but to intervene. Some libertarians, for example, will regard Smith's view of the state's role in education as excessively interventionist. Many communities might conclude all too quickly that they cannot resolve a problem, and that intervention by a "higher" community is indispensable.

Preventing such slippage means that any attention to subsidiarity must have at its core an emphasis on the need for people—if they are to grow as free and responsible persons—to exercise their unique capacity for free choice. This is at least half the point of subsidiarity. It is not just about helping others more effectively and efficiently; it is also concerned with protecting human liberty as something valuable in itself, and as a precondition for integral human development.

It is difficult to dispute that subsidiarity's consistent application to something like the welfare state in contemporary America and Europe would result in a considerable reduction in the number and scope of state welfare programs. Obamacare, for instance, would be hard to justify under these criteria. Subsidiarity would not result in the complete termination of state welfare functions; there will always be some situations that may require state intervention. The face of America's welfare state, however, would be changed forever.

Two other effects would follow from the application of Smith's vision of the state's economic tasks, combined with a consistent adherence to subsidiarity properly understood.

First, the opportunities for European-like insider-outsider dynamics would be curtailed. In an economic culture marked by adherence to subsidiarity and Smithian principles, there would be fewer opportunities and incentives for businesses to seek corporate welfare, for unions to seek legal privileges, or for politicians to use welfare to establish tame voting constituencies.

The same retraction of the state would produce a second effect that is perhaps even more challenging for Americans: a realization that maintaining freedom requires us to take more direct responsibility for those in need. The application of Smithian principles and subsidiarity to government intervention would not in itself cause the disappearance of all social and economic problems. Indeed, *everyone*, at different stages of life, needs varying levels of assistance; not everyone will have the personal resources to manage on their own, or even with their immediate family's assistance.

Here it becomes clear that the values underpinning subsidiarity and Smithian principles cannot be limited to liberty in the sense of noninterference. While liberty does indeed require us to take responsibility for ourselves, America's commitment to freedom has never been understood as absolving us from our concrete responsibilities to others. As *The Wall Street Journal's* William McGurn wrote, the argument of American "conservatives" with American "liberals" is not about whether people ought to help those in need. The issue concerns the *how*: How do we "balance our care for fellow citizens without wrecking the economy, ruining families, or giving birth to more soulless bureaucracies?"⁹

Market economic cultures have never implied that those in need should be abandoned to their fate. The market-oriented medieval economy of England, for example, teemed with private (invariably religious) associations focused on addressing such problems. Henry VIII's dissolution of the monasteries between 1536 and 1541 was not only one of history's greatest acts of theft; it destroyed a large, privately funded, and relatively efficient private system of hospitals, education, and charity. As James Bartholomew illustrated, the old, the infirm, and the poverty-stricken without families were suddenly stripped of a major support system that the state struggled to replace in England.¹⁰

For civil society to resume these and similar welfare functions in today's Europe would require nothing less than a revolution in the way many Europeans think about these problems. Given the widespread assumption throughout Western Europe that the state should be the primary educator, health-care giver, counselor, job supplier, and social security provider, it is hard to see such changes transpiring in most European countries. America's capacity for renewal in this regard, however, is far from exhausted.

Back to Tocqueville

Though recalibrating the state's economic functions is essential, it is also insufficient for breathing new life into American economic culture. In many respects, reinvigorating a "Tocquevillian" civil-society approach to addressing problems that neither markets nor governments can resolve might be the only way of forestalling the development of proto-European tendencies to regard government as the primary means to address most social difficulties.

As Tocqueville noted and others subsequently confirmed, free-associational approaches to resolving problems are deeply ingrained in American civic culture. Despite the welfare state's steady expansion, it has not managed thus far to undermine America's position as the most generous in the world in the areas of private charity, private philanthropy, and voluntarism.

America's tax system does provide incentives in the form of deductions for various types of charitable contributions. Similar incentives are much rarer in most of Europe. But even if such incentives were to be abolished tomorrow in America, it is not clear that the private resources that allow many private secular and religious organizations to carry out their work of helping those in distress would disappear overnight. Though it might result in some reduction in charitable giving, the American philanthropic instinct may well be strong enough to persist without financial incentives. This, incidentally, is not a reason to abolish such incentives. To the extent incentives encourage bottom-up private solutions to social problems, rather than top-down bureaucratic approaches, they should generally be welcomed.

America's contemporary culture of private solutions to many problems is not without its own challenges. In the first instance, it engages only particular parts of American society.

Paradoxically, this does not equate to a division between those in a position to give time and capital and those who are not. In his book *Who Really Cares?*, Arthur Brooks illustrates that most of this private giving comes from (1) self-identified conservative Americans, and (2) those who actively practice a religious faith. Self-identified American liberals (in the sense of favoring extensive government intervention) and/or those with decidedly "secularist" outlooks apparently suffer from serious generosity deficits.[11] These trends were confirmed by a 2012 *Chronicle of Philanthropy* study which illustrated that "Regions of the country that are deeply religious are more generous than those that are not," and that many "discrepancies among states, cities, and neighborhoods are rooted in part in each area's political philosophy about the role of government versus charity."[12]

On reflection, this is not surprising. If you treat economic and social problems in an abstract rationalist manner and take the view that these are best solved by top-down solutions (attitudes characteristic of modern American liberalism), you are unlikely to view private bottom-up solutions favorably, but rather as obstacles to the state's intervention in these areas. Futhermore, if you assume—like many Europeans—that paying the taxes that fund welfare programs somehow fulfills your obligations to your neighbor in need, you have fewer reasons to involve yourself in voluntary activity.

As for the gap between secularists and religious believers, religious organizations have long played a disproportionately prominent role in America in addressing social and economic problems. This means that the statistical odds of those with secularist outlooks being involved in private giving (and voluntary action) is smaller.

Moreover, many religions—most notably Judaism and Christianity—emphasize *personal* giving to and *personal* assistance of those in need as a catagorical imperative of adherence to the precepts of that faith. Neither atheism nor agnosticism acknowledge or articulate such responsibilities.

A second obstacle to a revitalization of civil-society solutions to social and economic difficulties in America is the extent to which many American private charitable organizations have become financially reliant on government contracts. At first glance, this seems unproblematic. Does it really matter who provides the financial resources?

Resoundingly, the answer is yes. There is much evidence to suggest that government contracts gradually change—and not always for the better—the culture of private welfare groups. Government contracts come with strings attached. Provisions requiring adherence to regulations designed to produce accountability for the expenditure of taxpayers' money invariably accompany government funding. Armies of accountants, lawyers, and managers are consequently employed by church agencies, for example, to ensure that the provisions of such regulations are met. As one church charity director stated, "What government agencies don't understand is that the more they regulate us, the more we have to spend what little money we get on business people and secretaries."[13]

Then there is the issue of mission distortion. To compete for such contracts, some American private welfare groups take on tasks that have little to do with their original purpose, and for which they are not especially well equipped to pursue. They begin to fashion their welfare priorities in ways that seek to maximize their chances of obtaining government contracts. They consequently lose a sense that they should be determining their *own* welfare priorities, not all of which will always accord with governments' wishes. The more private welfare agencies choose to accept such contracts, the more precarious becomes their ability to think and act independently in the face of social and economic challenges.

But at an even more basic level, an ongoing challenge for the reenergizing of a robust American civil society is acceptance of a hard reality: that trying to address severely asocial behavior such as drug dependency, or equally tough issues such as long-term care for the disabled, usually demands a great deal of often thankless work over long periods of time. In some respects, it is simply easier to abdicate one's personal and financial responsibility for the care of a profoundly disabled relative to the state, or to imagine that we can only *really* assist those in need by lobbying for state welfare programs.

In crisis, the cliché goes, we find opportunity. Instead of lamenting the welfare state's demise, as is the rule in much of Europe, Americans could engage in a genuine Renaissance about the *whys* and *hows* of taking care of those whose needs are not or cannot be met by the workings of the market economy. If Americans recognize, for example, that poverty is more than a material phenomenon, and that it also has moral, even spiritual dimensions (precisely those areas of human life that welfare states have never been good at, or frankly interested in addressing), genuine progress in diminishing these problems may well occur.

A Culture of Free Enterprise

The suggested reorientation of state economic interventions and the associated revitalizing of civil society involves more than structural change. The principle of subsidiarity, for instance, involves a concern for liberty. Likewise, Tocquevillian solutions to social and economic problems involve treating other people as individual persons, with dignity, rather than just another mouth to feed.

This attention to values is just as essential when it comes to revitalizing the culture of *free* enterprise, which is central to market economies. For if values are as core to economic culture as this book suggests, Americans need to be clear about the value choices they must make if they want to avoid economic Europeanization. Here are five of the most important of such choices.

1. Wealth creation over wealth redistribution

Following the Great Recession, many European governments moved, albeit reluctantly, toward policies of austerity. Not only did this translate into some efforts to restrain public spending, it also implied that governments had to temporarily renege on their part of the European social contract and restrain their pursuit of a key objective of Social Europe: greater equity in economic outcomes.

A prosperous economy requires not just wealth creation, but also recognition that policies of "spreading the wealth" in the name of equality can diminish the incentives for people to create wealth in the first place. Economists argue about the point at which tax levels and state redistribution begin to disincentivize entrepreneurs and businesses from embarking on new ventures. What they don't really dispute is that there *is* a point when it starts to dampen the pace of wealth creation. In private correspondence with the British-Australian economist Colin Clark, Keynes suggested that the figure of "25% percent [of GDP] as the maximum tolerable proportion of taxation may be exceedingly near the truth."[14]

According to the economist and historian of the Federal Reserve Alan Meltzer, one of the twentieth century's economic lessons is that "Transfers, grants and redistribution did little to raise living standards in Asia, Latin America and Africa." Meltzer also illustrated that just one percent of growth equates, within a generation, to a 25 percent increase in per capita income. Conversely, a low growth rate, Meltzer noted, "significantly lowers real wages and living standards for *everyone*, which in turn lessens tax receipts and resources for redistribution."[15]

Wealth creation is not the be-all and end-all of human existence. But if Americans want a dynamic, growing economy that avoids the negative impact of European-like redistributive policies, they need to prioritize *economic liberty* and allowing people to pursue their self interest in the marketplace over efforts to equalize economic outcomes through state-engineered redistributions.

But doesn't this give license to the "greed is good" mentality? No doubt some Americans will see it that way. Self-interest, however, is a much more complex phenomenon than commonly depicted.

Noneconomists ranging from medievals such as Aquinas to ancients such as Aristotle have recognized that the prospect of attaining and keeping property for oneself motivates people to work harder. They also have observed, however, that owning things in common (the ultimate redistribution) negatively impacts *personal responsibility*. People start assuming someone else will be motivated enough to create wealth in the first place and then take care of what has been created.

America has a long history of aligning self-interest with the common good. In the 1830s, Tocqueville noted that self-interest, properly understood, was the way by which Americans combated radical individualism. They did not equate self-interest with selfishness. In America, Tocqueville wrote, everyone—rich and poor—believed that "by serving his fellows, man serves himself and that doing good is to his private advantage."[16]

This is not mere selfishness. For one thing, it reflects the fact that creating wealth requires us to be attentive to what *others*—i.e., consumers—want or might desire. To be a radical individualist obsessed with oneself is to be a very poor wealth creator.

The moral value of wealth creation, however, goes beyond aligning self-interest with others' needs. Successful and consistent wealth creation requires certain moral habits including prudent risk-taking, foresight, courage, and tenacity. The development of such virtues makes us better human beings than would their opposite: recklessness (or timidity), shortsightedness, cowardice, and laziness.

More generally, the business of creating wealth helps us to engage our minds, intellects, and insights in order to make something new that did not previously exist. To this extent, wealth creation underscores a truth as old as the very first chapter of the very first book of the Bible. Humans are, *by nature*, creative beings. Through work and entrepreneurship, humans *can create value* for existing and potential consumers.

Of course, not everything created by entrepreneurs (e.g., pornography) should be valued. Certain products or services may even merit prohibition. But the emergence of morally destructive industries and activities is primarily a problem of the surrounding moral culture and bad individual choices—it cannot be attributed to entrepreneurship itself. There is still every reason to encourage people to see the process of creating something new which is valued by others as being, in principle, a good thing, and a confirmation of our uniqueness as human beings.

Without question, there are trade-offs here. Economic liberty produces greater amounts of wealth, but also, in some instances, greater wealth disparities. Even if everyone's material state of life gets better, it would be naïve to imagine such disparities will not facilitate a certain degree of envy. And envy, as well as more noble motives such as a concern for justice, can help fuel political pushes for extensive wealth redistributions, which as Europe's experience illustrates, often produce new political, cultural, and economic problems.

But does robust economic liberty translate into less security? As we have seen throughout this book, many Europeans reached this conclusion a long time ago. Writing in 1950, Walter Eucken lamented that in Europe "It is now usual to regard security and freedom as antithetical. Security is said to require a renunciation of freedom. Modern man is believed to be indifferent to freedom. What he wants above all is security."[17] However, Eucken went on to state, without freedom, one does not have security. Instead, one has dependency—and dependency is a form of insecurity, insofar as one is subject to the whims of state officials, corporatist hierarchs, and trade union officials. To this one may add that without the wealth creation that comes from economic freedom, entire societies are perpetually insecure in terms of their ability to meet their material needs, and even their capacity to provide a minimal safety net becomes questionable.

Indeed, a prioritization of economic liberty does not mean that the state cannot engage in *any* redistribution whatsoever. To address those gaps that neither families nor civil society can fulfill, either on a temporary or permanent basis, the state will have to perform some basic welfare functions. To do so, the state needs to tax some people. Even a night-watchman or minimal state needs to be paid for. And while Americans might argue about the size, scale, and form of taxation, few would argue that *all* tax is theft. Adam Smith used the phrase "easy taxes" to describe one of the preconditions for prosperity. He never said "no taxes."

Strict adherence to the principle of subsidiarity would, however, apply a brake to those who would use the tax system as a means to pursue redistributions in the name of economic equality, at the expense of private wealth creation and economic freedom. Moreover, the strong civil society described above would reduce the state's need to call on the private resources of citizens to address issues of poverty and marginalization, because many citizens would *already be using their own resources* to grapple with such problems.

Prioritizing wealth creation over redistribution is not simply a matter of examining each and every social welfare program and assessing whether or not it is compatible with subsidiarity and a Smithian view of the state's economic responsibilities. It also requires Americans to take a stand against corporate welfare—a subject that received considerable attention following the much-publicized 2011 bankruptcy of the solar manufacturer Solyndra, which had received a loan of $528 million, approved by the Department of Energy, from the Federal Financing Bank. As reported by *New York Times* journalists Eric Lipton and John Broder, Solyndra paid Washington lobbyists $1.8 million, and employed lobbying firms with connections to the Obama administration and congressmen, while its bid was being reviewed by the Department of Energy.[18]

Corporate welfare is, after all, a form of redistribution. It redistributes risk in a given society based on an individual's or company's ability to persuade government officials to back a project, rather than selling their wares in the marketplace. Corporate welfare seeks, as Arnold Kling and Nick Schulz state, "to insulate entrepreneurs from downside risks and thereby increase the incentive to attempt new businesses that have poor prospects."[19] The absence of market disciplines, however, invariably results in much larger losses for the overall economy. Over the long term, corporate welfare incentivizes businesses to lose their capacity to adapt to changes in the marketplace, while simultaneously increasing their ability to extract resources from the state.

In 2012, corporate welfare accounted for almost one hundred billion dollars of federal government spending for that fiscal year[20] in the form of loans, bailouts, and subsidies for large corporations, small businesses, and industry groups. Many of these businesses and industries have close relationships with federal and state politicians. This is exemplified by the Troubled Assets Relief Program (TARP), created in late 2008 to aid financial institutions *in extremis*. In a study analyzing the allocation of TARP funding, two Michigan economists found a strong correlation between the possibility of receiving TARP funding and a company's level of connectedness to members of congressional finance committees.[21] American history, however, is littered with such examples of collusion between business and governments, ranging from the Crédit Mobilier scandal of the 1870s to the political favoritism and influence-peddling that marred the activities of the Department of Housing and Urban Development during the 1980s,[22] to the $3.7 billion in financing received by the Enron Corporation from government agencies such as the U.S. Trade and Development Agency and the Export-Import Bank.[23]

Invariably, many of these provisions were publicly justified by the givers and receivers as somehow being in the national interest. But as Smith once commented, "I have never known much good done by those who affected to trade for the public good."[24] The challenge for Americans is to acknowledge business-politician collusion as an instance of European-like soft corruption that produces higher prices for consumers, undermines value creation in the marketplace, and facilitates unwholesome relationships between politicians and businesses.

Circumventing this situation is not simple. The more American companies invest in the business of political entrepreneurship, the less likely they are to favor the type of market liberalization that shifts the incentives back toward meeting consumer demand. Nor do those politicians, who derive their own benefits from the patronage system implicit to corporate welfare, have any strong interest in winding back these neo-mercantilist trends.

If American businesses are seriously interested in placing a premium on liberty and wealth creation in America's economic culture, one step forward would be for them to voluntarily swear off the practice of corporate welfare and other rent-seeking habits such as lobbying for regulations, tax breaks, and tariffs that hurt their competitors. By all means, businesses should defend themselves against competitors who cynically employ political influence in an effort to drive them out of the marketplace. It takes, however, another type of courage to tell your shareholders and employees that the days of cuddling up to Senator Leveraged and Congressman Influential are over.

Extracting themselves from the sticky web of government patronage or refusing to contemplate seeking corporate welfare might well prove economically costly—at least in the short term—for many American companies. They would, however, no longer be open to the charge of behaving in ways not dissimilar to public-sector unions. They would also have the satisfaction of knowing they are back in the business of creating wealth, instead of the less digni-fied endeavor of perpetually trying to live at everyone else's expense.

2. Accountability and transparency: truth over falsehood

One of the oldest and primary justifications for people keeping most of the profits from their business endeavors is that they have taken risks and/or invested capital that others have not. There is, however, another side to this dimension of a culture of free enterprise: If the endeavor fails, then you are expected to bear the loss. At issue is *accountability* for one's decisions.

Dealing with the fallout of business failure is not a simple matter. Over the centuries, Western countries have developed sophisticated bankruptcy laws attempting to ensure that, as far as is possible, the claims upon any remaining resources by those affected by the failure—creditors, investors, employees—are justly adjudicated.

European economic culture has gone a long way toward breaking the link between economic freedom and responsibility for one's actions. Numerous European businesses continue to be propped up by the state, instead of being allowed to quietly fold. Whether it is companies that refuse to modernize (either because they are heavily subsidized or terrified of possible union retaliation) or entire nations that quietly presume someone else will pick up the tab for their wel-fare state, the result is a growth of what is known as *moral hazard.*

Moral hazard is a term commonly used to describe those situa-tions where a person or institution is effectively insulated from the possible negative consequences of their choices. When individuals and institutions believe someone else will pay for the cost of failure, they will often persist with courses of action they would otherwise abandon. In the business world, it means companies are more likely to take risks they would not otherwise take, especially with capital entrusted to them by others: the higher the extent of the guarantee, the greater is the risk of moral hazard.

America is hardly immune to this problem. The downfall of the mortgage lenders Fannie Mae and Freddie Mac is a prominent example. Implicit to their lending policies was the assumption that, as government-sponsored enterprises with lower capital requirements than private institutions, they could always look to the federal government for assistance if an unusually high number of their clients defaulted. In 2007, the Nobel Prize-winning economist Vernon Smith warned that Fannie Mae and Freddie Mac had always been understood as "implicitly taxpayer-backed agencies."[25] Hence they continued what are now widely recognized as their politically driven lending policies until both were placed in federal conservatorship in September 2008.

If American citizens and governments decide to take moral hazard seriously, they would seek to identify those state structures, policies, and practices that create incentives for people to take excessive risks with their own and other peoples' assets. They would then do what they could to minimize these instances of moral hazard. They would also insist that there must be limits to which entrepreneurs and businesses can be protected from the prospect of failure.

In this connection, Americans should demand renewed emphasis on transparency. Imperfect knowledge is a fact of life. Nevertheless, the market's ability to hold individuals, businesses, and governments accountable for their choices—and reward or punish them accordingly—is undermined when individuals, businesses, and governments are less than candid about the risks they have undertaken and liabilities they have incurred. The results of Greece's lack of transparency with regard to its public finances in the 2000s are plain for all to see.

3. Justice: rule of law over the rule of men

Rule of law, it hardly need be said, is crucial for establishing accountability for the success or failure of entrepreneurs and businesses. Over the last century, economists and legal scholars from different schools of thought have also concluded that rule of law is indispensable for sustained economic development. As another Nobel Economics laureate, Friedrich Hayek, once wrote: "There is probably no single factor which has contributed more to the prosperity of the West than the relative certainty of the law which has prevailed here."[26]

But maintaining and promoting rule of law means that Americans should recognize that rule of law is not a morally neutral institution. The very idea of the rule of law is partly derived from the conclusion that it is *reasonable* and *good* to limit arbitrary power.

In his influential 1980 book, *Natural Law and Natural Rights*, John Finnis argued that legal systems embody the rule of law to the extent that:

- rules are prospective rather than retroactive and not impossible to comply with;
- rules are promulgated, clear, and coherent with respect to each other;
- rules are sufficiently stable to allow people to be guided by their knowledge of the content of the rules;
- the making of laws applicable to specific situations is guided by rules that are promulgated, clear, stable, and relatively clear;
- those charged with the authority to make and administer rules are accountable for their own compliance with the rules, and administer the law consistently.[27]

When we look at these conditions, we realize there is a great deal more than simply a concern for efficiency going on here. Each of them embodies a type of inner moral logic that flows from the realization that it is *reasonable* and *just* to treat people in one way and *unreasonable* and *unjust* in other ways. Unless a law is clear, coherent, and officially recognized, it is not reasonable, and therefore unjust.

This commitment to the nonarbitrary application of law is indispensable if we are to establish the stability and certainty of legal process needed by a culture of free enterprise. People will not take economic risks if they believe their wealth may be subject to arbitrary seizure, or if they lack confidence in the legal system's ability to provide relatively just resolutions to, for example, contract disputes. A legal environment in which governments reconfigure the rules governing commerce on an almost daily basis will deter potential investors from making decisions. Similarly, the inconsistent administration of property and contract law will make most people hesitate before risking their capital.

Faltering in the rule of law is usually associated with failed states or emerging dictatorships. Compared to countries such as Hugo Chávez's Venezuela or the near anarchy of 1990s Somalia, America exemplifies a country in which rule of law prevails over the "rule of men." Yet rule of law embraces more than the absence of tyranny or anarchy. Likewise, the willingness of European politicians to simply ignore treaty obligations about debt and spending in the 2000s, and then circumvent legal barriers to bailouts and ECB debt purchases, demonstrates how rule of men can manifest itself in less than obvious fashions. From this perspective, there are several reasons to worry that the rule of law in America is weaker than it should be.

In late 2010, Robert Samuelson observed that signs of undue risk adverseness were creeping into the American economy. Among other symptoms, Samuelson cited a 50 percent decline between 2007 and 2009 in the amount raised by venture capital funds; a reduction in the number of stock market investors; and the fact that of all new job hires, approximately half were from temporary-hire firms—a clear sign of employers' hesitations about full-time hires.[28]

Given the severity of the 2008 Great Recession, such trends were not surprising. But another element in play was the degree of *uncertainty* characterizing the American investment climate.

In everyday speech, the phrases "risk" and "uncertainty" are used interchangeably. But as the Chicago economist Frank Knight demonstrated in his famous 1921 book, *Risk, Uncertainty, and Profit*, they are different phenomena.[29]

In economic terms, Knight explained, risk concerns those probabilities that can be reasonably measured. This is expressed in terms such as "there is a 40 percent risk that the gold price will collapse this year." Measurable risks are thus no deterrent to the making of economic choices. They can actually help us adjust our economic choices so as to be consistent with our responsibilities, resources, and opportunities. The same measurements allow us to distinguish between prudent risk-takers and the reckless, and reward them appropriately.

Uncertainty, by contrast, involves risks that cannot be quantified. It can occur either because of the sheer complexity of a given situation or because the subject matter cannot be reasonably measured.

A good example of the workings of uncertainty is America's present taxation system. As one 2010 *Wall Street Journal* report noted: "The U.S. tax code is slowly being turned into a temporary patchwork of provisions that need to be addressed every year or two, depriving individuals and businesses of the predictability they need for long-range plans."[30]

How does this manifest itself in practice? One needs look no further than those tax provisions that require annual renewal. The temporary extension of the Bush tax cuts at the end of 2010 was negotiated on the proviso that they would either be extended in two years' time, or allowed to lapse. At the time, there was much comment that this arrangement exacerbated uncertainly about income-tax rates after December 2012. Fewer pundits, however, observed that there were approximately 141 tax provisions *already* requiring annual renewal. That was up from fewer than a dozen in the 1990s. Which of these would be renewed? Which would not? As the end of the year draws closer, taxpayers and investors can start to quantify the odds of extension or expiration of these tax provisions. Prior to this, such calculations were extremely difficult.

This is *precisely* the type of uncertainty that deters prudent people from investing, especially over the long term. In America's case, the degree of uncertainty may well be heightened by the gradual impact upon the economy of another factor: a notable weakening of several conditions that make up vital elements of the rule of law. Once again, the U.S. Internal Revenue Code illustrates the point.

In February 2010, the Internal Revenue Code consisted of 9,834 sections, each section being subject to the official interpretations found in the federal tax regulations issued by the Treasury Department, many of which have themselves been shaped by various court decisions.

Supplementing the Internal Revenue Code is the Internal Revenue Bulletin (IRB), which is issued weekly, and described by the Internal Revenue Service as "the authoritative instrument for the distribution of all forms of *official* IRS tax guidance." The IRS cautions, however, that "Rulings and procedures reported in the IRB do not have the force and effect of Treasury tax regulations, but they may be used as precedents."[31] The precise force of these precedents remains unspecified.

A tax code of this size and complexity, and subject to so many sources of potentially conflicting official and semi-official explanations, is bound to embody significant contradictions. It also offers considerable scope for *arbitrary* decision-making. The same tax code is likely to be impossible for large numbers of law-abiding citizens and businesses to understand and comply with—not to mention difficult for conscientious civil servants to administer justly. As a result, it is likely many people may simply choose to forgo any number of potentially wealth-creating opportunities for fear of violating the law.

Further muddying such rule-of-law problems is the sheer volume of law directly shaping American economic life. The 2010 Obamacare legislation, for instance, amounted to 2,700 pages. Not far behind it in length was the Dodd–Frank Wall Street Reform and Consumer Protection Act, which sought to overhaul financial regulation: a mere 2,300 pages.

More than a few legislators confessed to never having read very much of either piece of legislation. Nor should we assume any great familiarity on their part with the thousands of pages of legislation which these acts superseded, integrated, or reinterpreted. The possibility that many laws governing health care and financial services were subsequently rendered unclear, inconsistent, and impossible to comprehend is high.

The amount of legislation affecting the health-care and financial industries is now so great that even good American judges with no interest in judicial activism are very likely issuing rulings affecting these sectors of the economy that are ad hoc and arbitrary in nature. Judicial arbitrariness need not always proceed from the desire to use one's judicial authority to advance private ideological agendas. Arbitrariness can also occur because of a prevailing incoherence of legal principles, legislation, and precedents, in the midst of which judges often cannot help being arbitrary if they are to make any decisions at all.

Of course, the extent to which the different conditions of rule of law prevail in any society is usually a matter of degree. Human fallibility alone means that rule of law can only be imperfectly realized.

Imperfection, however, is one thing; decline and erosion quite another. If America is going to retain its economic place in the world—a preeminence underpinned by its edge in the realms of entrepreneurship, risk-taking, and venture capital—attention to these troubling rule-of-law issues is indispensable. The rule of law, and the value commitments justifying it, is hard enough to build. Once lost, it may be gone forever.

4. *Property rights over* dirigisme

Rule of law and the protection of property rights have always been strongly associated with each other in Anglo-American economic culture. But that same culture has not justified private property simply because it provides incentives to take risks, and is an efficient way of organizing the ownership of wealth. Private property has always been understood as linked to a number of value commitments. These include recognition that economic and political *freedom* requires people to be able to own and use personal resources as they see fit. Thus, by definition, the private possession and use of property helps limit the state's control of the economy.

Second, the existence and enforcement of property rights inspire *trust*. They generate confidence that the person with whom you are contracting is actually entitled to sell you his property. Property rights also facilitate trust between strangers, because their recognition by law means there is a *peaceful* means of adjudicating disputes. This encourages people to venture forth to use, buy, and sell different property rights. As Smith understood, when people "are secure of enjoying the fruits of their industry, they naturally exert it to better their condition, and to acquire not only the necessaries, but the conveniences and elegancies of life."[32]

Of course, private-property rights are not absolute. We are not free, for instance, to use our property to end other people's lives. Measures such as taxation are justified, in part, by the need to finance particular state institutions such as courts, which protect, among other things, property rights.

But as we have seen, one characteristic of Europe's economic culture is the readiness—even eagerness—to significantly limit property rights. This stands in stark contrast to the manner with which many Europeans almost recklessly apply the language of rights to many welfare and social programs. In Europe, this relentless relativizing of property rights has helped to clear the way for ongoing tax increases and the welfare state's growth.

Restrictions on property rights in America have not reached European proportions. This is partly because the state's share of GDP in America remains, for the moment, smaller than in most European nations. Nonetheless, much of America *has* lost sight of the moral and economic value of property rights. In this respect, much of the erosion of property rights has actually been propelled by business interests. One example of this is the issue of *eminent domain.*

If governments are going to build various forms of public infrastructure, some people's property rights occasionally have to be overridden. Likewise, in wartime, there may be instances where the state needs to appropriate the private ownership of particular goods and services. In these cases, there is a relatively clear justification for the state's invocation of its sovereignty to take such measures, at least on a temporary basis.

Such exercises of eminent domain are not revolutionary, and long predate the American founding. It has always been understood that governments are normally required to compensate owners for their loss. As the Fifth Amendment of America's Constitution states: "nor shall private property be taken for public use, *without just compensation*" (emphasis added). The compensation is meant to underline the fact that appropriation for public use is not to be understood as a license for outright confiscation.

Notwithstanding this conditionality, property rights in America *have* been corroded by the steady expansion of eminent domain's meaning since 2000, most infamously in the 2005 Kelo case.[33] Here the Supreme Court ruled that the City of New London in Connecticut could, by virtue of invoking eminent domain, take what was termed "non-blighted private property" and transfer the property for a dollar a year to a private developer. This invocation was made on the grounds that the City of New London's desire to increase its municipal revenues was legitimate. Ironically, the proposed redevelopment permitted by *Kelo v. City of New London* never transpired. Despite the expenditure of millions of taxpayer dollars on the redevelopment, nothing was constructed on the confiscated land—it was all for nothing.

The Kelo case was a classic instance of government-business collusion against other private actors in order to realize specific short-term objectives: i.e., profits for a *particular* company and increased revenue for a *particular* local government authority. The damage to property rights, both in terms of the liberty they protect and the long-term economic productivity they incentivize, was considerable—so much so that many American state governments enacted laws to prevent similar situations from ever arising in their jurisdictions.

It may well be that many Americans have become so accustomed to local, state, and federal government circumscribing the rights associated with their property that they simply don't notice how these are being interfered with, until confronted with something as blatant as *Kelo*. But some Americans' acceptance of such usurpations of property rights also reflects a tendency by many of the same Americans to believe that governments, looking at society and the economy from the top down, somehow know what would be the most optimal use of everyone's possessions. Such mind-sets ascribe to governments an almost divine knowledge of the present and the future. They are also, as Europe's experience demonstrates, deeply detrimental to market economic cultures.

5. Hope over fear: openness versus defensiveness

The fifth value essential to a culture of free enterprise might be described as *openness*. Perhaps the best way to understand this is to consider its opposite: an attitude of *defensiveness*.

However noble might have been their original purposes, there is little question that European guilds of the medieval and early modern period quickly became exercises in economic defensiveness.

Many of the European social model's distinctive features—*dirigisme*, neo-corporatism, subsidies, tariffs, national champions, strong labor-market regulation—likewise betray a yearning for very high levels of protection against life's uncertainties.

This defensiveness manifests itself in a resistance to economic change, the implementation of widespread regulatory frameworks to try to "manage" innovation, distrust in the ability of individuals and communities to assume responsibility for themselves, and a lack of confidence in the ability of European businesses to be competitive on international markets. But perhaps above all, the defensiveness of much of Europe vis-à-vis the rest of the world reflects an undercurrent of fear: fear of failure, fear of the future, even fear of the rest of the world.

An economic culture underpinned by such defensive ways of thinking may be able to resist external influences and internal pressures for change for some time. But no matter how many subsidies or tariffs are applied to a given product, the business or nation that enjoys and maintains a comparative advantage in producing and/ or distributing that product will usually and eventually overtake its competitors. Defensiveness also diminishes long-term business flexibility, produces more expensive and lower-quality products for consumers, compromises employees' long-term economic future, and encourages governments to become involved in areas of the economy they have no business entering. In the long run, economic cultures characterized by defensiveness become difficult to sustain, as much of Europe has belatedly discovered.

Militarily speaking, the opposite of defense is attack. This, however, is not what openness entails. In economic terms, openness concerns the creation of *space* for individuals and groups to innovate, experiment, invest where they choose, take risks, and succeed. This implies dismantling, as far as possible, internal and external impediments to innovation and investment.

Openness is also about a willingness to allow failure, instead of encouraging entrepreneurs and businesses to seek a crony capitalist solace in the state's embrace. Not only does this help prevent the establishment of de facto monopolies by existing businesses, it also lets new market entrants know they will not have to compete against the government as well as established companies.

This need to allow failure also illustrates that a commitment to openness is not about the mindless embrace and promotion of the new, simply because it is different. Many new products and services fail in the marketplace. Much wisdom is contained in the saying that, of every ten ideas dreamed up by an entrepreneur, perhaps one will have traction in the market.

Openness thus embodies a conservative dimension. It is preconditioned upon and tempered by virtues such as prudence and temperance, as well as the practical insights acquired through experience that enable us to identify what risks are worth taking and what are not, and which products and services are worth purchasing and which are not. Generally speaking, open markets are far better places in which to make such assessments than the offices of civil servants.

This is not to deny the trade-offs associated with openness. These involve accepting that the creative destruction of today will generally make life economically better for the next generation. Openness implies the willingness to trade off immediate and even medium-term stability for long-term prosperity, long-term rising living standards, and long-term adaptability.

A good example is the development of the automobile. In the initial stages, cars could only be afforded by the very wealthy. They also spelled doom for the horse-and-buggy industry. Yet within less than a generation, people with modest incomes could afford to purchase cars. The car industry also quickly created millions of new jobs that more than compensated for the loss of horse-and-buggy positions. Should these advances in technology and economic quality of life have been prevented to preserve the horse-and-buggy industry? Economically speaking, the response is surely a deafening *no*.

Another trade-off is accepting that those who have taken the risk of pioneering an economic change will, at least in the short term, benefit disproportionately, as will those who can immediately afford to buy the new or improved good or service. Other people (such as horse-and-buggy repairers) will, through no fault of their own, find themselves confronting upheaval in their lives. This means that if Americans want the benefits of openness, they must accept that one side effect will be a considerable degree of economic inequality. Contemporary Western Europe, however, provides us with numerous examples of what happens when governments and citizens chose to trade off openness, growth, and liberty in return for protection, stability, and equalization of economic outcomes.

But openness should not be understood as simply a means to an end or a necessary cost of doing business. It has its own moral value that ought to be taken seriously.

First, openness is predicated squarely on the principle of free association. This, we recall, is central to the critique leveled by both medieval theologians and modern market-oriented economists against guild-like restrictive practices. Their point was and is that, provided the purpose is not criminal, people should be free to associate in the marketplace with whom they want on mutually agreeable conditions, and free to part ways when they consider it necessary to do so. The guild-corporatist dimension of European economic culture has long sought to strictly corral such freedoms.

Second, and less obviously, openness is grounded in a willingness to be humble. An open economy requires entrepreneurs and businesses to be ready to acknowledge mistakes, to accept the verdict of consumers and investors, and to start again—instead of blaming others and clamoring for the state to bail them out and limit access to "their" market. Open economies also rely upon politicians being modest enough to accept the limits of government action in the economy, not to mention the counterproductive effects of many interventions. The persistent meddling of so many European politicians and civil servants in their economies, despite all the evidence of the negative consequences of such policies, bespeaks not only of a failure to learn: It also suggests arrogance.

Economic Culture, Human Flourishing, and a Civilization of Natural Liberty

Wealth creation, accountability, rule of law, property rights, openness, hope: All were characteristics highlighted by Tocqueville as prominent features of the American economy he encountered in the 1830s. But Tocqueville also noticed something else. As perhaps his most discerning biographer, André Jardin, notes: "[O]ne of the first surprises for Tocqueville . . . in New York was that at gatherings during the evening one would rub shoulders with men who had spent the day in an office or a bank—lawyers, businessmen, bankers. The pleasures of society came at the end of a day in which they had waged a fierce battle for profit."[34]

Such a state of affairs shocked Tocqueville. The salons of his native France were dominated by men holding public office and gentlemen of leisure devoted to disinterested scholarship. Captains of industry and aspiring entrepreneurs were largely absent from such gatherings.

This tells us something about the disdain with which much of 1830s Europe regarded the world of business. But it also reveals something about America: that it was not as materialistic as many Europeans supposed, and as some Europeans today continue to assume. The pursuit of prosperity for its own sake, Tocqueville found, was not all-consuming of Americans' lives, despite the republic's unabashedly commercial character. Achieving economic success and wealth gave many Americans the time and material resources to pursue other, less material goods: fine conversation, the pursuit of the humanities and natural sciences, philanthropy, charitable works, prayer, the cultivation of the arts, an appreciation of beauty, and their children's education.

It is a vision somewhat at odds with the rough-and-ready frontier imagery often associated with nineteenth-century America. Nevertheless, it is very consistent with the lives and aspirations of many of America's founders. The richest and most economically successful Founding Father of them all (and the last to depart this world, in 1832), Charles Carroll of Carrollton, exemplifies this.

Charles Carroll inherited great wealth. But as a successful businessman in his own right, he multiplied his holdings several times over. On his journeys throughout America, Carroll was forever identifying new trade routes and taking notes about what crops might be suitable for particular pieces of land. He also invested heavily in private economic projects designed to produce public works such as canals.

Yet none of these interests, and the time and energy they consumed, prevented Carroll from cultivating literary and other aesthetic interests. Nor did they inhibit him from a long-term involvement in public affairs, whether as a representative in several legislatures, a political commentator writing under a pseudonym, a learned discussant of America's emerging constitutional framework, or a fighter for religious liberty.

In signing the Declaration of Independence, Carroll put far more at risk, economically speaking, than any other signer. But his lack of hesitation in doing so demonstrated something else: Carroll's conviction that more was at stake in America's dispute with Britain than just taxes, and that some things are more important than money.[35]

Arthur Brooks has it exactly right when he points out that the endgame of America's economic system and its culture of free enterprise is *not* the endless acquisition of wealth. The goal, he stresses, is *human flourishing*. This idea is as old as Aristotle, but deeply integral to the American experience, and the aspirations contained in the immortal phrase *life, liberty, and the pursuit of happiness*.

No doubt, part of the happiness may be found in pursuit of some of the wide-ranging and often very uneconomic interests of a Thomas Jefferson, Benjamin Franklin, or Charles Carroll. But other realizations of happiness may occur through pursuit of the means that allow us to engage such interests: in the development, for example, of the moral and practical habits that are crucial to success in America's economic culture.

In much of Europe, a contrary attitude has long been characteristic of its economic culture: If people are to lead fulfilling lives, then—as far as is consistent with maintaining the minimal incentives required to encourage wealth creation—many people need to be provided with things and protected from risk. In policy and institutional terms, this translates squarely into the European social model.

There is little evidence that such policies actually help to make people happy. Why? Because people who are always given things know they have not, as Brooks noted, *earned* what they have been given. As evidence, he pointed to studies that underscore correlations between unearned income and dissatisfaction with life. Lottery winners—those suddenly *given* an enormous sum of money—generally tend to become unhappy over time. Other studies illustrate that welfare recipients are generally less happy than those who earn the same income, but not through a welfare payment.[36]

Obviously, we should not read too much into these studies. As the saying goes, correlation is not causality. They do, however, suggest that those economic cultures that prioritize institutions and policies focused upon redistribution, in an effort to realize the value of greater equality and stability, are less successful at helping people to flourish than they ought to be. "Money," as another wealthy American founder, Benjamin Franklin, wrote, "never made a man happy yet, nor will it." But *how* one achieves wealth most certainly *does* seem to matter when we think about something as profoundly unmaterialistic as human happiness.

The truth is that economic cultures more or less in thrall to the values associated with progressive economic equalization tend to have rather materialistic views of human flourishing. Collectivist systems—those that systematically redistribute wealth to a degree even many Western Europeans find disturbing—are an extreme example. The American Founding Fathers wrote more aptly than some of them realized when they associated the word "liberty" with the phrase "the pursuit of happiness." The exercise of freedom—including economic freedom—is *where* much of the happiness-making occurs. The downside may be less economic security. But while some economic security is important, it is not all-important. Nor is it enough for human happiness.

This further underscores the truth that if Americans want to resist economic Europeanization, they must do more than engage in policy battles. The fight to take back America's economy from those who have sought to realize the social democratic dream over the past eighty years must be more than an argument about the relative efficiency of markets versus mixed economies. It must have a moral dimension. Man does not live by efficiency alone. Life is about much more than maximizing utility.

As a society, America must consciously choose *not* to cut off its economic culture from the roots from which it came. And those roots are certainly European. These same roots have been shaped and deepened for more than two hundred and thirty years through distinctly American experiences—so much so that not even politicians as savvy as Franklin Roosevelt or Lyndon Johnson were able to pull them out completely.

Sadly, there are no guarantees that these roots will persist in America. Economic cultures are like plants: Once torn up from their roots, they can die quickly. Creating the values that promote market economic cultures—let alone the institutions that enhance and protect them over the long term—is extremely difficult. History is littered with failures to do so.

Americans can, however, cultivate what they have been given: as a sacred trust, and as part of that broader civilization of natural liberty to which Adam Smith's *The Wealth of Nations* pointed, and whose heritage is grounded deeply in what we should unashamedly call European civilization. If they choose to do so—and choose they must Americans can have confidence that, whatever happens to Europe, something of Western civilization will not only have been saved: It will also have been transformed anew.

Notes

Prologue

1. These figures are found in Martin Gilbert, *First World War* (London: HarperCollins, 1994), 541.

2. John Maynard Keynes, *The Economic Consequences of the Peace* (London: McMillan, 1919), 20.

3. Ibid., 23.

4. Ibid., 157.

Chapter 1: We're Becoming Like Europe

1. Edmund L. Andrews, "Greenspan Concedes Error on Regulation," *The New York Times*, October 23, 2008, http://www.nytimes. com/2008/10/24/business/economy/24panel.html.

2. Leon Mangasarian, "U.S. Losing Finance Superpower Status, Germany Says," *Bloomberg*, September 25, 2008, http://www.bloomberg. com/apps/news?pid=newsarchive&sid=ahUuZ8Z5rkDA&refer=germany.

3. Elitsa Vucheva, "'Laissez-faire' capitalism is finished, says France," *EUObserver*, September 26, 2008, http://euobserver.com/9/26814.

4. Daniel Henninger, "The We're-Not-Europe Party," *The Wall Street Journal*, May 13, 2010, http://online.wsj.com/article/SB1000142405274870 3339304575240591350076252.html.

5. Yuval Levin, "Beyond the Welfare State," *National Affairs*, March 21, 2011.

6. Ibid.

7. Joseph Stiglitz, "To choose austerity is to bet it all on the confidence fairy," *The Guardian*, October 19, 2010, http://www.guardian.co.uk/commentisfree/cifamerica/2010/oct/19/no-confidence-fairy-for-austerity-britain.

8. See Arthur C. Brooks, *The Battle: How the Fight between Free Enterprise and Big Government Will Shape America's Future* (New York: Basic Books, 2010), 7–19.

9. Anne Sorock, "*Occupy Wall Street: Short-Selling America*," marketing research report, The Frontier Lab, December 2011, 6.

10. Arnold Kling and Nick Schulz, *From Poverty to Prosperity: Intangible Assets, Hidden Liabilities and the Lasting Triumph over Scarcity* (New York: Encounter Books, 2009), 2.

11. A.M.C. Waterman, "'New political economies' then and now: Economic theory and the mutation of political doctrine," in *The New Political Economies: A Collection of Essays from around the World*, ed. Laurence S. Moss (Oxford: Blackwell, 2002), 13–40.

12. Kling and Schulz, *From Poverty to Prosperity*, 149.

13. Douglass North, "Economic Performance through Time," Prize Lecture to the memory of Alfred Nobel, December 9, 1993, http://nobelprize.org/nobel_prizes/economics/laureates/1993/north-lecture.html.

14. [My emphasis.]

15. Edmund S. Phelps, "Economic Culture and Economic Performance: What light is shed on the Continent's problem?," Perspectives on the Performance of the Continent's Economies, conference of CESifo and the Center on Capitalism and Society, Venice, July 21–22, 2006, 2.

16. Ibid., 4.

17. Kling and Schulz, *From Poverty to Prosperity*, 204.

18. Edmund S. Phelps, "Macroeconomics for a Modern Economy," Prize Lecture to the memory of Alfred Nobel, December 8, 2006, http://

nobelprize.org/nobel_prizes/economics/laureates/2006/phelps_lecture. pdf.

19. Phelps, "Economic Culture and Economic Performance," 15.

20. See Directorate-General Communication, *Entrepreneurship in the EU and Beyond* (Brussels: European Commission, 2009), http://ec.europa.eu/enterprise/policies/sme/facts-figures-analysis/eurobarometer/fl283_en.pdf.

21. Dennis L. Bark, *Americans and Europeans: Dancing in the Dark— On Our Differences and Affinities, Our Interests, and Our Habits of Life* (Stanford, CA: Hoover Institution Press, 2007), 9.

22. Paul Krugman, "Can Europe Be Saved?" *The New York Times*, January 12, 2011, http://www.nytimes.com/2011/01/16/magazine/16Europe-t.html?_r=2&pagewanted=1.

23. See Indermit Gill and Martin Raiser, *Golden Growth: Restoring the Lustre of the European Economic Model* (Washington, DC: The World Bank Group, 2011), http://siteresources.worldbank.org/ECAEXT/Resources/258598-1284061150155/7383639-1323888814015/8319788-1326139457715/fulltext_overview.pdf.

24. This North-South divergence theme pervades *every* section of Gill and Raiser's exhaustive study of contemporary European economic life.

25. "Languages," European Commission, http://ec.europa.eu/education/languages/languages-of-europe/index_en.htm.

26. For the reality and extent of convergence since World War II, see Gill and Raiser, *Golden Growth*, 71–81.

27. Paul Laity, "Uncomfortable Truths," *The Guardian*, May 17, 2008, http://www.guardian.co.uk/books/2008/may/17/politics1.

Chapter 2: Free Markets, Guilds, and the State

1. Alexis de Tocqueville, *Democracy in America*, trans. Arthur Goldhammer (New York: Library of America, 2004), 464–465.

2. Alexis de Tocqueville, *Recollections: The French Revolution of 1848*, ed. J. P. Mayer and A. P. Kerr (New Brunswick: Transaction Publishers, 2002), 7.

3. Tocqueville, *Democracy in America*, 184.

4. Ibid., 246.

5. Alexis de Tocqueville, *Journey to America*, trans. George Lawrence (New Haven: Yale University, 1959), 271.

6. See Tocqueville, *Democracy in America*, 731–732.

7. Ibid., 642.

8. See Tocqueville, *Recollections*, 146–165.

9. See Richard Swedberg, *Tocqueville's Political Economy* (Princeton: Princeton University Press, 2009), 167.

10. See Seymour Drescher, *Tocqueville and Beaumont on Social Reform* (New York: Harper and Row, 1968), 131.

11. Tocqueville, *Recollections*, 5.

12. Exemplifying this line of thought was Alban de Villeneuve-Bargement, *Économie politique chrétienne, ou recherches sur la nature et les causes du paupérisme en France et en Europe*, 3 vols. (Paris: Paulin, 1834).

13. Eric Jones, *The European Miracle: Environments, Economics and Geopolitics in the History of Europe and Asia* (Cambridge: CUP, 2003), xii.

14. Ibid., xviii.

15. Ibid., xii.

16. Ibid., xxxii.

17. See ibid., xvii–xxxvii.

18. Ibid., xxxvii.

19. See ibid., xxvii.

20. See Edwin S. Hunt and James M. Murray, *A History of Business in Medieval Europe, 1200–1550* (Cambridge: CUP, 2006).

21. See Robert S. Lopez, *The Commercial Revolution of the Middle Ages, 950–1350* (Cambridge: CUP, 1995).

22. See Hunt and Murray, *A History of Business in Medieval Europe*, 3.

23. Jones, *European Miracle*, xxix.

24. See Rodney Stark, *The Victory of Reason: How Christianity Led to Freedom, Capitalism, and Western Success* (New York: Random House, 2005).

25. Phelps, "Economic Culture and Economic Performance," 5.

26. See Antony Black, *Guild and State: European Political Thought from the Twelfth Century to the Present* (New Brunswick: Transaction Publishers, 2003), 32.

27. See ibid., 16.

28. See ibid., 8–11.

29. See Lopez, *Commercial Revolution*, 128.

30. See ibid., 129.

31. See Black, *Guild and State*, 86–95.

32. Ibid., 32. See also C. W. Bynum, "Did the twelfth century discover the individual?," *Journal of Ecclesiastical History* 31 (1980): 1–17.

33. See Black, *Guild and State*, 41.

34. See A. Mcfarlane, *The Origins of English Individualism: The Family, Property and Social Transition* (Oxford: Oxford University Press, 1978), 163. See also John F. McGovern, "The Rise of New Economic Attitudes—Economic Humanism, Economic Nationalism—During the Later Middle Ages and the Renaissance, A.D. 1200–1500," *Traditio* 26 (1970): 217–254.

35. See, for example, Bartolus of Sassoferrato, *Commentaries on the Digest* (Turin: 1577), 47.22.4. Here the medieval jurist insisted that guilds were not permitted to make "a law by which another is prejudiced, as for instance if they make a law that only certain persons and no others can exercise that craft."

36. For scholastic critiques of guilds and monopoly practices, see Raymond de Roover, *Business, Banking, and Economic Thought in Late Medieval and Early Modern Europe,* ed. Julius Kirshner (Chicago: University of Chicago Press, 1974), 273–305.

37. See Lopez, *Commercial Revolution*, 127.

38. On the legal significance of Christendom and the manner in which it broke up, see Samuel Gregg, "Legal Revolution: St. Thomas More, Christopher St. German, and the Schism of Henry VIII," *Ave Maria Law Review* 5, no. 1 (2007): 173–205.

39. For the theory and practice of absolutism, see H. M. Scott, ed., *Enlightened Absolutism: Reform and Reformers in Later Eighteenth-Century Europe* (Ann Arbor, MI: University of Michigan Press, 1990).

40. See Jean Bodin, *De Republica Libri Sex* (Paris: 1576), 327–346.

41. See Philippe Minard, *La fortune du colbertisme: état et industrie dans la France des Lumières* (Paris: Fayard, 1998).

42. See George V. Taylor, "Types of Capitalism in Eighteenth-Century France," *English Historical Review*, 79 (1964): 496.

43. See Samuel Gregg, *The Commercial Society: Foundations and Challenges in a Global Age* (Lanham, MD: Lexington Books, 2007), 10–14.

44. See Peter Groenewegen, *Eighteenth-Century Economics: Turgot, Beccaria and Smith and their Contemporaries* (London: Routledge, 2002).

45. See Christopher Hill, *Puritanism and Revolution: Studies in Interpretation of the English Revolution of the 17th Century* (London: Mercury Books, 1962), 28.

46. See T. S. Hamerow, *The Social Foundations of German Unification, 1858–1871*, vol. 2, *Struggles and Accomplishments* (Princeton: Princeton University Press, 1972).

47. Émile Durkheim, *Leçons de sociologie: physique des mœurs et du droit* (Paris: Presses Univ. de France, 1969), 63.

48. G. H. D. Cole, *Self-Government in Industry* (London: Hutchinson Educational, 1971), 6.

Chapter 3: Toward the European Social Model

1. *Le Figaro*, March 16, 2005.

2. Barry Eichengreen, *The European Economy Since 1945: Coordinated Capitalism Since 1945* (Princeton: Princeton University Press, 2007), 4.

3. Jean Lacouture, *De Gaulle*, vol. 2, *The Ruler: 1945–1970* (London: HarperCollins, 1991), 66.

4. Charles de Gaulle, *La Voix du Nord*, October 2, 1944.

5. See Mark Gilbert, "Mario Monti and Italy's Generational Crisis: Rome's Economic Solutions Don't Solve Its Political Problems," *Foreign*

Affairs, February 14, 2012, http://www.foreignaffairs.com/articles/137200/mark-gilbert/mario-monti-and-italys-generational-crisis.

6. Walter Eucken, *This Unsuccessful Age or The Pains of Economic Progress* (London: William Hodge and Company Ltd, 1951), 57.

7. John Maynard Keynes, *Collected Works of John Maynard Keynes*, vol. 4, *A Tract on Monetary Reform*, ed. D. Moggridge (London: Macmillan, 1971), 65.

8. John Maynard Keynes, *Collected Works of John Maynard Keynes*, vol. 27, *Activities 1940–46. Shaping the Post-War World: Employment and Commodities*, ed. D. Moggridge (London: Macmillan, 1980), 322.

9. Wilhelm Röpke, "Marshall plan and economic policy," reprinted in Wilhelm Röpke, *Against the Tide*, trans. Elizabeth Henderson (Chicago: Regnery, 1969), 127–128.

10. Wilhelm Röpke, "The formation and use of capital," reprinted in Röpke, *Against the Tide*, 165.

11. Robert Skidelsky, *Keynes: The Return of the Master* (New York: Public Affairs, 2009), 104.

12. "Neoliberal" is used here as a catch-all phrase. Eucken, Böhm, and the "ordoliberals" associated with the University of Freiburg focused specifically upon the rules governing market life, whereas Röpke, Müller-Armack, and Rüstow (often called "neoliberals" or "sociological liberals") complemented an attention to rules with reflection on sociological questions.

13. Alexander Rüstow, *Freedom and Domination: A Historical Critique of Civilization*, ed. D.A. Rüstow (Princeton: Princeton University Press, 1980), 455–456.

14. See Franz Böhm, *Wettbewerb und Monopolkampf* (Berlin: Heymann, 1933), 323.

15. Ibid., 291–94.

16. Walter Eucken, *Grundsätze der Wirtschaftspolitik* (Tübingen: J.C.B. Mohr, 1952), 41–55.

17. Wilhelm Röpke, *Is the German Economic Policy the Right One?*, reprinted in Horst Wünsche, ed., *Standard Texts on the Social Market*

Economy, trans. Derek Rutter (Stuttgart and New York: Gustav Fisher, 1982), 37–48.

18. Ibid., 47.

19. See Protokoll des Parteitages der Sozialdemokratischen Partei Deutschlands: Abgehalten zu Erfurt vom 14. bis 20. Oktober 1891 [Minutes of the Party Congress of the Social Democratic Party of Germany: Held in Erfurt from October 14–20, 1891] (Berlin: Verlag der Expedition des Dowarts Berliner, 1891): 3–6.

20. See, for example, Eichengreen, *The European Economy Since 1945*, 40–47.

21. Larry Siedentop, *Democracy in Europe* (New York: Columbia University Press, 2001), 141.

22. See Dennis Bark and David Gress, *A History of West Germany*, vol. 1, *From Shadow to Substance 1945–1963* (Oxford: Blackwells, 1993), 396–397.

23. See Samuel Gregg, "Social Contracts, Human Flourishing, and the Economy," *Public Discourse*, June 22, 2011, http://www.thepublicdiscourse.com/2011/06/3424.

24. Richard W. Stevenson, "The Budget Debate Revealed," *The New York Times*, April 16, 2011, http://www.nytimes.com/2011/04/17/weekinreview/17deficit.html.

25. See, for example, Joseph Stiglitz, *Freefall: America, Free Markets, and the Sinking of the World Economy* (New York: W.W. Norton and Company, 2010).

Chapter 4: A Very Imperfect Union

1. See Independent Sector, *Giving and Volunteering in the United States 2001* (Washington, DC: Independent Sector, 2001), http://www.independentsector.org/uploads/Resources/GV01keyfind.pdf.

2. These figures may be found at http://www.nptrust.org/philanthropic-resources/statistics/ [accessed October 6, 2012].

3. See "They Work for Us," *The Economist*, January 22, 2011, http://www.economist.com/node/17929027.

4. For all these institutions and their functions, see http://europa.eu/institutions/index_en.htm.

5. See GAO, *Report to Congressional Addresses: Opportunities to Reduce Potential Duplication in Government Programs, Save Tax Dollars, and Enhance Revenue* (Washington, DC: GAO, 2011).

6. Winston Churchill, "Speech delivered at the University of Zurich, 19 September 1946" (Strasbourg: Council of Europe, 2005), http://assembly.coe.int/Main.asp?link=/AboutUs/zurich_e.htm.

7. Congress of Europe: The Hague, May 1948: *Resolutions* (London-Paris: International Committee of the Movements for European Unity, 1948), 5–7.

8. Robert Schuman, "Declaration of 9 May 1950," http://europa.eu/abc/symbols/9-may/decl_en.htm.

9. *Treaty Constituting the European Coal and Steel Community and Connected Documents* (Luxembourg: Publishing Services of the European Communities, 2011), 1–90, http://www.ena.lu/treaty_establishing_european_coal_steel_community_paris_18_april_1951-020301854.html.

10. Schuman, "Declaration of 9 May 1950."

11. *Treaty Establishing the European Economic Community and Connected Documents* (Luxembourg: Publishing Services of the European Communities, 2011), 5–183.

12. See Wilhelm Röpke, *The Economics of Full Employment* (1952), reprinted in Henry Hazlitt, ed., *The Critics of Keynesian Economics* (Lanham, MD: University Press of America, 1960), 362–386.

13. A. J. Nichols, *Freedom with Responsibility: The Social Market Economy in Germany 1918–1963* (Oxford: Oxford University Press, 1994), 244–246.

14. See Wilhelm Röpke, "Gemeinsamer Markt: ja - aber ohne Dirigismus," *Die Zeit*, December 12, 1957; and Nichols, *Freedom and Responsibility*, 346.

15. See Wilhelm Röpke, "Gemeinsamer markt und freihandelszone," *Ordo*, 10 (1958): 31–62.

16. Wilhelm Röpke, "Die wirtschaftspolitische tendenz der EWG," *Neue Zürcher Zeitung*, May 16, 1964.

17. Wilhelm Röpke, "European economic integration and its problems," *Modern Age* 8, no. 3 (1964), 236.

18. Wilhelm Röpke, "Europäische investitionsplanung—das Beispiel der Montanunion," *Ordo*, 7 (1955): 75–80.

19. Röpke, "European economic integration and its problems," 238.

20. Eichengreen, *The European Economy since 1945*, 335.

21. Ibid., 338–340.

22. *Treaty on European Union/Protocol on Social Policy* (1992), http://www.unifi.it/relazioni-internazionali-studi-europei/upload/sub/Protocol_on_social_policy.pdf.

23. Felix Gilbert and David Clay Large, *The End of the European Era: 1890 to the Present* (London: W.W. Norton & Company, 2009), 596–7.

24. Ibid.

25. See Bark, *Americans and Europeans*, 172.

26. See Judy Dempsey, "Rival views on EU are out in the open," *International Herald Tribune*, June 20, 2005.

27. See *Directive 2006/123/EC of the European Parliament and of the Council of 12 December 2006 on services in the internal market*, http://eur-lex.europa.eu/LexUriServ/LexUriServ.do?uri=OJ:L:2006:376:0036:0068: EN:PDF.

28. See Gill and Raiser, *Golden Growth*, 120.

29. See Riva Froymovich, "EU Aims to Boost Worker Mobility Throughout Region," *The Wall Street Journal*, April 13, 2011, http://online.wsj.com/article/SB10001424052748703518704576258501173219510.html.

30. Mario Monti, *A New Strategy for the Single Market at the Service of Europe's Economy and Society* (2010), 37 and 3, http://ec.europa.eu/bepa/pdf/monti_report_final_10_05_2010_en.pdf.

31. Ibid., 107.

32. See *Charter of Fundamental Rights of the European Union*, http://www.europarl.europa.eu/charter/pdf/text_en.pdf.

33. See European Commission, *Your Guide to the Lisbon Treaty* (Luxembourg: Publications Office of the European Union, 2009), 5, http://ec.europa.eu/publications/booklets/others/84/en.pdf.

34. Ibid., 3.

35. Ibid., 8.

36. Ibid.

37. Jürgen Stark, "Fit for the future? Towards a lean and efficient public sector," given at the conference "Fiscal Policy Challenges in Europe" organized by the German Ministry of Finance and Centre for European Economic Research, March 23, 2007, http://www.ecb.int/press/key/date/2007/html/sp070323_1.en.html

38. Ibid.

39. Ibid.

40. Ibid.

41. Ibid.

42. Václav Klaus, "The Euro Zone Has Failed," *The Wall Street Journal*, June 1, 2010, http://online.wsj.com/article/SB1000142405274870 4875604575280452365548866.html. Klaus qualified his remarks by noting that he was "speaking about 'normal' countries, e.g. countries without wars or revolutions."

Chapter 5: Insiders and Outsiders

1. See interview with Prime Minister George Papandreou, *CNN Money*, January 28, 2011, http://www.cnn.com/2011/BUSINESS/01/28/greece.prime. minister.davos/index.html?eref=rss_latest&utm_source=feedburner&utm_ medium=feed&utm_campaign=Feed%3A+rss%2Fcnn_latest+%28RSS%3A +Most+Recent%29.

2. Jürgen Habermas, *The Crisis of the European Union: A Response* (Cambridge: Polity, 2012), 52.

3. Gregory Viscusi, "French senators get lessons in the realities of business," *International Herald Tribune*, October 18, 2006, http://www. nytimes.com/2006/10/18/business/worldbusiness/18iht-senate.3207045.html.

4. See Charles Murray, *Coming Apart: The State of White America, 1960–2010* (New York: Crown Forum, 2012), 46–68.

5. See Patience Wheatcroft, "No breaching the Eurocrats' Paywall," *The Wall Street Journal*, November 25, 2010, http://online.wsj.com/article/SB10001424052748703572404575634940075930992.html.

6. See Takis Michas, "Greece's Bailout Brinkmanship," *The Wall Street Journal*, June 21, 2011, http://online.wsj.com/article/SB1000142405270230382310457639152270884I218.html?mod=WSJ_Opinion_LEFTTopOpinion

7. See Marcus Walker and Alkman Granitsas, "Germany Insists on Greek Budget Controls," *The Wall Street Journal*, February 1, 2012, http://online.wsj.com/article/SB10001424052970204740904577195180019183416.html?mod=googlenews_wsj.

8. See Kerin Hope, "Greek parliament debates austerity bill," *Financial Times*, February 12, 2012, http://www.ft.com/intl/cms/s/0/cdf94132-5578-11e1-9d95-00144feabdc0.html#axzz1mJiVy9iK.

9. See Brian Carney, "Fear and loathing in Athens," *The Wall Street Journal*, February 14, 2012, http://online.wsj.com/article/SB10001424052970204795304577221100541160824.html?mod=WSJ_Opinion_LEFTTopBucket.

10. Hans-Jürgen Schlamp, "A Dream Job with a Cash Guarantee," *Der Spiegel*, September 24, 2010, http://www.spiegel.de/international/europe/0,1518,719450,00.html.

11. Ibid.

12. Theodore Dalrymple, "Austerity in the U.K.," *City Journal* 21 (3), 2001, http://city-journal.org/2011/21_3_otbie-uk-govt-spending.html.

13. See Zoé Shepard, *Absolument dé-bor-dée! ou le paradoxe du fonctionnaire—Comment faire les 35 heures en . . . un mois !* (Paris: Albin Michel, 2010).

14. See, for example, Ruben Vives, "Bell council seeks resignations of 3 city officials," *Los Angeles Times*, July 21, 2010, http://www.latimes.com/news/local/la-me-721-bell-20100721,0,3475382.story.

15. See Delphine Chayet, "Une haute fonctionnaire poursuivie pour un pamphlet," *Le Figaro*, July 2, 2010, http://www.lefigaro.fr/

actualite-france/2010/07/01/01016-20100701ARTFIG00696-une-haute-fonctionnaire-poursuivie-pour-un-pamphlet.php.

16. See Roger Cohen, "Divided We Grumble: Europe's Loss of Focus," *International Herald Tribune*, June 9, 2004.

17. See Emmanuel Martin, "Paris vs. Reality: The French government proposes austerity for everyone except the state," *The Wall Street Journal*, August 31, 2011, http://online.wsj.com/article/SB1000142405 311190419940457653824261650016.html?mod=WSJEUROPE_hpp_ MIDDLEFourthNews.

18. See Bureau of the Census, "2010 Public Employment and Payroll Data State Governments," in *2010 Annual Survey of Public Employment and Payroll*, http://www2.census.gov/govs/apes/10stus.txt.

19. See Bureau of the Census, "2010 Public Employment and Payroll Data Local Governments," in *2010 Annual Survey of Public Employment and Payroll*, http://www2.census.gov/govs/apes/10locus.txt.

20. See Arthur Brooks, "Slouching Towards Athens: The Obama agenda and the Europeanization of America," *The Wall Street Journal*, June 25, 2010, http://online.wsj.com/article/SB10001424052748704764404 57528645165310987 6.html?mod=WSJ_hp_mostpop_read.

21. Siedentop, *Democracy in Europe*, 135–6.

22. Cited in Karim Tadjeddine, "'A duty to modernize': Reforming the French civil service," *McKinsey Quarterly*, April 2010, http://www. mckinseyquarterly.com/Public_Sector/Government_Regulation/A_duty_ to_modernize_Reforming_the_French_civil_service_2780.

23. Department for Business, Innovation and Skills, *Trade Union Membership 2009* (London: BIS, 2009), http://stats.bis.gov.uk/UKSA/tu/ TUM2009.pdf.

24. OECD, *Trade union density in OECD countries, 1960–2011*. Online OECD employment database, http://www.oecd.org/employment/ labourstatistics/onlineoecdemploymentdatabase.htm#union. For the decline in union membership, see Gill and Raiser, *Golden Growth*, 295.

25. See "The Battle Ahead," *The Economist*, January 6, 2011, http:// www.economist.com/node/17851305.

26. See "Public Sector Workers: (Government) Workers of the World Unite!," *The Economist*, January 6, 2011, http://www.economist.com/node/17849199.

27. See Alberto Alesina and Francesco Giavazzi, *The Future of Europe: Reform or Decline* (Cambridge, MA: MIT Press, 2008), 58.

28. "Surrender, Italian Style: The unions water down Monti's labor reforms," *The Wall Street Journal*, April 6, 2012, http://online.wsj.com/article/SB10001424052702303299960457732590281624654.html?mod=WSJ_Opinion_AboveLEFTTop. See also Christopher Emsden, "Italy Official Seeks Culture Shift in New Law," *The Wall Street Journal*, June 27, 2012, http://online.wsj.com/article/SB1000142405270230487030457749080387 4875894.html?mod=WSJ_hps_LEFTTopStories.

29. See Mark Landler, "Volkswagen Corruption Trial Includes Seamy Testimony," *The New York Times*, January 16, 2008, http://www.nytimes.com/2008/01/16/business/16bribe.html.

30. See Eichengreen, *The European Economy*, 401; and Ricardo J. Caballero, Kevin Cowan, Eduardo Engel, and Alejandro Micco, "Effective Labor Regulation and Microeconomic Flexibility," NBER Working Paper No. 10744, 2004.

31. See Gill and Raiser, *Golden Growth*, 175.

32. See Gregory Viscusi and Mark Deen, "Why France Has So Many 49-Employee Companies," *BloombergBusinessWeek*, May 3, 2012, http://www.businessweek.com/articles/2012-05-03/why-france-has-so-many-49-employee-companies. The *Code du Travail* may be found at http://www.legifrance.gouv.fr/affichCode.do?cidTexte=LEGITEXT000006072050&dateTexte=20120502.

33. See Eurostat, "April 2012: Euro area unemployment rate at 11.0%," 81/2012–1 June 2012, http://epp.eurostat.ec.europa.eu/cache/ITY_PUBLIC/3-01062012-AP/EN/3-01062012-AP-EN.PDF.

34. See Fiona Govan, "Spain's lost generation: youth unemployment surges above 50 per cent," *Daily Telegraph*, January 30, 2012, http://www.telegraph.co.uk/news/worldnews/europe/spain/9044897/Spains-lost-generation-youth-unemployment-surges-above-50-per-cent.html.

35. See Mathieu von Rohr and Helene Zuber, "The Rage of the 'Indignants': A European Generation Takes to the Streets," *Der Spiegel*, June 7, 2011, http://www.spiegel.de/international/europe/0,1518,767032,00.html.

36. See Gill and Raiser, *Golden Growth*, 292.

37. See "Spain's economy: split personality," *The Economist*, July 9, 2011, http://www.economist.com/node/18929032.

38. Gill and Raiser, *Golden Growth*, 274.

39. See, for example, Katharina Peters, "Spanish Youth Part of the Lost Generation," *Der Spiegel*, August 6, 2010, http://www.spiegel.de/international/europe/0,1518,699467,00.html.

40. See "Q&A: ECB President Mario Draghi," *The Wall Street Journal*, February 23, 2012, http://blogs.wsj.com/eurocrisis/2012/02/23/qa-ecb-president-mario-draghi/.

41. See Samuel Gregg, "Europe's Not-So-Revolutionary Youth," *American Spectator*, June 22, 2011, http://spectator.org/archives/2011/06/22/europes-not-so-revolutionary-y/.

42. See Wolfgang Kasper and Manfred E. Streit, *Institutional Economics: Social Order and Public Policy* (Cheltenham, UK: Edward Elgar, 1998), 326.

43. See Alesina and Giavazzi, *The Future of Europe*, 80.

44. Ibid., 127–128.

45. See, for example, Brian Riedl, *Still at the Federal Trough: Farm Subsidies for the Rich and Famous Shattered Records in 2001*, Heritage Foundation Backgrounder #1542, 2002, http://www.heritage.org/Research/Reports/2002/04/Farm-Subsidies-for-the-Rich-amp-Famous-Shattered-Records-in-2001.

46. See, for example, Timothy P. Carney, "Obama's green subsidies attract do-gooder bandits," *Washington Examiner*, February 27, 2011, http://washingtonexaminer.com/obamas-green-subsidies-attract-do-gooder-bandits/article/111008#.UHCMSK7Z2So; and "Haley Barbour and corporate welfare," *Washington Examiner*, February 22, 2011, http://washingtonexaminer.com/haley-barbour-and-corporate-welfare/article/141216.

47. See, for instance, Timothy P. Carney, "Immelt, Daley, and Obama's antipathy to free markets," *Washington Examiner*, January 23, 2011, http://washingtonexaminer.com/immelt-daley-and-obamas-antipathy-to-free-markets/article/109710. See also Jeff Gerth and Brady Dennis, "How a Loophole Benefits GE in Bank Rescue: Industrial Giant Becomes Top Recipient in Debt-Guarantee Program," *The Washington Post*, June 29, 2009, http://www.washingtonpost.com/wp-dyn/content/article/2009/06/28/AR2009062802955_pf.html.

48. See Alesina and Giavazzi, *The Future of Europe*, 84.

49. See "Can anything perk up Europe?" *The Economist*, July 10, 2010, http://www.economist.com/node/16539326.

50. See European Commission, *Entrepreneurship in the EU and Beyond*, 2009.

51. See "State aid: Commission adopts new state aid Framework for Research, Development and Innovation," November 22, 2006, http://europa.eu/rapid/pressReleasesAction.do?reference=IP/06/1600&type=HTML&aged=0&language=EN&guiLanguage=en.

52. Gill and Raiser, *Golden Growth*, 49.

53. See Tocqueville, *Democracy in America*, 625–626.

Chapter 6: Soft Despotism

1. *Stenographische Berichte über die Verhandlungen des Reichstages*, Bd. 075, 05.Legislaturperiode 04.Session 1884, 9. Sitzung am Donnerstag, 20.03.1884, 165.

2. See Gill and Raiser, *Golden Growth*, 21.

3. See James Bartholomew, *The Welfare State We're In* (London: Politico's Publishing, 2004), 50–52.

4. See J. McGowan, *American Liberalism: An interpretation for our time* (Chapel Hill, NC: North Carolina University Press, 2007).

5. Tocqueville, *Democracy in America*, 692.

6. See Dudley Baines, Neil Cummins, and Max-Stephan Schulze, "Population and Living Standards," in Stephen Broadberry and Kevin

O'Rourke, eds., *The Cambridge Economic History of Modern Europe*, Vol. 2, *1870 to the Present* (Cambridge: CUP, 2010), 394.

7. See the country list at the OECD website at http://www.oecd.org/countrieslist/0,3351,en_33873108_33844430_1_1_1_1_1,00.html.

8. See Alesina and Giavazzi, *The Future of Europe*, 7 and 17.

9. See P. H. Lindert, *Growing Public: Social Spending and Economic Growth Since the Eighteenth-Century* (Cambridge University Press, 2004), 20.

10. See the countries list at the OECD website at http://www.oecd.org.

11. See Gill and Raiser, *Golden Growth*, 331.

12. See Oskari Juurikkala, *Pensions, Population, and Prosperity* (Grand Rapids, MI: Acton Institute, 2007), 13.

13. See Gill and Raiser, *Golden Growth*, 21.

14. Ibid., 21.

15. See Edward Cody, "Europeans shift long-held view that social benefits are untouchable," *The Washington Post*, April 24, 2011, http://www.washingtonpost.com/world/europeans-shift-long-held-view-that-social-benefits-are-untouchable/2011/02/09/AFLdYzdE_story.html.

16. See Court of Justice of the European Union Judgment in Case C-78/11, Luxembourg, June 21, 2012, http://curia.europa.eu/juris/document/document.jsf?text=&docid=124190&pageIndex=0&doclang=en&mode=req&dir=&occ=first&part=1&cid=4288828.

17. See Juurikkala, *Pensions, Population, and Prosperity*, 17.

18. See Bartholomew, *The Welfare State We're In*, 65.

19. See Juurikkala, *Pensions, Population, and Prosperity*, 18.

20. See Jonathan Gruber and David Wise, "Social Security Programs and Retirement around the World: Fiscal Implications. Introduction and Summary," NBER Working Paper No. 11290, 2005.

21. See, for example, Alesina and Giavazzi, *The Future of Europe*, 6–7.

22. Baines, Cummins, and Schulze, "Population and Living Standards," 396–7.

23. Wilhelm Röpke, "Robbing Peter to pay Paul: on the nature of the welfare state," reprinted in Röpke, *Against the Tide*, 204.

24. See Bartholomew, *The Welfare State We're In*, 314.

25. Wilhelm Röpke, *A Humane Economy: The Social Framework of the Free Market*, trans. Elizabeth Henderson (Wilmington DE: ISI Books, 1998), 167.

26. Wilhelm Röpke, *Civitas Humana: A Humane Order of Society*, trans. C. S. Fox (London: William Hodge and Company, 1948), 147.

27. Röpke, "Robbing Peter to pay Paul," 206.

28. "Staring into the Abyss," *The Economist*, July 8, 2010, http://www.economist.com/node/16536898?story_id=16536898&fsrc=rss.

29. See Cody, "Europeans shift long-held view that social benefits are untouchable."

30. Röpke, *Civitas Humana*, 94.

31. Peter Sloterdijk, "Die Revolution der gebenden Hand," *Frankfurter Allgemeine*, June 13, 2009, http://www.faz.net/artikel/C30717/die-zukunft-des-kapitalismus-8-die-revolution-der-gebenden-hand-30074630.html.

32. See Cody, "Europeans shift long-held view that social benefits are untouchable."

33. See James Shields, *The Extreme Right in France: From Pétain to Le Pen* (London: Routledge, 2007), 272.

34. Russell Shorto, "Marine Le Pen: Is this the most dangerous woman in France?," *Observer*, June 26, 2011, http://www.guardian.co.uk/world/2011/jun/26/marine-le-pen-far-right.

35. See Timo Soini, "Työväenpuolue ilman sosialismia," *Helsingin Kokoomus*, August 14, 2010, http://www.helsinginkokoomus.fi/sitenews/view/-/nid/6506/ngid/12/.

36. All the figures for the preceding three paragraphs may be found at the OECD Tax Database, http://www.oecd.org/document/60/0,3746, en_2649_34533_1942460_1_1_1_1,00.html#pir.

37. All these figures for average wage earnings may be found at the OECD's Center for Tax Policy and Administration, http://www.oecd.org/ctp/taxpolicyanalysis/taxingwages.htm.

38. Gill and Raiser, *Golden Growth*, 52.

39. See David Wessel, "The Numbers Inside a Hot-Button Issue," *The Wall Street Journal*, August 5, 2012, http://online.wsj.com/article/SB 10000872396390444246904577571042249868040.html?mod=WSJ_hpp_ LEFTTopStories. The same article illustrates that when it comes to the top 5 percent of earners' share of income and taxes, they averaged 22.6% of income and paid 28.5% of taxes in the 1980s; 25.3% of income and 34.3% of taxes in the 1990s; and 28.4% of the income and 40.3% of the taxes in the 2000s. As Wessel notes, this does not mean that the better-off are living on less. In raw dollars, they are both earning more and paying more taxes.

40. Ibid.

41. Paul Hannon, "Odds Stacked Against Latest EU Pact," *The Wall Street Journal*, February 15, 2011, http://online.wsj.com/article/SB100014 24052748703584804576144230148510492.html?mod=WSJEurope_hpp_ MIDDLETopStories.

42. See Alberto Alesina, Dorian Carloni, and Giampaolo Lecce, "The Electoral Consequences of Large Fiscal Adjustments" (October 2010), http://www.economics.harvard.edu/faculty/alesina/files/Electoral%2 BConseq%2Bof%2BLge%2BFiscal%2BAdjust.pdf.

43. See Paul R. Ehrlich, *The Population Bomb* (New York: Ballantine Books, 1968), 1.

44. Karl Gunnar Persson, *An Economic History of Europe: Knowledge, Institutions and Growth, 600 to the Present* (Cambridge: CUP, 2010), 54–56.

45. See Baines, Cummins, and Schulze, "Population and Living Standards," 404–406.

46. Ibid., 404–407.

47. United Nations Department of Economic and Social Affairs, Population Division, *World Population Prospects: The 2010 Revision*, CD-ROM Edition (2011).

48. Ibid.

49. Ibid.

50. Ibid.

51. Ibid.

52. See "Europe's other crisis: recession is bringing Europe's brief fertility rally to a shuddering halt," *The Economist*, June 30, 2012, http://www.economist.com/node/21557774.

53. See "Virility symbols: American fertility is now lower than that of France," *The Economist*, August 11, 2012, http://www.economist.com/node/21560266.

54. See Nicholas Eberstadt, "The Demographic Implosion," *Foreign Affairs* 89, no. 6 (2010), 62.

55. See Gill and Raiser, *Golden Growth*, 314.

56. Ibid., 23.

57. Jean-Claude Chesnais, *Le crépuscle de l'Occident* (Paris: Laffont, 1995), 61.

58. See Gabriel Stein, "The Economic, Political and Financial Implications of Ageing Populations," *Economic Affairs* 28, no. 1 (2008), 24.

59. See Gill and Raiser, *Golden Growth*, 280.

60. John Maynard Keynes, "Some economic consequences of a declining population," *Eugenics Review*, 29, no. 1 (1937), 16.

61. Ettore Gotti Tedeschi, "Faced with deflationary prospects: A new model of leadership," *L'Osservatore Romano*, November 4, 2011, http://www.osservatoreromano.va/portal/dt?JSPTabContainer.setSelected=JSPTabContainer%2FDetail&last=false=&path=/news/editoriali/2011/254q11-Un-nuovo-modello-di-leadership.html&title=A%20new%20model%20of%20leadership&locale=en.

62. Stein, "The Economic, Political and Financial Implications of Ageing Populations," 24.

63. See Gill and Raiser, *Golden Growth*, 356.

64. Stein, "The Economic, Political and Financial Implications of Ageing Populations," 25.

65. Ibid., 24.

66. Ibid.

67. Ibid.

68. Michel Schooyans, *Le Crash Démographique* (Paris: Fayard, 1999), 42.

69. See Eberstadt, "The Demographic Implosion," 62–63.

70. See Schooyans, *Le Crash Démographique*, 25–28.

71. See Michele Boldrin, Mariacristina De Nardi, and Larry E. Jones, "Fertility and Social Security," NBER Working Paper No. 11146, 2005, www.nber.org/papers/w11146.

72. See Issac Ehrlich and Jinyoung Kin, "Social Security and Demographic Trends: Theory and Evidence from the International Experience," *Review of Economic Dynamics*, 10, no. 1 (2007): 55–77.

73. See Jeffrey B. Nugent, "The Old Age Security Motive for Fertility," *Population and Development Review* 11, no. 1 (1985): 75–98.

74. Juurikkala, *Pensions, Population, and Prosperity*, 36.

75. Baines, Cummins, and Schulze, "Population and Living Standards," 404–415.

76. Philip Booth, "Review: The Political Economy of Social Security in Aging Societies," *Economic Affairs* 28, no. 1 (2008), 83.

77. See von Rohr and Zuber, "The Rage of the 'Indignants'," http://www.spiegel.de/international/europe/0,1518,767032,00.html.

78. See Philip Booth, "Held to Ransom—A Public Choice Analysis of the UK State Pension System," *Economic Affairs* 28, no. 1 (2008): 4–5.

79. See ibid., 8.

80. This scenario is outlined in Nicholas Misoulis, "Demographic Effects on Economic Growth and the Consequences for the Provision of Pensions," *Economic Affairs* 28, no. 1 (2008): 29–34.

81. See Booth, "Held to Ransom," 9.

82. See "Reforming Zapatero," *The Economist*, February 5, 2011, http://www.economist.com/node/18073408.

83. See Gill and Raiser, *Golden Growth*, 364.

84. Office of Management and Budget, *Fiscal Year 2012: Historical Tables—Budget of the US Government*, 48, http://www.whitehouse.gov/sites/default/files/omb/budget/fy2012/assets/hist.pdf. This figure includes Social Security; Medicare; Education, Training, Employment, and Social

Services; Health; Income Security; and Veteran's Benefits and Services. Education includes grants for higher, secondary, and primary education. This amounted to 3.6 percent of overall spending in human resources in 2009. See ibid., 55.

85. Ibid., 51.

86. Ibid., 55.

87. Ibid., 50.

88. Ibid., 55.

89. Ibid.

90. Nicholas Eberstadt, "A Nation of Takers: America's Entitlement Epidemic," August 2012, http://www.templetonpress.org/book/nation-takers.

91. William Beach and Patrick Tyrrell, *The 2012 Index of Dependence on Government* (Washington, DC: Heritage Foundation, 2012), http://www.heritage.org/research/reports/2012/02/2012-index-of-dependence-on-government.

92. See Robert Rector, "Obama's attack on 'Workfare'," *National Review Online*, August 8, 2012, http://www.nationalreview.com/articles/313350/obama-s-attack-workfare-robert-rector.

93. This is drawn from Eberstadt's analysis of the disability payment data in "A Nation of Takers," August 2012. His source is U.S. Social Security Administration, *Annual Statistical Report on the Social Security Disability Insurance Program, 2011, Disabled Beneficiaries and Nondisabled Dependents*, Table 1: Number, December 1960–2011, selected years, http://www.ssa.gov.

94. Ibid.

95. Beach and Tyrrell, *2012 Index of Dependence on Government*.

96. See David Wessel, "The Numbers Inside a Hot-Button Issue."

97. Congressional Budget Office, *Long-Term Analysis of Plan 2 of the President's Commission to Strengthen Social Security*, July 21, 2004, 5, http://www.cbo.gov/ftpdocs/56xx/doc5666/07-21-CraigLetterUpdated.pdf.

98. See Congressional Budget Office, *The Budget and Economic Outlook: Fiscal Years 2012 to 2022*, January 2012, Appendix D, 122, http://www.cbo.gov/ftpdocs/126xx/doc12699/01-31-2012_Outlook.pdf.

99. Peter Ferrara, "America's Expanding Welfare Empire," *Forbes*, April 22, 2011, http://blogs.forbes.com/peterferrara/2011/04/22/americas-ever-expanding-welfare-empire/.

100. See Neil King Jr. and Scott Greenberg, "Poll Shows Budget-Cuts Dilemma," *The Wall Street Journal*, March 3, 2011, http://online.wsj.com/article/SB10001424052748704728004576176741120691736.html.

101. Robert Samuelson, "Welfare State Stasis," *The Washington Post*, February 14, 2007, http://www.washingtonpost.com/wp-dyn/content/article/2007/02/13/AR2007021301091.html.

102. See Robert Samuelson, "Who Rules America? The AARP," *Real Clear Politics*, February 21, 2011, http://www.realclearpolitics.com/articles/2011/02/21/who_rules_america_the_aarp_108960.html.

103. Samuelson, "Welfare State Stasis."

104. See Robert W. Fairle, *Kauffman Index on Entrepreneurial Activity 1996–2010* (Kansas City: Ewing Marion Kauffman Foundation, 2011), http://www.kauffman.org/uploadedFiles/KIEA_2011_report.pdf.

105. These figures are taken from United Nations Department of Economic and Social Affairs, *World Population Policies 2005* (New York: United Nations, 2006). They involve some approximation for illegal immigrants who are, by definition, difficult to count.

106. Felix Gilbert and David Clay Large, *The End of the European Era, 1890 to the Present* (New York, W.W. Norton and Company, 2009), 549.

107. Esther Ben-David, "Europe's Shifting Immigration Dynamic," *Middle East Quarterly* Spring (2009), 16, http://www.meforum.org/2107/europe-shifting-immigration-dynamic.

108. Ibid., 18.

109. See Gill and Raiser, *Golden Growth*, 309.

110. See Alesina and Giavazzi, *The Future of Europe*, 35.

III. See, for example, B. R. Chiswick, "The Effect of Americanization on the earnings of foreign-born men," *Journal of Political Economy* 86, no. 5 (1978): 897–921; and Gill and Raiser, *Golden Growth*, 309.

112. See Gill and Raiser, *Golden Growth*, 316.

113. See Yann Algan, Christian Dustmann, Albrecht Glitz, and Alan Manning, "The economic situation of first and second-generation immigrants in France, Germany and the United Kingdom," *The Economic Journal* 129, February (2010): F4–F30.

114. See Gill and Raiser, *Golden Growth*, 295.

115. See Richard Boudreaux and Paulo Prada, "Exodus of Workers From Continent Reverses Old Patterns," *The Wall Street Journal*, January 14, 2012, http://online.wsj.com/article/SB10001424052970203550304577137174048327642.html?mod=WSJ_hps_editorsPicks_3; and Geoffrey Rogow and James Glynn, "Australia's Booming Economy and Shortage of Workers Attract Greeks," *The Wall Street Journal*, January 14, 2012, http://online.wsj.com/article/SB10001424052970203899504577127821001713042.html.

Chapter 7: Deficits, Debt, and Deception

1. David Marsh, *The Euro: The Politics of the New Global Currency* (New Haven: Yale University Press, 2009), 40.

2. See ibid., 126–128.

3. See Articles 104 and 121 of the Treaty of Maastricht, http://eur-lex.europa.eu/LexUriServ/LexUriServ.do?uri=CELEX:11997E104:EN:NOT, and http://eur-lex.europa.eu/LexUriServ/LexUriServ.do?uri=CELEX:12002E121:en:HTML.

4. See Article 123 of the Treaty of Lisbon, http://www.lisbon-treaty.org/wcm/the-lisbon-treaty/treaty-on-the-functioning-of-the-european-union-and-comments/part-3-union-policies-and-internal-actions/title-viii-economic-and-monetary-policy/chapter-1-economic-policy/391-article-123.html.

5. See Christopher Caldwell, "Euro Trashed: Europe's rendezvous with monetary destiny," *Weekly Standard* 16, no. 14 (2010), http://www.weeklystandard.com/articles/euro-trashed_522123.html.

6. "Greece admits fudging euro entry," *BBC*, November 15, 2004, http://news.bbc.co.uk/2/hi/business/4012869.stm.

7. José Manuel González-Páramo, "The reform of the Stability and Growth Pact: an assessment," conference on New Perspectives on Fiscal Sustainability, Frankfurt, October 13, 2005, http://www.ecb.int/press/key/date/2005/html/sp051013.en.html.

8. "EU states accused of 'hiding' deficits," *Financial Times*, October 6, 2005.

9. Andrei Khalip, "Portugal opposition says deficit underestimated," *Reuters*, November 21, 2010, http://uk.reuters.com/article/2010/11/21/uk-portugal-opposition-deficit-idUKTRE6AK0QZ20101121.

10. "The Lisbon Irony: Europe's growth problems aren't the fault of central bankers," *The Wall Street Journal*, April 7, 2011. http://online.wsj.com/article/SB10001424052748704013604576248803314545230.html?mod=WSJ_Opinion_AboveLEFTTop.

11. Alesina and Giavazzi, *The Future of Europe*, 155.

12. See Antonis Kamaras, "The Origins of the Greek Financial Crisis," *Foreign Affairs*, December 13, 2011, http://www.foreignaffairs.com/features/letters-from/the-origins-of-the-greek-financial-crisis.

13. See Robert Samuelson, "Europe at the Abyss," *Real Clear Politics*, May 30, 2010, http://www.realclearpolitics.com/articles/2011/05/30/europe_at_the_abyss_110025.html.

14. Ibid.

15. See ibid.

16. "Germany and the euro: We don't want no transfer union," *The Economist*, December 4, 2010, http://www.economist.com/node/17632957.

17. See Andrew Willis, "Van Rompuy: Eurozone will bail out Greece if needed," *EU Observer*, February 12, 2010.

18. See Andrew Willis, "Merkel: Spain can access aid if needed," *EU Observer*, June 15, 2010.

19. Andrew Willis, "Plans emerge for 'European monetary fund'," *EU Observer*, August 2, 2010.

20. See Samuel Gregg, "Truth, Lies and Euros," *American Spectator*, June 8, 2011, http://spectator.org/archives/2011/06/08/truth-lies-and-euros; and Patricia Kowsmann, "Portugal Spending Cuts Questioned," *The Wall Street Journal*, May 25, 2011, http://online.wsj.com/article/SB100 014240527023040665045763452401041119096.html?mod=WSJEUROPE_ newsreel_world.

21. Wolfgang Münchau, "A grand bargain that cannot end the crisis," *Financial Times*, March 28, 2011, 9.

22. See Oliver Marc Hartwich, "A plan that will damage Europe," *Business Spectator*, March 17, 2011, http://www.cis.org.au/media-information/opinion-pieces/article/2515-a-plan-that-will-damage-europe%3E%C2%A0.

23. See Charles Forell, Patricia Kowsmann, and Costas Paris, "Greece Gets New Bailout as U.S. Nears Brink," *The Wall Street Journal*, July 22, 2011, http://online.wsj.com/article/SB1000142405311190355490457645931 0597648944.html.

24. "Emergency Repairs," *The Economist*, May 11, 2010, http://www.economist.com/node/16106575.

25. See European Central Bank, "Objective of monetary policy," http://www.ecb.int/mopo/intro/objective/html/index.en.html.

26. See Hugh Carnegy, "Hollande calls for ECB growth mandate," *Financial Times*, March 18, 2012, http://www.ft.com/intl/cms/s/0/ f82369ee-70f1-11e1-a7f1-00144feab49a.html?ftcamp=published_links/rss/ ftfm_investment-strategy/feed//product#axzz1pUmsPTsA.

27. "France Versus the ECB," *The Wall Street Journal*, April 16, 2012, http://online.wsj.com/article/SB10001424052702304432704577347720195 376872.html

28. John Taylor, "Central banks are losing credibility," *Financial Times*, May 11, 2010, http://www.ft.com/intl/cms/s/0/eedbe85c-5d2a-11df-8373-00144feab49a.html#ax.

29. See "Interview mit Bundesbankpräsident Axel Weber," *Börsen-Zeitung*, May 11, 2010.

30. "Emergency Repairs," *The Economist*.

31. See "Top German quits ECB over bond-buying row," *Reuters*, September 9, 2011, http://www.reuters.com/article/2011/09/09/us-ecb-stark-idUSTRE7883DF20110909.

32. Jean-Claude Trichet, "Building Europe, building institutions," (speech on receiving the Karlspreis 2011, Aachen, June 2, 2011), http://www.ecb.int/press/key/date/2011/html/sp110602.en.html.

33. "Russian or Belgian roulette?," *The Economist*, July 21, 2011, http://www.economist.com/blogs/charlemagne/2011/07/euro-zone-crisis-summit.

34. See Alexandra Hudson and Christian Plumb, "Euro states must give EU more power: German finance minister," *Reuters*, November 12, 2011, http://mobile.reuters.com/article/idUSTRE7AB0IA20111112?irpc=932.

35. See David Román, "Spain Parties Signal Change on Deficit," *The Wall Street Journal*, August 23, 2011, http://online.wsj.com/article/SB10001424053111903327904576525963452423284.html?mod=WSJEUROPE_hpp_MIDDLETopNews.

36. See Pablo Domínguez and David Román, "Controversy Spices Up Spain's Autumn of Discontent," *The Wall Street Journal*, August 24, 2011, http://blogs.wsj.com/source/2011/08/24/constitution-controversy-spices-up-spains-autumn-of-discontent/.

37. See Irwin Stelzer, "Europe's Not Playing Ball With Merkel," *The Wall Street Journal*, February 7, 2011, http://online.wsj.com/article/SB10001424052748704858404576127960989229174.html?mod=WSJEurope_hpp_LEFTTopStories; and Barry Eichengreen, "An Ever Closer Union," *Foreign Policy*, February 7, 2011, http://www.foreignpolicy.com/articles/2011/02/07/an_ever_closer_union.

38. See Irwin Stelzer, "Prepare for a European Union Divided in Two," *The Wall Street Journal*, March 21, 2010, http://online.wsj.com/article/SB10001424052748704433904576212331884145752.html?mod=WSJEurope_hpp_LEFTTopStories.

39. See "The divisiveness pact," *The Economist*, March 12, 2011, http://www.economist.com/node/18330371.

40. Marcus Walker, "Budget Treaty: Neither Panacea Nor Poison," *The Wall Street Journal*, January 31, 2012, http://online.wsj.com/article/SB10001424052970203920204577193020562230202.html.

41. See *Treaty on Stability, Coordination and Governance in the Economic and Monetary Union* (2012), paragraph 3, http://www.european-council.europa.eu/media/579087/treaty.pdf.

42. See William Boston, David Roman, and Gabriele Parussini, "EU Leaders Sign Fiscal Pact," *The Wall Street Journal*, March 2, 2012, http://online.wsj.com/article/SB10001424052970203986604577256862951941608.html. Eventually, Spain negotiated a compromise. The very fact, however, that there was a negotiation raised questions about whether the new rules were actually rules, or simply starting points for further discussion. See Victor Mallet, "Spain wins more time for deficit cuts," *Financial Times*, March 13, 2012, http://www.ft.com/intl/cms/s/0/8d188386-6d05-11e1-ab1a-00144feab49a.html#axzz1poRQ2eNC.

43. See William Boston, Laurence Norman, and Matina Stevis, "Germany Pushes for EU Budget Control Over Greece," *The Wall Street Journal*, January 28, 2012, http://online.wsj.com/article/SB10001424052970204573704577189061997582228.html.

44. Cited in Walker and Granitsas, "Germany Insists on Greek Budget Controls."

45. See ibid.

46. See Office of Management and Budget, *Fiscal Year 2012*, 21–23.

47. See Department of the Treasury, "The Debt to the Penny and Who Holds It," http://www.treasurydirect.gov/NP/BPDLogin?application=np. This figure is constantly updated.

48. See Congressional Budget Office, *Budget and Economic Outlook: An Update*, August 2011, http://www.cbo.gov/ftpdocs/123xx/doc12316/Update_SummaryforWeb.pdf.

49. See Congressional Budget Office, *The Budget and Economic Outlook: Fiscal Years 2012 to 2022*, January 2012, http://www.cbo.gov/doc.cfm?index=12699.

50. See Congressional Budget Office, *The 2012 Long-Term Budget Outlook*, June 5, 2012, http://www.cbo.gov/publication/43288.

51. Congressional Budget Office, *An Update to the Budget and Economic Outlook: Fiscal Years 2012 to 2022*, August 22, 2012, http://www.cbo.gov/publication/43539.

52. See Carmen M. Reinhart and Kenneth S. Rogoff, "Growth in a Time of Debt," *American Economic Review* 100, no. 2 (2010): 573–78, http://www.nber.org/papers/w15639.

53. See Manmohan S. Kumar and Jaejoon Woo, "Public Debt and Growth," *IMF Working Paper 10/174* (Washington, DC: IMF, 2010), 2, http://www.imf.org/external/pubs/ft/wp/2010/wp10174.pdf.

54. See CBO, *Budget and Economic Outlook: Fiscal Years 2012 to 2022*.

55. See Mehmet Caner, Thomas Grennes, and Fritzi Koehler-Geib, "Finding the Tipping Point: When Sovereign Debt Turns Bad," *Policy Research Working Paper 5391* (Washington, DC: World Bank, 2010), 11, http://siteresources.worldbank.org/INTDEBTDEPT/Resourc es/468980-1238442914363/5969985-1295539401520/ 9780821384831_ch03.pdf.

56. See Stephen G. Cecchetti, M. S. Mohanty, and Fabrizio Zampolli, "The Real Effects of Debt," Bank for International Settlements paper prepared for symposium sponsored by the Federal Reserve Bank of Kansas City, Jackson Hole, Wyoming, August 25–27, 2011, http://www.bis.org/publ/othp16.pdf.

57. Martin Feldstein, "Europe Needs the Bond Vigilantes," *The Wall Street Journal*, April 4, 2012, http://online.wsj.com/article/SB1000 14240527023034047045773060139799928438.html?mod=WSJ_Opinion_ LEFTTopOpinion.

58. In 2012, projections for gross federal spending were estimated to be 57 percent of all government expenditures (http://www.usgovernmentspending.com/total_2012USrt_13rs5n). Direct federal revenues were estimated to be 49 percent of all government revenues (http://www.usgovernmentrevenue.com/total_2012USrt_13rs5n).

59. See, for example, Tami Luhby, "Bailing out the states: How it will work," *CNN Money,* January 29, 2009, http://money.cnn.com/2009/01/29/news/economy/help_for_states/index.htm.

60. See Gill and Raiser, *Golden Growth*, 24.

61. Paul Hannon, "Amid EU's Open Borders, Workers Stay Put," *The Wall Street Journal*, July 5, 2011, http://online.wsj.com/article/SB10001424052702304803104576425793648428566.html?mod=WSJEurope_hpp_MIDDLETopStories.

62. Ibid.

63. See Gill and Raiser, *Golden Growth*, 23.

64. Ibid., 23.

65. Willem F. Duisenberg, acceptance speech, International Charlemagne Prize of Aachen for 2002, May 9, 2002, http://www.ecb.int/press/key/date/2002/html/sp020509.en.html.

Chapter 8: Globalization: The Last Frontier

1. Anthony Browne, "We cannot hide. EU must accept globalisation or we are nothing," *London Times*, October 24, 2005.

2. See Owen Fletcher, "EU Aims to Seal Deal With Beijing," *The Wall Street Journal*, January 7, 2011, http://online.wsj.com/article/SB10001424052748704415104576065384259344432.html?mod=googlenews_wsj.

3. Annalyn Censky, "Foreigners bought more U.S. debt in November," *CNN Money*, January 18, 2011, http://money.cnn.com/2011/01/18/markets/bondcenter/treasuries/index.htm?iid=EL.

4. For a sketch of this scenario, see Dambisa Moyo, *How the West Was Lost: Fifty Years of Economic Folly and the Stark Choices Ahead* (New York: Farrar, Straus and Giroux, 2010), 190–191.

5. Adam Smith, *An Inquiry into the Nature and Causes of the Wealth of Nations*, reprinted in R. H. Campbell and A. S. Skinner, eds., *The Glasgow Edition of the Works and Correspondence of Adam Smith*, vol. 2 (Indianapolis IN: Liberty Fund, 1776/1981), Book IV.iii.c, 11–12.

6. Ibid., Book IV.ii, 12.

7. Wilhelm Röpke, *L'économie mondiale aux XIXe et XXe siècles* (Genève: Publication de l'institut universitaire de hautes études internationales, 1959), 11–27.

8. Wilhelm Röpke, "European free trade—the great divide," *The Banker* September (1958), 12.

9. Ibid., 17.

10. Wilhelm Röpke, "Political enthusiasm and common sense: some comments on European economic integration," *Modern Age* 2, no. 2, (1958), 171.

11. Ibid., 171.

12. See European Commission (Trade), *EU & WTO: The Doha Round* (2010), http://ec.europa.eu/trade/creating-opportunities/eu-and-wto/doha/.

13. See Commission Regulation 0861/2010 of October 5, 2010, *Official Journal of the European Union*, L 284–October 29, 2010, http://eur-lex.europa.eu/LexUriServ/LexUriServ.do?uri=OJ:L:2010:284:0001:0887:EN:PDF.

14. Ibid., 133.

15. Daniel Griswold, *Mad About Trade: Why Main Street Should Embrace Globalization* (Washington, DC: Cato Institute, 2009), 148–149.

16. Herman Van Rompuy, "Europe in the New Global Game," *The Economist: The World in 2011*, December 2010, 97.

17. See "Going Dutch: The polder model is under attack," *The Economist*, October 7, 2004, http://www.economist.com/node/3270777.

18. Röpke, "European economic integration and its problems," 240.

19. See U.S. Environmental Protection Agency: Agriculture, "Demographics," http://www.epa.gov/oecaagct/ag101/demographics.html.

20. See Daniel Mitchell, "Corporate Tax Rates Are Falling in Europe. Why Not in the U.S.?" *Forbes*, July 1, 2010.

21. Thomas Molloy, "Ireland's low corporate tax helped fuel banking crisis, claims Merkel," *The Independent*, February 24, 2011, http://www.

independent.ie/national-news/irelands-low-corporate-tax-helped-fuel-banking-crisis-claims-merkel-2554023.html.

22. Leigh Phillips, "Corporate Tax Rates Fall Again in Europe," *Business Week*, June 29, 2010, http://www.businessweek.com/globalbiz/content/jun2010/gb20100629_855797.htm.

23. See Ambrose Evans-Pritchard, "German jobs miracle as Latin unemployment soars," *Daily Telegraph*, January 31, 2012, http://www.telegraph.co.uk/finance/financialcrisis/9052931/German-jobs-miracle-as-Latin-unemployment-soars.html.

24. See Klaus F. Zimmerman, "Germany's Second Chance," *The Wall Street Journal*, April 14, 2011, http://online.wsj.com/article/SB10001424052748703730104576260693050432986.html.

25. "Lemon Aid," *The Economist*, July 8, 2010, http://www.economist.com/node/16542836.

26. "The neighbours fall out," *The Economist*, July 8, 2010, http://www.economist.com/node/16539414.

27. "France's lost decade," *The Economist*, February 3, 2011, http://www.economist.com/node/18073390.

28. "A machine running smoothly," *The Economist*, February 3, 2011, http://www.economist.com/node/18061718.

29. See "A great burden for Zapatero to bear," *The Economist*, January 20, 2011, http://www.economist.com/node/17965525.

30. Ronald Kessler, "Obama Could Learn From Sweden's Labor System," *Newsmax*, April 6, 2011, http://www.newsmax.com/RonaldKessler/Obama-Sweden-socialist-capitalism/2011/04/06/id/391944.

31. Ibid.

32. See James Bartholomew, "Krona capitalism," *Spectator*, July 9, 2011.

33. Gabriel Sahlgren, *Schooling for Money: Swedish Education Reform and the Role of the Profit Motive* (London: IEA, 2010), http://www.iea.org.uk/sites/default/files/publications/files/Schooling%20for%20money%20-%20web%20version_0.pdf.

34. See Bartholomew, "Krona capitalism."

35. Ronald Kessler, "Obama Could Learn From Sweden's Labor System."

36. See Gill and Raiser, *Golden Growth*, 325.

37. Bartholomew, "Krona capitalism."

38. George W. Bush, Statement by the President, December 4, 2003, http://www.america.gov/st/washfile-english/2003/December/20031204160 328ikceinawzao.8047296.html.

39. See Stephen Greenhouse, "Tire Tariffs are Cheered by Labor," *The New York Times*, September 14, 2009, http://www.nytimes.com/2009/09/15/business/15labor.html.

40. "Split in organized labor over immigration," *Associated Press*, June 21, 2007, http://www.msnbc.msn.com/id/19352537/ns/politics/.

41. See Gill and Raiser, *Golden Growth*, 62–63, 251.

42. Ibid., 242.

43. Ibid., 63.

44. See Heritage Foundation, *2012 Index of Economic Freedom*, http://www.heritage.org/index/ranking.

45. Soumitra Dutta, ed., *The Global Innovation Index 2012* (Fontainebleau: INSEAD, 2012), http://globalinnovationindex.org/gii/main/fullreport/index.html.

46. Charles Wolf, Jr., "The Facts about American 'Decline'," *The Wall Street Journal*, April 13, 2011, http://online.wsj.com/article/SB1000 142405274870441510457625129272225228886.html?mod-WSJ_Opinion_ LEADTop.

47. Ibid.

48. See "Red tape rising," *The Economist*, January 22, 2011, http://www.economist.com/node/17961890.

49. Robert E. Lucas, Jr., "The U.S. Recession of 2007–201?," Milliman Lecture, University of Washington, May 19, 2011, http://www.econ.washington.edu/news/millimansl.pdf.

Chapter 9: How America Can Have a Non-European Future

1. For the data associated with this poll, see "Market troubles," *The Economist*, April 6, 2011, http://www.economist.com/blogs/ dailychart/2011/04/public_opinion_capitalism; and Globescan, "Sharp Drop in American Enthusiasm for Free Market," April 6, 2011, http:// www.globescan.com/news_archives/radar10w2_free_market/.

2. Václav Klaus, "The Crisis of the European Union: Causes and Significance," *Imprimis* 40, no. 7/8 (2011), 5.

3. See Brian Blackstone, "Euro Zone Expands, at Two Speeds: Growth Gap Widens; Northern Nations Power Ahead but Southerners Struggle," *The Wall Street Journal*, May 14, 2011, http://online.wsj.com/ article/SB10001424052748703864204576320650448030890.html?_ nocache=1305379288758&mg=com-wsj.

4. See, for example, Timo Soini, "Why I Don't Support Europe's Bailouts," *The Wall Street Journal*, May 9, 2011, http://online.wsj. com/article/SB10001424052748703864204576310851503980120. html?mod=WSJ_newsreel_opinion; and Marcus Walker, "Is Germany Turning Into the Strong Silent Type?" *The Wall Street Journal*, June 27, 2011, http://online.wsj.com/article/SB10001424052702304259304576373281798293222.html.

5. See Felix Rohatyn, *Bold Endeavors: How Our Government Built America, and Why It Must Rebuild Now* (New York: Simon & Schuster, 2009).

6. Thomas Aquinas, *Summa Contra Gentiles* (Notre Dame, IN: University of Notre Dame Press, 1997), III, c.71, n.4.

7. John Paul II, *Centesimus Annus*, 1991, paragraph 48, http://www. vatican.va/holy_father/john_paul_ii/encyclicals/documents/hf_jp-ii_ enc_01051991_centesimus-annus_en.html.

8. See Smith, *Wealth of Nations*, Book V.i.2d.

9. William McGurn, "After the Welfare State," *The Wall Street Journal*, April 5, 2011, http://online.wsj.com/article/SB10001424052748703

806304576242960277394774.html?_nocache=1302365541505&mg=
com-wsj.

10. See Bartholomew, *The Welfare State We're In*, 27–28.

11. See Arthur C. Brooks, *Who Really Cares: The Surprising Truth
About Compassionate Conservatism* (New York: Basic Books, 2006); and
Arthur C. Brooks, ed., *Gifts of Time and Money: The Role of Charity in
America's Communities* (Lanham, MD: Rowman & Littlefield, 2005); and
Ben Gose, "Charity's Political Divide," *The Chronicle of Philanthropy*,
November 23, 2006, http://philanthropy.com/article/Charitys-Political-
Divide/54871/.

12. See Emily Gipple and Ben Gose, "America's Generosity Divide,"
The Chronicle of Philanthropy, August 19, 2012, http://philanthropy.com/
article/America-s-Generosity-Divide/133775/.

13. Cited in Joe Loconte, "The 7 Deadly Sins of Government
Funding for Private Charities," *Policy Review: The Journal of American
Citizenship*, March/April (1997), 29.

14. Cited in Colin Clark, *Taxmanship: Principles and Proposals for the
Reform of Taxation* (London: IEA, 1964), 21.

15. See Allan H. Meltzer, "Welfare State or Start-Up Nation," *The
Wall Street Journal*, June 15, 2011, http://online.wsj.com/article/SB1000
1424052702304432304576369933829499132.html?mod=WSJ_Opinion_
LEADTop [my emphasis].

16. Tocqueville, *Democracy in America*, 525.

17. Eucken, *This Unsuccessful Age*, 64.

18. See Eric Lipton and John Broder, "In Rush to Assist a Solar
Company, U.S. Missed Signs," *The New York Times*, September 22,
2011, http://www.nytimes.com/2011/09/23/us/politics/in-rush-to-assist-
solyndra-united-states-missed-warning-signs.html?pagewanted=all.

19. Kling and Schultz, *From Poverty to Prosperity*, 190.

20. See Tad DeHaven, "Corporate Welfare in the Federal Budget,"
Policy Analysis no. 703, July 25, 2012 (Washington DC: Cato Institute,
2012), 3–5.

21. See Ran Duchin and Denis Sosyura, "TARP Investments: Financials and Politics," University of Michigan Working Paper, February 24, 2009, http://apps.olin.wustl.edu/FIRS/PDF/2010/1591.pdf.

22. See Ted DeHaven, "HUD Scandals," Downsizing the Federal Government, Cato Institute, June 2009, http://www.downsizinggovernment.org/sites/default/files/hud-scandals.pdf.

23. See Jim Valette and Daphne Wysham, "Enron's Pawns: How Public Institutions Bankrolled Enron's Globalization Game," Institute for Policy Studies, March 22, 2002, 4, http://www.csub.edu/~mault/enronpawns.pdf.

24. Smith, *Wealth of Nations*, Book IV.ii.9.

25. Vernon L. Smith, "The Clinton Housing Bubble," *The Wall Street Journal*, December 18, 2007.

26. Friedrich A. Hayek, *The Constitution of Liberty* (London: Routledge & Kegan Paul, 1960), 208.

27. See John Finnis, *Natural Law and Natural Rights* (Oxford: OUP, 1980), 270–273.

28. See Robert Samuelson, "The Flight from Risk," *The Washington Post*, December 13, 2010, http://www.realclearpolitics.com/articles/2010/12/13/the_flight_from_risk_108220.html.

29. See Frank Knight, *Risk, Uncertainty, and Profit* (1921), http://www.econlib.org/library/Knight/knRUP.html.

30. John D. McKinnon, Gary Fields, and Laura Saunders, "Temporary Tax Code Puts Nation in a Lasting Bind," *The Wall Street Journal*, December 14, 2010, http://online.wsj.com/article/SB10001424052748703963704576005960558986604.html?KEYWORDS=uncertainty.

31. Internal Revenue Service, *Tax Code, Regulations and Official Guidance*, http://www.irs.gov/taxpros/article/0,,id=98137,00.html.

32. Smith, *Wealth of Nations*, III.iii.12.

33. Supreme Court of the United States, *Kelo v. City of New London 545 U.S. 469* (2005), http://www.law.cornell.edu/supct/html/04-108.ZO.html.

34. André Jardin, *Tocqueville: A Biography*, trans. Lydia Davis with Robert Hemenway (Baltimore and London: John Hopkins University Press, 1998), 109.

35. For an accessible and comprehensive study of Charles Carroll, see Bradley J. Birzer, *American Cicero: The Life of Charles Carroll* (Wilmington, DE: ISI Books, 2010).

36. See Brooks, *The Battle*, 77–81.

Index

of market entry, 152
of modern welfare state,
169–172
of pensions, 180–182
of population decline, 178–180
Council of the European
Community, 106–107
Crèvecoeur, J. Hector St. John de,
27–28
cuddle capitalism, xix
cultural reality, 8–9
culture
economic. *See* economic
culture
economy and, 9–10
European vs. American
attitudes toward, 16–20
market. *See* market culture
Cuomo, Andrew, 130
currency dilemma (EU). *See*
monetary union (EU)

Daladier, Édouard, 98
D'Alema, Giuseppe, 125
D'Alema, Massimo, 125
Dalrymple, Theodore, 134
Daniels, Anthony, 134
De Officiis (Cicero), 45
Debré, Michel, 138
debt and deficits, 174, 187. *See also*
monetary union (EU)
defensiveness, openness vs.,
295–299

Delors, Jacques, 91–94, 105, 125,
202
Delors Report, 202
Democracy in America
(Tocqueville), 32–33, 161
Democratic Party (U.S.), 141
The Demographic Winter, 176
demographics, 175–180
dependency, 282
despotism, soft. *See* welfare state,
modern
Deutsche Börse, 255
dirigisme, 22, 85, 88, 104–105, 128–
129, 132, 151, 243–245, 293–295
disability benefits, 159, 166, 186
disaster response, 39
divine right of kings, 48
Dodd-Frank Wall Street Reform
and Consumer Protection Act of
2010, 292
dollar, U.S., 255–256
Draghi, Mario, 146
Drescher, Seymour, 35
Du Contrat Social (Rousseau), 87
Duisenberg, Willem, 227
Durkheim, Émile, 56, 58
dynasticism, 125–126

Eberstadt, Nicholas, 177, 180, 185
École Nationale d'Administration
(ENA), 138
Economic and Monetary Union,
104, 219

347